STEVE JUDD was born in July 1955. He found his first astrological tables in 1977 and then spent years learning astrological basics. Self-taught, he is on the cutting edge of modern astrological developments in the last quarter of a century. In July 2005, Steve was awarded the MA in Cultural Astronomy and Astrology from the Sophia Centre at Bath Spa University, the eleventh person in the world at that time to hold this qualification. Since the late 90s, Steve's client database has evolved exponentially. He has a loyal following, with many clients returning for regular updates, as well as a large presence on YouTube, with over 80,000 subscribers. Steve is advancing public knowledge and awareness of astrology like no other before him in modern times.

In forty-five years of study and practise as an astrologer, Steve has developed unique ways of interpreting the horoscope. He covers all pertinent areas involving health patterns, children, residence, family, finances, community, career, philosophy and relationships, as well as working extensively with astrolocation. Steve's ability to define and explain past situations from an impersonal and objective perspective gives him the potential to expand on current situations and then explore and project into possible options for the future.

For more information, visit:
www.stevejudd.co and www.astrobabbleproductions.com

I0099926

Books by Steve Judd

The Bedroom Astrologer (SilverWood Books 2023)

The Lore of

PLUTO

RESHAPING THE VOID

STEVE JUDD

SilverWood

This edition published in 2023 by SilverWood Books
Previously published in 2014

SilverWood Books Ltd
14 Small Street, Bristol, BS1 1DE, United Kingdom
www.silverwoodbooks.co.uk

Copyright © Steve Judd 2023

ISBN 978-1-80042-266-7 (paperback)
Also available as an ebook

British Library Cataloguing in Publication Data
A CIP catalogue record for this book is
available from the British Library

Page design and typesetting by SilverWood Books

THE LORE OF PLUTO

RESHAPING THE VOID

Contents

Preface

Today, the 13th of February 2013 I step into the unknowable. As I write these words Pluto in the heavens is exactly opposite my Cancerian Sun, hopefully opening the doorway into the deeper workings of the universe and acting as a portal for my own personal transformation. I dedicate this book to the transformative urge that permeates the whole of evolution, accepting that I can never comprehend the depths of the Hadean experience and hoping that by acting as a conduit for the regenerative process this offering will bring a more contemporary perception of Pluto.

Today, the 31st of August 2014, with the Moon, Mars and Saturn all conjunct in Scorpio I finish this book and openly embrace and accept the more feminine side of Pluto that has shown itself to me in the last eighteen months. Hopefully, the reader will also gain a more complete and thorough understanding of this most mysterious of astrological influences.

The following clients actively contributed towards this book and my thanks go to them: Alison, Alla, Amanda, Amy, Ana, Angela, Ann, Anne, Bodil, Catherine, Christine, Clare, Diana, Dorinda, Elaine, Geoff, Hala, Heather, Jennifer, John, Kate, Kimberly, Linda, Maria, Mary, Matt, Michael, Michelle, Mimi, Noah, Ralph, Richard, Roma, Ruth, Ruya, Shahz, Sharon, Sheila, Sujatin, Teresa, Terry, Tracey, Tracy, Trish, Yvonne.

There are astrologers to whom I owe thanks for their input in my life. These include Michael York, Patrick Curry, Bernadette Brady, Nick Campion and Sue Farebrother. Particular thanks go to Liz Greene who gave inspiration when it was most needed. Grateful thanks must also go to the people without whom this book could never have happened: Karen and James without whom none of this would have happened, Joanna, my editor and friend, and Emily who kept me in order at the start.

Section One: The Mechanics

1

The discovery, naming and symbols of Pluto

By the time of the early-mid nineteenth century and with the discovery of Uranus firmly established, astronomers had come to the inescapable conclusion that irregularities in the orbit of Uranus could only be caused by the gravitational influences of another large body or other bodies elsewhere in the solar system and from the resultant calculations and observations the planet Neptune was eventually discovered in 1840. After this and during the following years astronomers continued making more calculations and after further decades of observation, the majority of them concluded that there had to be another large body outside of the orbit of Neptune which was causing irregularities or perturbations in the orbital patterns of both Uranus and Neptune. The search for the elusive 'Planet X' became an enthusiastic cause for many astronomers at the end of the nineteenth and beginning of the twentieth century, assuming almost Holy Grail like proportions in the modern astronomy of the times.

In 1894 Percival Lowell, an agnostic pacifist from a rich Boston family who travelled the world extensively in his youth for purposes of self-discovery and anthropology, decided to establish a private astronomical observatory in Flagstaff, Arizona from where he made many recordings and drawings of the surface of Mars. It was from these recordings that Lowell started to postulate the existence of the 'canals on Mars' as being evidence of intelligent life. This may or may not be connected to the fact that also at this time H.G. Wells was writing 'The War of the Worlds' which was published in 1898, although there is no written record of Lowell and Wells having actually met. Lowell's ideas of there being life on any other planet in the solar system did not endear him to the astronomical community of the time, being seen as 'of the lunatic fringe' and he was considered an outsider at least and derided as delusional by many of his peers.

When not looking at Mars and in his spare hours Lowell dedicated time and energy to solving the problem of the outer planetary orbital irregularities eventually concluding that there had to be another large planetary body in a certain position in the heavens that would explain these irregularities in the orbital patterns of Uranus and Neptune. Lowell worked extensively with William Pickering, another American astronomer of repute and between them they proposed a number of areas of the night sky where they believed the new planet would be found. This belief in a large undiscovered planet outside the orbit of Neptune became a passion for Lowell and from 1905/6 onwards he made his search for the mysterious 'Planet X' his prime focus which if and when found would finally explain the supposed orbital discrepancies. When Pluto was completely eliminated from the reasons for the outer planetary perturbations in 1978 another search was initiated only finally and permanently closing in 1989 when the Voyager flyby of Neptune enabled much more accurate measurements to be made. These new measurements corrected older calculations and proved the orbital patterns of Neptune to be more regular than previously supposed thus eliminating the supposed perturbations and removing the need for the existence of 'Planet X.' This does however raise the question of why Lowell and Pickering chose to look for Planet X in the same area of the heavens as Pluto was eventually found. Modern astronomers choose to believe this was coincidental.

Lowell died in 1916 without any success or mainstream astronomical recognition, officially through ill health although many of his colleagues stated at the time that they felt his failure to find Planet X had depressed him and lowered his vitality. In later years it was discovered that faint images of Pluto were on plates taken by his observatory in 1915 but that the images were so small that it eluded his attention. After Lowell's death a decade long battle ensued between his foundation and his widow over the Flagstaff observatory's legacy which only concluded in 1925 after the involvement of other members of his family, notably his brother. After a period of re-modernisation and an upgrade to the telescopes the observatory started work again in 1928 and in 1929 the observatory director at the time gave the (seemingly minor) job of locating Lowell's Planet X to a young aspiring astronomer named Clyde Tombaugh.

Tombaugh ignored Lowell's chosen area of search having reviewed his work and instead made the decision to search the plane of the ecliptic and the areas around it looking for Pluto through the band of the zodiac signs. Over the course of 1929 he took over two million photographs of different constellations, always the ones opposite where the Sun was at the time so that he would be able to better capture retrograde motions. Photographs taken of the constellation of Gemini in late January 1930 were evaluated in February and Pluto's position was determined some two degrees away from where Lowell originally estimated Planet X would be. In later years when Pluto's orbit was accurately calculated, it was discovered that Pluto orbits the Sun in a different plane to the rest of the planets in the solar system and it is only similarly placed by plane to the rest of the planets for two periods of approximately five years out of every two hundred and forty eight. It was during one of these brief five year periods that Tombaugh found Pluto. After further checks and confirmations, news of the new planet's discovery was announced on March 13, 1930. Once the discovery of the new planet had been announced, other observatories began to check their back catalogue of photographs and it was realised that up to fifteen earlier photographs of Pluto had been taken unknowingly before its discovery the earliest of which is recorded as being in 1909. Upon the discovery of the new planet, a quest for a suitable name for that planet began, a quest that was to have long and unforeseen implications and that story is worth recounting in detail if only to confirm or refute a number of urban myths about the naming of Pluto.

A popular story told in astrological circles over the 1960's through to the middle of the 1980's was that upon discovering the existence of the new planet on a number of telescopic plates that he had taken earlier that month, Clyde Tombaugh went home to his family and announced that he had just discovered a new planet and was stuck for a name as to what to call it. The urban myth states that one of Tombaugh's young children had just been watching the first of the Walt Disney Mickey Mouse cartoons, featuring a large dog. According to the myth, when asked about what to call the new planet that child turned round to their father and said 'call it Pluto daddy,' ostensibly after the name of the dog in the Disney movie. However as in most cases urban myth turns out to be exactly that, myth and this is precisely the case here. The simplest of research quickly established that in the first few Disney movies the featured dog went by the name of Rex and that it was only changed to Pluto by Walt Disney himself in 1932. In later interviews, Ben Sharpsteen, the main animator for Disney at that time stated that there was no clear explanation for the name change that he was aware of and that it 'just occurred' without forethought or plan.

As already stated, the discovery of the new planet was announced to the world on 13th March 1930 and the echoes of this discovery reverberated around the globe within twenty four hours. At the time of the announcement Clyde Tombaugh urged his superiors to find a name for the new planet before either someone else did or before they were inundated with suggestions. Sure enough, within days the Lowell Observatory, which being the location of Pluto's discovery had the honour of naming it, was inundated with thousands of different names for the new planet. Constance Lowell, (who had stymied the re-opening of the observatory for a decade after Lowell's death by laying claim to his discoveries and assets) suggested the names Zeus, Percival (after Lowell) and Constance (after herself) all of which were rejected by the observatory.

In the UK, the Times newspaper carried a report of the new planets' discovery the following day on the 14th of March 1930. Falconer Madan, a former librarian at the Bodleian library at Oxford University whose brother Henry was the science master at Eton and had suggested the names of Phobos and Deimos for the moons of Mars, read the story of the new planet's discovery and mentioned it to his eleven year old granddaughter Venetia who already had a smattering of Greek and Roman mythological understanding. She suggested the name Pluto, considering it at the time as being the Roman god of the underworld who was able to make himself invisible and Madan forwarded the suggestion to astronomer Herbert Hall Turner, who cabled his American colleagues at the Lowell Observatory. The people at the observatory showed the name to Clyde Tombaugh, who liked the proposal because it started with the initials of Percival Lowell, the original proposer of the Planet X hypothesis.

Venetia Birney's choice of Pluto along with the names Cronos and Minerva were put forward on a short list of three to every member of the Lowell Observatory and at the end of the voting process on March 24th 1930 it was found that Pluto had received every single vote. As a result the name of the new planet was formally announced to the world on May 1st 1930 and to quote the New York times of May 25th1930: *"Pluto, the title of the Roman gods of the region of darkness, was announced tonight at Lowell Observatory here as the name chosen for the recently discovered trans-Neptunian body, which is believed to be the long-sought Planet X."* Credit for the factual establishment and verification of the naming of Pluto and Venetia Birney's involvement should go to Alex Trenoweth, an American astrologer living in England who ascertained the true facts of Pluto's naming shortly before her (Birney's) death in April 2009 aged ninety.

As we have already learned, the orbital plane of Pluto is at a considerable variation to the orbital plane of the rest of the planets in the solar system with the two different planes intersecting for no more than five years at a time and that Pluto was discovered at such a time. This discovery was hailed in the astronomical community as both the answer to the existing issues of orbital discrepancies and as the logical next step in the ongoing exploration and development of the known solar system and beyond. Over the following decades Pluto's reputation amongst the global astrological community also grew and a set of astrological meanings were derived from years of statistical observation and analysis. However, come the 1980's and the consequent astronomical confirmation that the orbital perturbations of the outer planets were not caused by Pluto, the nature of its status as a planet began to be questioned by those astronomers who considered it too small, too far away and too insignificant to count as a planet. In addition to these factors, the knowledge that Pluto orbits the Sun in a different plane than the rest of the planets in the solar system also casts doubt on its viability for full planetary status.

During the 1990's and the first decade of the new century there was an exponential growth in the quality of both earth-based and orbital telescopic observation platforms. From these came much more detailed information and it was gradually realised that Pluto was just one of a number of similar sized objects orbiting the Sun outside of the orbit of Neptune at a distance of some twenty to fifty AU's (Astronomical Units: the distance from Earth to Sun, c.96 million miles, is one AU) in a type of ring formation similar but different to the asteroid belt but orbiting in a different plane of the ecliptic to the rest of the solar system. This became known as the Kuiper belt, named after one of its discoverers and was rapidly found to hold a number of Pluto sized objects at least one of which (Eris) was found to be larger in size than Pluto although its orbit is far more erratic. The Kuiper belt is not to be confused with either the belt of the Centaurs (Chiron etc) that orbit between Jupiter and Neptune or with the Oort cloud some fifty times further out than the Kuiper belt and theoretically the origin and home of the comets. The development of these astronomical discoveries caused astronomers worldwide to re-assess the status of Pluto as a planet and in 2006 its planetary status was removed and the International Astronomical Union designated it as a Kuiper belt object, a decision that continues to reverberate to this day with a number of challenges to that decision and at least three states in the USA refusing to accept the IAU's ruling.

It is worth noting that there seems to be an underlying force or power here that does its very best to be inconspicuous but that manifests in very large terms over long periods of time. This phenomenon becomes more evident at the time of a planet's discovery and the development of corresponding archetypes of human existence that come into conscious play at the time of that discovery. Some examples may serve to demonstrate this theory, so looking at the pre – Plutonian discoveries of Uranus and Neptune and the post – Plutonian discovery of Chiron may give some insightful clues about how the interaction between new planets, their naming process and the simultaneous birthing of new archetypes actually works.

In the early 1780's the world was a changeable place and in 1781 William Herschel discovered Uranus from his back garden in Bath, UK. Ever aware of the niceties and influences of the time he immediately named his discovery Georgium Sidus after the king at the time, but quite quickly this name was abandoned in most circles and was replaced briefly by the name Herschel after its discoverer. Bearing in mind that in the late 1700's the world was a very tempestuous place, the name Uranus surfaced out of the collective and became accepted by the end of the 1780's. It was the time of Goethe, Voltaire, Mozart and Kant, as well as the birth time of people such as Faraday who revolutionised ideas around power and electrical generation.

This was the time of Captain Cook circumnavigating the world, when Britain was establishing itself in India whilst at the same time the American revolution was in full swing, and the French revolution was just around the corner. It marked a new beginning and approach to the social order, towards the use of more mechanical processes, an innovative approach to art and community as well as a burgeoning growth in the awareness of the rights of the individual. These times brought the phenomena that in time have come to be associated with Uranus, those of independence, freedom and liberty, madness and uniqueness, innovation and novelty as well the capacity for sudden change and drama, all mixed with a heady blend of electricity and adventure. Put simply, Uranus was discovered at the time of the greatest period of social revolution the world has ever known, and the events and developments surrounding the time of its discovery reverberate to this day.

Some sixty years later the planet Neptune was discovered in ways and times that are still to this day vague: the discovery was made by two separate people very close to each other in time, one in the UK and the other in France and the nebulousness of its discovery perhaps served as an advanced metaphor for its eventual governances. When Neptune was discovered, it was the time of the Chinese opium wars as well as seeing the first commercially organised brewing of alcohol at a large level, which perhaps is an indicator of Neptune's more challenging sides concerning the nature of addiction and avoidance. It was the time of the onset of mesmerism, photography and the start of major oil production fuelling the growth of the Industrial revolution that was ongoing at the time and again, the hypnotic, elusive and slippery sides of Neptune are shown here. Of course, it was also the time of the onset of spiritualism as well as the time of the writings of the Communist Manifesto by Marx and Engels, themes which over the years can be seen in Neptune's more altruistic nature and its attitudes towards the ideas of larger community.

In a similar light the discovery of Chiron, the first of the Centaurs orbiting between Jupiter and Neptune, has brought its own set of archetypes into common parlance only since Charles Kowal identified it astronomically on 1st November 1977. On the positive side of things, it is only since Chiron's discovery that the ongoing holistic revolution has gathered pace. Before its discovery, who had heard of words like aromatherapy, homoeopathy, astrology, integrated medicine, nutritional advice, lifestyle management and reflexology? It is only since the discovery of Chiron that simultaneously attitudes towards health and lifestyle have changed substantially in the lives of those who have embraced a holistic lifestyle. Only since the late 1970's have individuals had the objective capacity to look at themselves and their relationships and interactions with others in ways that open them up to new holistic ways of being. Recent therapeutic advances in self-development have opened fields where individuals can now deal with areas of self-sabotage, self-worth and feeling devalued as well as address areas where the need for greater assimilation, integration and self-acceptance is desired. The idea of embracing the worthless one within and accommodating it within one's nature, nurturing and protecting the challenged side of oneself as opposed to attempting to eradicate it has gathered momentum in recent decades and is now mainstream as opposed to being on the radical fringe of alternative health.

When looking at the discoveries of Uranus, Neptune and Chiron from an astronomical perspective and then measuring those discoveries against the gestalt and zeitgeist of the times, it can be seen how the corresponding events and social developments of those times dramatically affected the ways in which the planets were given meaning by the astrologers of the era in which the planets in question were discovered. A comparable situation is discovered in the case of Pluto but here the analogy is much stronger and powerful.

When Pluto was discovered in 1930 the USA was in the collective grip of the biggest crime wave that the world had ever seen until that time, with mob warfare almost the norm as gangs of heavily armed men fought for possession of turfs, status and power in the cities. This turf war was initiated by immigrant Italian families but rapidly escalated to involve mobsters of all types and nationalities and this sudden upsurge of crime nationwide was rapidly christened that of the 'criminal underworld' by the US media of the times, a very fitting title considering Pluto's domain.

Simultaneously these times saw a sudden upsurge in the new and developing techniques of psychology and psychotherapy, primarily those of Jung and his contemporaries and followers but also with a remnant of Freudians. Since the discovery of Pluto, the ideas of psychology and psychotherapy have taken hold of the collective consciousness in ways that simply would have been unthinkable and could not have happened even as recently as the late 1800's. It was in the very early 1930's at the time of Pluto's discovery that people such as Oppenheimer, Heisenberg, Pauli, Fermi and Teller were interactive, leading to the first papers on quantum mechanics whilst Rutherford was defining and splitting the neutron at the same time. Shortly after this Glenn Seaborg named the latest new element Plutonium following the theme of naming new elements after recently discovered planets such as Uranium and Neptunium. This was also the time of rampant inflation and economic meltdown in the western world, the subsequent rise of fascism worldwide and the lead up to World War 2 when the most destructive force ever unleashed in warfare, the atomic bomb, was dropped on Japan.

With the splitting of the neutron, the emergence of both psychology and quantum mechanics and the corresponding rise of both fascism and the criminal underworld it can be clearly seen that the time of the discovery of Pluto carried in it a number of strong Plutonian archetypes, even though those archetypes had not been established at the time and could only be seen in retrospect!

Within a few years of Pluto's discovery its orbital pattern had been both projected and confirmed and accurate paths of its orbit were published in the first Plutonian ephemerides. These ephemerides used a symbol for Pluto that consisted of a circle with a dot in the centre, like the Sun's symbol but with a cross above the circle (this symbol has also been used in the past for Mars and Uranus). Within a matter of just a couple of years this had been superseded by the more postmodernist symbol for Pluto that came to be accepted in the 1940's through to the 1960's and 1970's.

This symbol was the blending of the capital letters P and L mixing the two together and giving the capital P a horizontal support going to the right from the base of its vertical. Astrologers accepted it worldwide for two primary reasons. Firstly, it was immediately recognisable as Pluto with the combined P and L obviously standing for the first two letters of the planet's name and secondly the letters PL were also acknowledged as the initials of Percival Lowell the person credited with the initial postulation of Pluto's existence.

However, as the 1970's developed so the recognition and understanding of Pluto's astrological correspondences and meaning evolved, and as the meaning of Pluto from an astrological perspective became steadily clearer and stronger so the tacit acknowledgement that the PL symbol was not up to scratch or sufficiently deep or profound enough became louder. It was noted that the astrological planetary symbols from the Sun out to Neptune used various combinations of the dot, circle, line, crescent and cross and the question of why Pluto did not conform to this pattern became asked increasingly frequently as Pluto became accepted as a serious astrological influence. As the 1980's started, a new symbol for Pluto emerged in classically underworld ways from the collective unconscious of astrological thought.

This new symbol incorporated classical astrological symbolism, being the circle nestling in an upturned crescent which in turn is on top of the cross. Esoteric astrologers describe this as the circle of soul being contained in and supported by the crescent of spirit both superimposed over the cross of matter, suggesting that by working up through the material world of matter and possessions the individual can attain a greater spiritual understanding of the way that the world works and aspire to some type of transformative soul elevation and evolution whilst retaining their notion of individuality and identity. This system of understanding is also complementary to the alchemical principle of transformation that Pluto is so representative of in that the individual always starts from the lowest and basest of beginnings and endeavours and aspires to increasingly refined processes of transformation, transmutation and ultimately alchemical purification often through periods of intense challenge and sometimes pain. As astrology moved into the 1980's and 1990's so the new symbol for Pluto rapidly gained ground and nowadays it is increasingly rare to see the PL symbol used in horoscopes in today's astrological world.

2

The astrononomy of Pluto

Pluto was initially classified at the time of its discovery as the ninth planet from the Sun until it was redesignated as a dwarf planet in 2006 along with other small solar system objects all occupying the Kuiper belt some 20-50 AU from the Sun. Pluto's orbital pattern is not circular, more ovoid and it ranges from as close to the Sun as 29.7 AU and as far as 49.3AU. Pluto is at its closest to the Sun whilst in the astrological constellations of Scorpio and Sagittarius spending an average of some eleven years in each sign whilst it is at its furthest in the signs of Taurus and Gemini where it can easily spend over thirty years in each sign. Pluto's orbital rotation around the Sun is in a plane that is highly elliptical when compared to the rest of the planets in the solar system, only crossing that plane for two periods of five years out of every 248 (Pluto's orbital cycle). It was during one of those five year periods that Tombaugh found Pluto. Pluto's orbital cycle of 248 years relates almost perfectly with Neptune's orbital period of 164.8 years in a 2:3 ratio that seems stable for the long term as Pluto goes round the Sun twice for every three times that Neptune does so.

Pluto's orbit is so unusual that occasionally for 20 years out of every 248 it comes within the orbit of Neptune and is closer to the Sun, although due to the different orbital planes the risk of collision is absolute zero. This transit last happened between the years 1979 and 1999 and astrologers have related this time to that of the power of transformation as symbolised by Pluto coming within the boundaries of the imagination as symbolised by Neptune.

Pluto's mass appears to be approximately one five hundredth of that of the Earth. It takes somewhere between six and seven days to spin on its axis although its poles are nearer the equator than they are to the north/south axis in a similar fashion to that on Uranus, which means that during the period of Pluto's solstice one quarter of the planet is in perpetual darkness whilst another quarter is in perpetual sunlight. As far as is currently known Pluto is approximately 60% rock of some type and 40% ice and most of that ice is nitrogen although there are also traces of both methane and carbon. The visible colour of Pluto has changed from black and white with isolated orange hues when first photographed in the early 1990's to black and white with increasing red patches tinged with orange in the last twenty years. To give an idea of its relative size, whilst Pluto is about twice the mass and size of the dwarf planet Ceres it is still considerably smaller than a number of planetary Moons, such as Neptune's Triton, Saturn's Titan, Jupiter's Europa and the Earth's Moon.

Recent telescopic discoveries of Pluto indicate that it has its own family of moons. Furthest out is the moon Hydra, just outside the minor 'moonlet' Kerberos. This is in turn just outside the orbit of Nix, which is the third moon out from Pluto. Inside the orbit of Nix is the moonlet Styx and then closest to Pluto lies the major moon Charon. Recent observations of the Pluto system have confirmed that Charon's pull on Pluto is practically as strong as Pluto's pull on Charon. This results in these two points performing a dance where they constantly keep the same face shown towards each other, pulling each other out of what should be a perfect orbital pattern. Instead, their dance is like that of the edges of a doughnut where Charon goes round the outside edge of the doughnut and Pluto goes round the inside edge, both circling around a point in space that is void and empty and making this a binary planetary system. Recently a number of astrologers have drawn inference to this fact, pointing out that there is nothing at the centre of the Plutonic system and thus alluding to emptiness and the void as being represented here amid the Plutonian darkness.

It should be noted that in July 2015 the space probe New Horizons will perform a flyby of Pluto and its moons and from that it is hoped that more accurate measurements and photographs can be made which should then help humanity understand a great deal more about this quiet and remote part of the solar system.

The New Horizons craft, a piano shaped object, is the fastest man made object ever constructed. On its journey to Pluto the New Horizons spacecraft passed the orbit of Neptune on 25th August 2014 – exactly twenty five years to the day since Voyager 2 passed at its closest to Neptune and sent information back to Earth that would see the start of the demise of Pluto as a planet in the eyes of astronomers. At the time of writing New Horizons is 90% of the way from the Earth to Pluto, travelling at fifteen kilometres per second and is scheduled to interact with the Pluto system on 15th July 2015.

3

The mythology of Pluto

It is immediately clear upon studying the mythology of Pluto that there are a number of varied factors involved, not least the origin of the archetype of Pluto in the first place. Mythology is just that, myth and myth is constantly changing as cultural attitudes towards history and modern translations of old stories become more prevalent. What was accepted as embedded archetypes of mythological understanding even thirty years ago is now seen as outmoded and outdated. With the accelerating increases in education and technological techniques for understanding antiquity even the new models of today will be seen as old fashioned within fifteen years. What is without doubt is that knowledge of what has become western astrology and potentially mythology as well spread from Mesopotamia through Egypt across to Crete and from there into Greek and Roman culture over millennia. Nevertheless, stories and myths must have a referential point of origin and most astrologers and mythologists agree that the embryonic myth of Pluto began in south-east Europe some three thousand years ago, although with a different name and job description.

Based on a contemporary early twenty first century perspective the first mention of Pluto comes from the struggle between the Olympians and the Titans. From Ouranus the sky god and Gaia the earth goddess came forth the Titans, many of whom were ugly or grotesque in some shape. Ouranus decided to imprison many of his children in Tartarus, especially the Gigantes (giants), the Hecatonchires who were hundred armed and fifty headed deities and the Cyclops, the monstrous single eyed deities. Gaia was repelled by the idea of having some of her children confined and tried to coerce others of the

Titans to act and rebel against their father but in the end only the youngest of them, Cronos, accepted the proffered sickle.

It was Cronos (later to become Saturn in Roman mythology) who wielded the sickle, castrating Ouranus and throwing his father's severed genitals into the ocean out of which according to most versions of Greek mythology arose the goddess Aphrodite. On his deathbed the mortally wounded Ouranus cursed Cronos wishing upon him the same fate as had befallen himself, a prophecy that was to resonate into the next generation.

According to many versions of the Greek myths Cronus was the least deformed of the Titans and upon acceding to the position of power that his father had held immediately imprisoned his other Titan brothers and sisters again in Tartarus, to be guarded by Campe the last of the she-dragons. Having secured his empire against his siblings Cronos set about establishing himself as the new pantheon head. He married his sibling Rhea and set about consolidating his empire. Ever mindful of the curse that his father had put on him, Cronos ensured that as soon as his children were born, he consumed them into himself so that they would not fulfil the prophecy of Ouranus. In an equivalent way to Gaia, her mother-in-law, Rhea did not hold with the idea of her husband consuming her children at birth and so set about remedying the situation. At the time that her sixth child Zeus was born, she managed to deceive Cronos into swallowing a hot stone thinking that it was Zeus and thus helped her son escape the misfortune of his five previous siblings. In later years Zeus/Jupiter grew and started leading a revolution against his father, which became known in time as the Titanomachy. He went to Tartarus, slaying Campe and freeing the remaining Titans, some of whom teamed up with Zeus and others with Cronos in the ensuing war between the Titans and the Olympians.

It was in the direct confrontation between Zeus/Jupiter and Cronos/Saturn that Zeus managed to wound Cronos in his belly and from that wound emerged his five siblings, Hestia, Demeter, Hera, Hades/Pluto and Poseidon/Neptune. Eventually the male members of these siblings banded together and overcame the Titans, casting Cronos into Tartarus for good measure and proceeded to cast lots for the firmament and real estate left behind after the wars. According to the Iliad, Zeus became the sky god and lord of the overworld, Poseidon became the sea god and ruled the domain of the waters and Hades became the lord of the underworld, the realm where souls went after death. It is after the events of the Titanomachy that Hades begins to lose the separate notion of individual identity and instead begins to assume the status of being a realm as opposed to a god. With this realm came the duties of collaborating with souls in the underworld, but also of defining how that underworld and the work in it was to be both manifested and managed. Tartarus became just one of the diverse levels of Hades, comparable to the ideas of Sheol in Hebraic texts and Christian ideas of hell and purgatory in later times.

The idea of Hades as a realm of experience as opposed to an individual entity gradually became the established reality, so the areas of Hades became more clearly defined in ways that speak of both the rewards and the penalties of life.

Hades was not initially all challenging work. The Garden of the Hesperides and variations on it throughout history is a kind of paradisiacal land where gods, heroes and martyrs are welcomed by nymphs and dryads, similar to the concept of Valhalla in Norse mythology and other stories from around the world. There are the Asphodel Meadows, a land of neutrality where the souls of those whose work is done go to rest in a dormant almost limbo-like state. There is the more well known area of Elysium. By the time of Homer (560 BCE) the idea of the Elysian Fields had developed. This was an area initially separate from Hades but quickly integrated, at first reserved for those related in some way to the gods but in later times also admitting those fortunate souls chosen by the gods as well as the righteous and the heroic. A number of Greek writers of the period postulated that the Elysian Fields existed somewhere to the west of Greece, although in some cases they were also called the Isle of the Blessed, again a place for the valiant who had passed over and whose souls needed sustenance. There may be connotations here with the legends emanating from ancient south-west England about Lyonesse and the Summer Land, places of myth and tranquillity where heroes rested after their valour. In many ways Elysium is the direct opposite of Tartarus, the land of the damned from which there is no escape.

Hades was boundaried by different rivers. The river Cocytus was the river of woe, lamentation and wailing, whilst the Phlegethon was the river of fire, burning and purifying all that it touched. The river Lethe was the force for forgetfulness and oblivion and all who entered its waters forgot their purpose. There were also the rivers Acheron and Styx. The river Styx is the boundary between the upper overworld and the lower underworld, famous for having Achilles totally immersed in it apart from his heel by which his mother held him. It is the river that could convey immortality, but it could equally be portrayed as a spiteful and hateful energy when not dealt with cleanly. The Styx and the Acheron are both seen as the main rivers in Hades with the other rivers flowing into them, with Charon (not to be confused with Chiron) the ferryman plying his trade on both rivers, according to which version of the mythology one reads. There needed to be a payment, whether that was by an obolus, or small coin placed in the mouth of the deceased, or by metaphorically paying the ferryman in some form. (In modern astronomy, Charon is the Moon that orbits Pluto in an almost binary fashion, guarding and protecting Pluto from visitation). Once the souls of the dead had passed over the river courtesy of Charon, they were often met on the opposite bank by Cerberus the three headed dog of Hades whose function was to stop the dead from leaving Hades whilst at the same time preventing the living from entering.

Hades should never be directly linked to the death and dying process, it was always the facilitator and the realm of the process not the event itself: this belonged firmly in the realm of others. Here is found one of the origins of the oldest myths of all worldwide, that of the three fates. Depending on which cultural basis one reads from, there is always a different version of this tale, from the English Fates to the German Norns, but in the Greek version of antiquity it is that of the Moirai. Clotho is the spinner, who was responsible for the thread of human life, spinning the life. Lachesis was the member of the triad who measured, weighed and determined the destiny and life path of the individual whilst Atropos wielded the cutters, effectively bringing the life span to an end. The actual physical process of mortal passage into the next world was broken down even further, into that involving either Thanatos who governed peaceful death or Keres who governed violent endings. All these different 'agents of death' operated within the confines and boundaries of Hades which by 500 BCE had become exclusively a realm of existence and no longer an individual deity. However, with all the different attendant forms of Hadean experience came a fear of dealing directly with that realm and by this time in history the name of Hades had become so tainted with the idea of death and the corresponding underworld that it was considered unfortunate to use it in any form.

As the name of Hades became proscribed, so the ideas of the wealth of the underworld being manifested began to surface, primarily through the trading in precious metals, stones and jewels that were being unearthed and mined at the time. The deity that ruled that element of deep wealth was named Plouton and it quickly became the name for the agent or intermediary of the underworld. Plouton (Pluto) quickly becomes disassociated with Hades as is best shown by different versions of the Persephone myth where in some stories Hades is the violent abductor whilst in others Pluto is the deep and wise husband. Homer described Hades as 'the god most hateful to mortals' whilst Plato preferred to use Plouton as the bringer of wealth because the name of Hades was too fear provoking. It is in the story of the abduction of Persephone that the different manifestations of Pluto begin to become glaringly obvious and the final mythological differentiation between Pluto and Hades becomes more permanent.

The earliest versions of the story of the abduction of Persephone seem to come from before the days of the Greek empire, from at least the Mycenaean period of c.1,000–1,500 BCE if not earlier. The origin of the mythology of Demeter and her daughter Persephone as the goddesses of the land and the grain goes back thousands of years to the original agrarian cultures of the time and over the ensuing centuries the mythology grew to the point of become an established tradition by the time of Minoan and Greek culture. Here is seen a classic example of the differences of the time regarding Pluto and Hades, in that in one version of the myth, from the Odyssey, Demeter gives birth to Ploutos, making him the brother of Persephone (whom she conceived with her brother, Zeus), whilst Demeter herself is one of the original six Olympians and along with Hades another of her brothers spent the early part of her life imprisoned within the confines of Cronos, her father. So, with Hades as her brother and Ploutos her son a clear difference between the two concepts of darkness and depth began to emerge.

What is also clear is that at the same time in Greek history/mythology some type of tragedy/story developed that exists today only in myth and metaphor involving permanent and ongoing conflict between Demeter and Hades. As two of the original six Olympians, there was never going to be a clear winner, and this conflict certainly involved the abduction of Persephone from Demeter's care. Most of the metaphorical and allegorical versions of the tale talk of Demeter and Persephone out walking in the meadows when the ground opens and the lord of the underworld emerges, whether Hades or Pluto, often with black horses, forcibly abducts Persephone from the protection of her mother and drags her back down into the underworld with the land sealing itself after their departure. However, the identity of the abductor raises a lot of different questions that need addressing to best understand the nature of both Persephone and Pluto and the relationship between them. What is agreed in all versions is that Persephone was held hostage for a considerable period of time probably as a pawn in some type of deep male/female power game between the archetypes of her mother and her uncle and that during this time of enforced separation between Demeter and Persephone, a gulf develops between them that became so empty and void that it started to reflect into other areas of Demeter's domain. So grief ridden was Demeter that she withdrew her energies, laying waste to the previously fertile farmlands that she was the patron of and creating a barren wasteland, uninhabitable and unusable.

Over time, as the land and its occupants withered and died the rest of the Olympians realised that soon they would have nothing left to govern and no-one to pray to them, so they solicited the two siblings to make their peace and in that light Zeus as the leader of the Olympians dispatched Hermes/ Mercury into Hades to negotiate with the lord of the underworld for the release of Persephone so that Demeter would be better and that the land would flourish once again. With his considerable communication skills Hermes negotiated the release of Persephone to the surface conditional on her periodic and cyclical return. Here once again, the myth diverges into different streams of fable and tale. In most versions, Persephone is given 'pomegranate seeds' by Hades/Pluto as a form of binding and some commentators have suggested that this implies Persephone was pregnant upon her return to the overworld. In similar but different forms of the myth, Persephone returned to the overworld and was joyfully reunited with her mother, the land blossomed and all was well, but then Persephone began a regular cycle of voluntary return into the underworld. The concurrent theme here is that the lord of the underworld somehow manages to entice Persephone back into regular visits to his domain, whether Persephone's return is voluntary or obliged. It is during these cyclical periods of return by Persephone that Demeter allegorically weeps for the loss of her daughter, only to rejoice again at the start of Spring as she returns. Similarly, many commentators have drawn allusions to the return of Persephone to the underworld and Demeter's withdrawal of support to the land in protest as a metaphor for the cycle of the seasons and there is specific reference in the Homeric 'Hymn to Demeter' of Persephone returning to the overworld on the first day of spring. Up to the abduction of Persephone the divergence between Hades and Ploutos/Plouton/Pluto had been a gradual affair with no clear sign of obvious distinction apart from the unwillingness to discuss Hadean affairs in public for fear of attracting unwelcome energies. However, when it comes to the story of Persephone then over the years two quite different versions of the tale have evolved, one involving the more violent Hadean archetype and other a more benign but still dominating influence as symbolised by the emerging Plutonic archetype.

In the first version of the tale, Persephone is violently abducted from in front of her mother by her uncle, the personification of Hades. Hades was the eldest of the original Olympiad being the first swallowed by his father but the last regurgitated, or at least this is the version told by his younger brother Poseidon in the Iliad. It may be that Hades felt that he was not given enough respect by his younger siblings and so created strife with them wherever possible. In this version, Persephone and her mother are picking flowers in the fields of Nysa when she is forcibly kidnapped. She is then taken to the Hadean underworld and impregnated, ensuring her constant return. Her mother, Demeter, is often described as dark cowled and scowling and there are versions of this story where Persephone was not obliged to return annually but that she did so by choice. Hades of course never left the underworld and consistently opposed those who would try and leave his domain. Here perhaps the argument between Hades and Demeter can be seen as a metaphor for the struggles between the matriarchal and the patriarchal power systems of the times, much as the mythological infidelities of both Zeus and his wife Hera also symbolically show the battle between the genders.

In a second version of the tale, where Pluto and Persephone are half siblings with the same mother but different father, Pluto is still seen as the abductor of Persephone from the safety and security of her mother's realm but once again there are hints, especially in Hesiod's Theogony, that Pluto being born of Demeter was not all bad and that perhaps this abduction was in fact a rescue. Although this then would make any union an incestual one there are nevertheless many versions of the story where Pluto and Persephone do marry Pluto becoming a stern but fair ruler of the underworld, alongside his bride.

There were temples to the two of them, whereas Hades has very few statues or visible manifestations of adoration or worship. Fragments remaining from inscriptions of the Eleusinian Mysteries suggest clearly that Pluto and Persephone are a divine couple who receive souls in the afterlife.

A summary of this myth is that it involves the fall of the matriarchy and the imposition of brutal male dominance as symbolised by the Hadean version of the myth and similar fables involving Zeus's dalliances. It also implies that by identifying with the power of the dark that both the masculine and the feminine archetypes become the epitome of the 'strong and silent' type, as perhaps suggested by the version of the myth that eulogises the teamwork of Pluto and Persephone. Viewed from a twenty-first century astrological perspective this myth has massive implications in our emerging understanding of the astrological meaning of Pluto as well as its impact on our current astrological delineations of Pluto's strengths and weaknesses in individual horoscopes. This is best mooted by postulating that in today's allegedly sensitive world astrologers are more likely to be able to differentiate between the hard core and harsh, sometimes sadistic and ruthless side that is best described as Hadean, as opposed to the more transformative and regenerative side of this energy, best described as Plutonic.

4

The 21st Century Pluto

During the first 65 years of Pluto's known existence both astronomers and astrologers agreed that Pluto was the next planet in the solar system out from Neptune, a tacit agreement that stood solid until the middle of the 1990's. By this time, the quality of both earth and satellite-based observation platforms and telescopes had started to improve exponentially as the corresponding technological revolution gathered pace and the information being received about the nature of Pluto was beginning to change a lot of people's minds, especially in the astronomical community. The writing was on the wall for the planetary status of Pluto from as early as the late 1980's, when the Voyager space probe completed a flyby of the planet Neptune on the 25th of August 1989. The results of that flyby, that the supposed orbital perturbations of Neptune did not in fact exist, eliminated the need for a larger invisible planet to be exerting a gravitational pull on Neptune and at the same time it was quickly being realised that even if that large invisible planet did exist it clearly was not Pluto. These results were verified, collated and presented to the International Astronomical Union who in 2006 rescinded Pluto's status as a conventional planet.

There were many reasons for this decision but primarily there were a few key factors. Firstly, it was realised that Pluto was just one of a large number of similar objects orbiting the Sun in a belt like formation which became known as the Kuiper belt and that Pluto was not even the largest object in that belt although it was the most regular in terms of orbital pattern. Secondly it was also quickly realised that this belt was orbiting the Sun at a tilted plane to the rest of the solar system's planetary plane of orbit, creating a different dynamic. Thirdly it was recognised with the help of recent telescopic advances that Pluto was marginally smaller than the Earth's Moon and when the fact that it is some four billion miles away is added to this size ratio and comparing these facts to other planetary parameters, the case for Pluto's planetary status can be seen as clearly questionable by current conventional astronomical standards. It is a small step from here to see how astronomers without any astrological knowledge can dismiss Pluto as insignificant and not a part of the solar system in the same way as any other more orthodoxically accepted planet.

Those same orbital telescopic platforms have also added to the ways in which Pluto is understood, not only by astronomers but also by astrologers. The recent discoveries of the last five to ten years of the Moon system of Pluto has surprised everyone especially as it seems from information known so far that the orbital resonance of Pluto's moons from Hydra, Kerberos, Nix, Styx and Charon through to Pluto at the apparent centre seems to follow numeric ratio to a fairly accurate degree in a way that has not been seen elsewhere in the solar system. Yet Pluto is not at the centre of this mini system. The size, distance and speed of Pluto's largest moon Charon has an unusual effect on Pluto. Charon pulls Pluto out of the potential centre of its own little system in a way that is like the outside and inside faces of a ring doughnut, or torus. This has been described as a barycentric system with an empty middle and as a binary system with two bodies orbiting each other. As a result of this exact and constant pull on each other both Pluto and Charon always present the same faces towards each other, their individual spin on their axis' is synchronised to always be constantly facing each other. This is similar but different to the Earth/Moon system where the Moon always presents the same face to the Earth but not vice versa. After all these observations but before any clear information or pictures of the Pluto system have arrived from the New Horizons probe due at Pluto on 15th July 2015, it is clear that the astronomers are right and that the Pluto system, small and far away and on a different orbital plane to anything else, bears no physical relation to any of the other much larger planetary systems that orbit the Sun. However, this statement directly conflicts with the observations of astrologers.

Since the time of the early 1930's astrologers have been placing Pluto in horoscopes and ascribing meaning to it and from those times to the late 1990's these definitions and practices continued to flourish and grow without any major deviation or challenge from outside of the global astrological community. So, it came as a sudden and considerable shock across the whole of the community when seemingly out of the blue Pluto was downgraded as a planet in the eyes of the International Astronomical Union. It could be said metaphorically that the sky had indeed fallen in on astrology. The reverberations of this announcement amongst astrologers seemed to follow a pattern worldwide initially of denial and then followed by confusion and uncertainty until a new paradigm began to emerge in the second decade of the 21st century. It has taken astrology and astrologers at least two decades to come to terms with this change in Pluto's astronomical status and many astrologers are still in some type of denial of the actual astronomy of the Pluto system.

At the time of writing (late August 2014) the dichotomy and the gulf between the two dimensional astrological Pluto as presented in horoscopic charts and the three dimensional astronomical Pluto as known and proven by telescopic observation appears to be growing steadily, giving some astronomers and other types of sceptics' ammunition in their refutation of astrology. However, as the astronomical understanding of the Pluto system grows so the correlations as well as the dichotomies between the astronomical and the astrological seem to be keeping pace with each other. In the last decade or so those astrologers who have taken on the new astronomy of Pluto have struggled to work out how the astrological Pluto has such a massive effect in the horoscope whilst it is puny in size, distance and conformity compared to the rest of the planets in the solar system. By all systems of orthodox and conventional astrological thought Pluto should not work. Even astrologers using contemporary explanations of Pluto have retreated into the purely psychological and allegorical, using metaphor and myth as their explanation, and have not attempted to bridge the growing gap between astronomical fact and astrological knowledge.

Astronomy and astrology have never really been that far apart in that they were always the same thing until the discovery and usage of the telescope and the time of Descartes. Astrology itself is nothing if not versatile and adaptable; it is the 'astro logos,' the knowledge of the stars continuing unstoppably in human culture. The accelerated development of new technological understandings of how the universe appears to work have revolutionised the planet within the last two decades. Humanity's ability to grasp concepts that would have been unthinkable even one generation ago is unmistakable evidence of human evolution in an accelerated way and it is not only technological evolution that is accelerating. As a steadily increasing population turns to modern methods of understanding to best guarantee its future, so attitudes towards spirituality and individual relationships with divinity are also changing at an accelerated rate, which in turn is changing perception and understanding at a more comprehensive and wide ranging level. Looking at this global change in both technology and consciousness and bringing it sharply back into focus on the issue of the status of Pluto, certain facts are unequivocal from an astrological perspective.

Regardless of how humanity's understanding of the astronomical mechanics of the solar system is portrayed the basic fact is that for well over fifty years successive generations of astrologers have worked with the emerging archetype of the astrological Pluto and have moulded, shaped and wrenched some type of understanding of its nature. Almost all astrologers would agree that to suddenly not use Pluto in a horoscope would detrimentally subtract from the greater horoscopic analysis to a major degree. It would also negate and invalidate half a century's worth of psychological insight and understanding into how both individual and global unconscious and subconscious factors affect long term patterns and outcomes. It is certain that astrologers are not going to just suddenly stop using Pluto on the say-so of the astronomical community. When viewed from a two dimensional perspective on a horoscope, Pluto clearly works. By changing that two dimensional view into a three dimensional one and seeing the variation of Pluto compared to the rest of the solar system, it is clear why it should not work. The question that astrologers and astrology face now is clear: how to equate the absolute certainty of the astrological Pluto as evinced by half a century of astrological statistics against the new astronomical paradigm of Pluto from a non-astrological perspective?

When astrologers point to a planet in someone's horoscope, they are referring to a ball of rock or gas that is orbiting the Sun on a parallel or parallel plane to all the other planets, i.e., on or close to the ecliptic, except the Pluto system. So the astrologer can point to the astrological Mars or Jupiter and then hopefully be able to take the client outside and show them that same planet or planets in the night sky, at the same time clearly showing the band of zodiac constellations (the ecliptic) that the Sun and planets pass through on their journey in the heavens. When the astrologer points to the position of Pluto in the horoscope and then tries to extrapolate that into a visual context, there is nothing there. This is not only because Pluto is too small to notice even with large amateur telescopes, but also because Pluto is rarely on the ecliptic instead being in a different angle to the Sun's apparent journey through the constellations than the other planets. So, unlike all the other planetary positions in the horoscope the position of Pluto bears little relation to its astronomical location. It is the idea of there being nothing in the place that the astrological Pluto occupies that is of interest here and especially so with the recent discoveries about the Pluto system from an astronomical perspective. It is now known that the Pluto system is a barycentric one where the gravitational influences of Pluto's moons, especially Charon, pull Pluto out of its central stationary point and cause the planet itself to orbit an empty point in the centre of the whole planetary system. At the heart of the Pluto system there is an empty space, a void, nothing. This is an important observation with potentially profound astrological implications.

When astrologers attempt to define Pluto in terms of effect and influence on an individual, they do so by using the astrological Plutonic parlance that has built up in the last half century. This parlance involves the use and acceptance of synchronicity, psychology, intuition, insight, metaphor and analogy in one's life to be able to relate to the non-logical or irrational side of both one's own and other people's nature. Pluto in the horoscope could be flippantly summarised as everything that one cannot think about, one's personal depths, the unconscious and the subconscious. These realms of personality are seen as 'dark' and 'invisible' by most people simply because they cannot be thought about rationally and are thus considered as being at least scary if not terrifying because of millennia of cultural conditioning. However, researchers of these transpersonal and unconscious states of being have become the 'enlightened' ones who bring light into the dark and reveal that there is nothing to fear in there and that darkness is only the absence of light. It is by going into one's own personal darkness or void that the individual becomes psychologically self-empowered and self-acceptant. That area of personal darkness is clearly symbolised by the position, house and aspect of Pluto in the individual chart.

The willingness to accept this 'void' that is deep at the base of oneself and that can never be clearly known or controlled shows the individual's personal link with the Pluto archetype and their willingness to accept the unconscious part of their nature as being valid and real. From this perspective, the validity of the astrological Pluto is thus extended into the realm of the astronomical. Clear correlation can be drawn between the presence of the void at the centre of the Plutonic planetary and moon system and the void that is at the heart of and representative of both one's own unconscious and the collective unconscious.

In terms of true Plutonic synchronicity and as some type of hint of things to come soon, a confirmation of the importance of Pluto was clearly demonstrated by a NASA press release on the 25th of August 2014, about the New Horizons spacecraft. This statement drew allusion to the 'amazing coincidence' that New Horizons passed the orbit of Neptune twenty five years to the day since Voyager 2 performed a flyby of the same planet. On the 25th of August 1989, the Voyager 2 spacecraft sent signals back to Earth that eventually provided conclusive proof that Pluto was not what it had been thought to be until that time and started the demise of its planetary status. On the 25th of August 2014, the New Horizons spacecraft passed the orbit of Neptune on its way to a rendezvous with the Pluto system on 15 July 2015. It is another coincidence for astronomers but an amazing synchronicity for astrologers that the Voyager flyby took place exactly in the middle of a twenty year period of February 1979–1999 when Pluto was inside Neptune's orbit and thus closer to the Sun. This co-incidental but massively synchronous event can be seen as the notion of Pluto transcending the limitations of the last twenty five years and giving humanity once again the chance to view the psychological future with depth, openness and confidence.

Section Two: The Astrology

5

Pluto through the signs

Although Pluto's existence has been known for less than one hundred years, in that time a number of different astrological translations of its meaning dependent on which sign of the zodiac it is in have been both postulated and published. The following sections list the influences of Pluto in each sign of the zodiac that it has inhabited since its discovery as well as the major developments in terms of manifest events and situations worldwide. Because of both the extreme distance of Pluto from the Sun and its irregular orbit, the time it spends in each sign of the zodiac is not consistent. However even at its shortest distance from the Sun, Pluto spends at least a decade in each sign of the zodiac which makes any translation of its influence according to its zodiac sign position a very generalised one. It is much easier to ascribe meaning in this context from a generational perspective than it is from an individual one. For more of a personal perspective, the house position of Pluto as well as the aspects that it makes to the other planets in the horoscope are much more significant than its sign position.

Pluto in Cancer 1913–1939

Pluto entered Cancer in July 1913 at a time where the entire world was in a fervent and fertile state, ready and ripe for a transformative process that would accelerate the evolution of humanity. In Europe, Western Asia and the Mediterranean it heralded the start of the Great War of 1914-1918 with millions of people dying and whole generations being wiped out. Immediately afterwards in what is now known as Russia the Bolshevik revolution brought about the emergence of communism into the world in a way that changed the political and economic landscape forever. The post-war emergence of the USA as a superpower led to a decade of North American consolidation of global power, primarily through financial and economic methods. During the period of Pluto being undiscovered in Cancer there was a major repositioning of power structures amongst the leading countries in the world at the time. One way of seeing this from a historical perspective is the establishing and consolidating of new global political power blocs, ignoring the growing needs of the individual in favour of the dominant global forces of the time and their hold on power. Alternatively, the emergence of the League of Nations, the precursor to the United Nations, laid the foundations for all voices to be heard and it was this need for everyone to have a voice that increasingly brought the disparity between people and their masters to the surface. As mentioned earlier, the time of Pluto's discovery and the lead up to this time was dominated worldwide by financial crisis, economic meltdowns and what has been labelled as 'the Great Depression,' with its attendant civil unrest and disorder.

Post Pluto's discovery the need for transformation at the global level became glaringly obvious to all but those responsible for the process of change. To a fundamentalist level the rise of the left in Russia, the right in Germany and the development of monetarism in the USA during the 1930's led the world to the brink of the second global war. Nationalism and xenophobia became the norm and the need to defend one's home and family, personal property, boundaries and nation became paramount. As the world teetered on the point of war again in 1939 Pluto, considering his job done, slipped unobtrusively into Leo.

Children born during this time grew into a world where everything was changing very fast around them and there was no long term stability except in the safety of home and family. It is the Pluto in Cancer generation who best extol the virtues of the nuclear family, the idea of Mum and Dad, two point two children, the home, garden and family, the mortgage, car and television and the apparent emotional security that this attitude engenders. This need for security remained and remains as strong as ever in the charts of people with this position which is why significantly more of them hold down long term jobs or relationships than most other generations because of the long term stability provided. The Pluto in Cancer generation tried to make all their group affiliations into their larger family in an unconsciously obsessional and compulsive way, whether those affiliations were professional, social or religious. This process was always done with a vestige and veneer of sentimentality as though they were bringing the sheep back into the fold in an all-encompassing way. As decades passed so in retrospect it is easy to describe the Pluto in Cancer generation as being security conscious and strongly protective with an emphasis on traditional tribal, national and family values. It can also be seen how these ingrained traditional attitudes towards family, role play within the family and the carrying of those values into the larger community accelerated the later urge for women's liberation, sexual freedoms and a higher divorce rate, transforming old attitudes towards family and security into a more futuristic pattern.

Post Pluto's discovery, the almost blind obedience to the nature of family and tribe/nation started to undergo a form of systematic review, resulting in the global war at the end of Pluto in Cancer but also personally in the feuding and breakages that began to develop between groups, families, collectives and individuals. Long established family traditions underwent renewal often with temporarily catastrophic results, although the transformations would always be seen as both necessary and positive, breakthrough or breakdown. The second global war obscured the real outcomes of Pluto in Cancer, which was the transformation of family and national structures and systems. The results of this transformation did not really begin to emerge until well after the end of the war. Pluto in Cancer, which some astrological commentators have referred to as the 'age of the breast,' has come to symbolise both the rise and the transformation of the role of the mother and the notion of mothering. It could be said that the demise of the nuclear family and traditional parent/ child relationships in the emerging twenty first century is the direct response to the over emphasis on family structure and security of 1913–1939 and the corresponding transit of Pluto through Cancer.

Pluto in Leo 1939–1957

This is the fabled group known as the 'baby boomers,' those who 'have never had it so good.' After the horrors of the mid twentieth century global war there was a recognition of some of the mistakes of the past and an acknowledgement that old ways of being were no longer appropriate for the emerging technological age. Leo is one of the more creative signs of the zodiac and with Pluto within its borders for twenty years the rebirth and transformation of various forms of creative endeavour became a trademark of the generation with this position.

During the two decades of this transit the development and use of nuclear energy became steadily more of a priority, both in terms of economic power and military might. To a considerable extent the emergence of Pluto into Leo was one of the two main defining astrological aspects of the second global war, the second being the conjoining of Jupiter, Saturn and Uranus in Taurus over 1940-1942. These two factors happening in fixed signs added to the degree of resilience, perseverance and stubbornness of both sides in the conflict and the early part of the 1940's is seen as one of the hardest periods of human history from an astrological perspective. Pluto in Leo may be seen at its most nihilistic during the dropping of atomic bombs on Nagasaki and Hiroshima in 1945. Post war and as Pluto moved into the middle decanate of Leo so the rebuilding of society began in a more creative way, with the Saturn/ Pluto conjunction of 1947 bringing with it both the United Nations and NATO and the determination to never be seen to allow things to get so bad again. It also saw the emergence of a more belligerent development of nation statehood, as perhaps indicated by the rise of both Israel and communist China, as well as Indian independence. By this time, the nature and the face of warfare had changed and instead of worldwide naked aggression, as Pluto moved into the second half of Leo a more recalcitrant and subversive energy became the norm and manifested in what is now known as the 'Cold War.' By the mid 1950's and Pluto's transit of the latter degrees of Leo the developing technological boom coupled well with the advancing age of imagination, as symbolised by the Uranus/Neptune square of 1953-1957, and gave the world an aspiring generation seeking both power and creativity in ways that would have seemed impossible and unimaginable to their parents in their childhood.

This was the time when every household was promised a car and a television as representative of the 'New Age' although it is also the time when the idea of the 'guru' or celebrity became more pervasive in contemporary society. Remember that Leo is the sign of the zodiac that is most associated with children and rock stars and throughout this period of Pluto's stay the tendency for more playful and childlike attitudes towards life in many people was only matched by the emergence of egotistic and omnipotent domineering attitudes in others. The 'baby boom' of the late 1940's and early 1950's is seen as a direct result of soldiers returning from war and wanting to create a new and beautiful life to replace the horrors and traumas of war. It is also at this time that civil rights and the rights of the child became a more manifest concern in the mass gestalt of humanity, as well as a much more tolerant attitude towards artistry and creativity. Of course, there was the archetypal Plutonian backlash as symbolised in the USA by McCarthyism, the suppression of the new in favour of the old born out of fear of change, but this did not really last too long in the face of Plutonian determination.

At the individual level Pluto in Leo provided a complete contrast to the more family orientated side of Pluto in Cancer with the breakdown of traditional family structures and the emergence of more alternative lifestyle choices, as perhaps best demonstrated by the emergence of rock and roll and other similar forms of youth culture in the 1950's. These are the people who became the hippies and permanently changed society's ideas towards love, sex and the raising and education of children, all classic Leonian archetypes. These are the people who opened doorways into the future that had been occluded to previous generations: Pluto in Leo people did not necessarily go through those doors, but they opened them for future generations to explore. This was the first generation to have a conscious awareness of their own destiny being in their own hands as opposed to the larger collective more so than any previous generation, demonstrated best by the emergence of the 'rock star' persona. The previous transit of Pluto through Leo was in the 1690's and early 1700's when John Locke wrote his essays on how governments only existed by voluntary agreements and that their first function was to protect the rights of individuals. The 20th century Pluto in Leo generation seems to have taken this message to heart. This generation is the first of the recent 'me' generations and opened doors into self-development that are still being explored. It is truly the first of the 'youth cultures' that exist routinely today. To quote the astrologer Bob Marks, *Pluto in Leo will always defy authority, unless, of course, they are the authority.*

Pluto in Virgo 1957–1972

This was the time of social experimentation, the 'swinging sixties' and the groups of people that changed the functional ways in which things were done forever, best immortalised by the name 'Generation X.' Social attitudes towards lifestyle management, nutrition, personal health and hygiene, morals and community care became more of a cause and a popular theme of the times. Astrologically this time is best remembered for the four year conjunction of Pluto with Uranus in Virgo over the period of 1963-1967, a time which both transformed and revolutionised society's attitudes towards itself and its structures most notably by the advent in the workplace of electronic culture and automatic technology and in the social world by the emergence of alternative lifestyles. There was a particularly strong time astrologically speaking when oppositions from both Saturn and Chiron together in Pisces in 1965 and 1966 to the Uranus/Pluto conjunction compressed the need for social change as well as the resistance to it and accelerated those concentrated urges in ways that couldn't be ignored or shunted under the carpet. It was the time of Woodstock and the Beatles and Stones: it was when people 'discovered' themselves in India or Peru and it was the time of the recreational drug explosion and the corresponding initial development of the ongoing consciousness revolution.

Pluto in Virgo was the time when people transformed their ideas of work and career. This was the beginning of the end for the meniality of the production line and the boredom of the checkout for most of these people. It is not that these jobs are too menial for these industrial obsessives: it is that their aspirations go way beyond the mundanity of the forty hour week and its attendant routine into something where they can truly demonstrate their efficiency and effectiveness.

During this time, many governments and other forms of authoritarian structures reeled under the sudden onslaught of the need for social change and found themselves hideously unprepared and initially resistant to this wave of change. The old 'power' tendency of Pluto in Leo was still dominant here as evinced by the might and ultimate failure of the American war machine against a much smaller foe in Vietnam, as well as the worldwide protests against both that military involvement and the old fashioned notion of military might still having domain over empire. Yet at the same time a growing cognisance of the need to pull together, to act and unite as a species collectively was being born at this time and because of these protests and other similar ones. It was out of the cognisance that steadily more people emerged to whom service, duty and responsibility for those less fortunate than themselves became gradually the norm. People with a strong Pluto in Virgo position are to be found at the forefront of new, emerging holistic and environmentally friendly technologies that are simplifying life at the daily level and improving conditions worldwide for humanity. Alternatively, others with this position will instead be concentrating on maintaining either their personal or the global status quo with increasing efficiency and effectiveness in an almost robotic or machine-like and dispassionate way, because order must be preserved at all costs!

As they age individuals with this aspect aspire to find a more holistic and integrated way of seeing and experiencing the world without having to conform to old stereotypes of belief or behaviour in ways that previous generations have done. Pluto in Virgo people are the ones who question not so much the authority but the nature of authority itself and as they have aged have become increasingly and willingly self-reliant rather than be at the behest of others. In general, these people have a more naturopathic attitude to life as opposed to allopathic: they tend to look for the cause rather than at the symptoms and have a more integrated attitude. Here is found the first generation who grew up with processed foods as opposed to organic, but here also are found the first 'food freaks,' those people at the forefront of the push for cleaner and healthier produce as well as a more natural approach to medicine. The 'packaging' of the world began properly during these times, as machines began to properly replace human labour.

Similarly, Pluto in Virgo brought with it an innovative approach to the idea of 'work' and whether that included job, career and goals alone, or whether it also included words like vocation, passion and enthusiasm. These are the people who want to be able to enjoy their work knowing that others get as much benefit from it as they do; they want to be able to get out of bed in the morning with a willingness in their step. This is why so many of them either end up in positions of management if not authority or else end up working for themselves. These people will go to the ends of the earth if it means that they can get things done properly no matter how difficult the things that emerge from the undergrowth. There is an oddly perverse side to this Pluto position in that it is strangely fascinated by the very pollution and corruption it is trying to cleanse and purify. A person with a strongly aspected Pluto in Virgo will be seen as the most orderly and efficient in terms of doing what they do but there is a need not to take this too far, lest the same individual be seen as obsessive or compulsive.

Pluto in Libra 1971–1984

Libra is the sign of the zodiac commonly associated with relationship patterns and Pluto is the planet that uses words like transformation, regeneration and rebirth as its mantras, so the journey of Pluto through Libra was going to change the ways in which individuals and collectives managed their relationship patterns. It would be fair to say that the potential destructive and dynamically transformative energies of Pluto do not appear to mesh well with the more delicate, elegant and diplomatic side of Libra unless there is a total willingness from the word go to embrace the ideals of equality not only in word but in every single action of one's life. Equality needs to be the consistent intention at a constant day by day level to avoid the pitfalls of Plutonic temptation and as both individuals and groups with this position weigh their options as time evolves so the need for greater transparency, equality and synergetic teamwork becomes apparent.

Collectively Pluto in Libra was known as the divorce generation, or even 'Generation Y,' a group who collectively questioned the need for orthodox and organised relationships as least as they had been presented as being. This is the generation who looked at historic and cultural ways of existing with 'other' and asked questions like 'why does it always have to be this way'? Until Pluto's entry into Libra families were supposed to stay together come what may and regardless of difficulty or problem which led to decades of unhappiness, misery and depression. Pluto's capacity for annihilation and destruction wreaked havoc in orthodox and conventional couples' lives, bringing the dawning awareness that a healthy interaction requires the participation of two willing and equal partners, a policy and philosophy that had been fundamentally absent in modern society until this time. Pluto in Libra people can never take too much for granted because to do so would only encourage complacency, one of Pluto's magnets for dramatic change. The days of convenience marriages and relationships started coming to an irrevocable end with this transit. In the outside world, the strongest and most obvious of the changing gender balance came when Margaret Thatcher became the first female Prime Minister of the UK and then declared war on Argentina.

50

Elsewhere the more elegant and glamorous side of Libra insinuated itself into Pluto's domain with the election of Ronald Reagan in the USA, an actor in the White House playing the biggest role of all.

At the personal level, the rights of the individual became more enshrined in law, especially those of women and children, and this in turn changed the nature of relationship patterns at the one to one level across the board. Divorce levels reached what was (for then) record highs. Despite the necessity of interacting with other and others at an equally based level to find healthy relationships, some of the Pluto in Libra generation people can sometimes act quite conversely. These are the people who want everything from those around them but as a test of other people's trust in them as opposed to a demand or requirement. For some of these people it can take many years to really trust someone and even then, there sometimes must be a life/death or other type of critical yes/no situation for these people to really trust others. There is a basic philosophy here that says, 'how can you help anyone else if you're not in good working order yourself,' but at the same time deliberately choosing not to remain an island and to mingle and mix with humanity despite its many apparent flaws.

This is the generation that is changing the model when it comes to establishing new patterns of family interactions. Here is found the changing roles within family with more fathers staying at home or where both parents are working, changes that have stayed permanent as time and Pluto has moved on. Here also can be found the origins of greater and broader tolerance to non-heterosexual people with alternative rights becoming a major theme in society during this transit with the emergence of same sex relationships and families.

Pluto in Scorpio 1984–1996

During the 1960s and 1970s, the few contemporary astrological textbooks that existed were dry, very orthodox and the interpretations of the influences of Pluto were still settling and consolidating. Nevertheless, astrologers around the world had agreed by the end of the 1970s on the rulership of Scorpio by Pluto at least to a shared degree with Mars if not totally on its own. And the imminent transit of Pluto through Scorpio was occupying the minds of the astrological community of the time in a way that was quite cautious, even scared. It was seen as the time of 'transform or die' to quote The Astrologer's Handbook.

This twelve year period of Pluto in Scorpio covered three other hugely significant astrological transits. This process began with the conjunction of Mars, Saturn and Uranus all passing together into Capricorn during mid-February 1988, was immediately followed by the conjunction of Saturn with Neptune in Capricorn throughout 1989 and was at a peak at the Uranus/Neptune conjunction, again in Capricorn in 1993. Immediately prior to Pluto's movement into Scorpio in November 1983 the world was a vastly different place to what it is now. Astrologically the previous twelve months had been dominated by a long conjunction of Saturn with Pluto at the end of Libra that in ways curtailed, obstructed and blocked the emerging signs of Plutonic transformation. Saturn flirted with the beginning of Scorpio before retrograding back into Libra and reporting to Pluto one last time and then finally the scene was set. By the end of 1983 and for the next two years both Saturn and Pluto were going to be passing through Scorpio and there would be no prisoners taken.

In terms of manifest developments there are two striking examples of this time. In the United Kingdom there was a near two year strike by the mining community of the country against the union reforms of Thatcherism. This involved pitched battles between mounted police and large groups of miners in ways that were almost reminiscent of the civil war, certainly the only time in living memory involving mounted charges on British soil. The astrological analogy is so clear here. The mining community, which suffered tremendous hardships in its struggle against reforms, was working in the dark bowels of the earth bringing the 'black stuff' from the depths of the underworld to the surface whilst Pluto and Saturn, the transformer and the rebuilder were entering Scorpio intent on reform. There was only going to be one ultimate winner there. In addition, this was also the time of the next chapter of the sexual revolution with AIDS and related phenomena. For a decade fear of sexually transmitted diseases reached a high not seen since the morally oppressive times of the 1950s and particularly in the non-heterosexual communities a culture of both ultra caution and its opposite, total hedonism emerged. Only as Pluto began to leave Scorpio in the mid 1990's was it seen that AIDS was not the terror or the killer it had been presumed to be and that properly managed many if not most sufferers continue to live a healthy lifestyle. One of the side effects of this was that a much more open and informed attitude towards contraception became obvious worldwide, especially in television and newspaper outlets. From mid-1988 to early 1991, Saturn was in its own sign of Capricorn whilst Pluto was in its own sign of Scorpio, a time strangely reminiscent of the time of writing of this book, with Pluto in Saturn's sign of Capricorn whilst Saturn is in Pluto's sign of Scorpio. It was during this influence at the very end of the 1980's and the corresponding conjunction of Saturn with Neptune that the first codings were postulated that would eventually become the internet. It was also the time of both the fall of the Berlin wall and of the Tiananmen Square massacre in China. Looking back on the period of 1989 and 1990, it can be seen as one of the most radical and forcibly transformative times in modern history, as dominoes seemed to tumble one after the other.

Politically Pluto's passage through Scorpio heralded changes that would have been inconceivable even a decade previously. Up until the early 1980's those people born since the end of the second global war had constantly lived in what became known as the Cold War with the knowledge that 'the bomb could drop' at any moment. However, it was as Pluto began to establish itself in Scorpio that this attitude suddenly changed with the rise to dominance of Mikhail Gorbachev in the Soviet Union. He brought with him the policies of 'glasnost' (openness and transparency, particularly appropriate considering the Plutonian times) and 'perestroika' (restructuring, again appropriate with Saturn in Scorpio at the time). This in a stroke defused the Cold War and was the start of the dismantling of the Soviet empire. Within five years of Gorbachev's rise to power countries annexed by the Soviets in the late 1940's had reclaimed their autonomy in a rising tide of rebellion and nationalism and by the time that Pluto left Scorpio for the final time in November 1995 the Cold War and the accompanying potential threat of nuclear annihilation had almost completely disappeared. However, as one threat receded so another developed. In 1990, many countries of the world united to engage the forces of Saddam Hussein and Iraq in the first Gulf war, a shot across the bows for times to come.

In terms of individual experience, the generations born with Pluto in Scorpio have become increasingly capable of yes/no, black/white decisions as their peer group reaches a degree of prominence. It is the generation that has changed the ways that value is manifested in the world and how money is managed. Individuals with a prominent Scorpionic Pluto have rewritten the rulebooks when it comes to words like efficiency, ruthlessness, incision and psychology.

Pluto in Sagittarius 1995–2008

By the end of Pluto's transit through Scorpio, astrologers around the world were reeling with the enormity of the manifestations of these times and wondering what was coming next. After the expectations of nuclear war had turned into nuclear peace and the global terror of sexual disease had become another in a line of virals and toxins that were steadily killing us, opinions of Pluto and its methodology were changing rapidly. Within the space of just over a decade the financial revolution and the accompanying technological boom had taken the world by storm and was accelerating fast. By seeking and identifying Pluto's influence at the subversive and hidden level in these events, astrologers suggested that the archetypal Sagittarian themes of higher education, religion, travel and law were next in line for transformation at the most basic of levels. In this light, the major astrological aspect of the times alongside Pluto entering Sagittarius is the corresponding movement of Uranus into Aquarius. With both big hitters moving from feminine Scorpio and Capricorn into masculine Sagittarius and Aquarius within a couple of months of each other, the sudden shift of emphasis towards technology and electronic community really began to take off at the start of 1996.

With the advent of the internet and increasingly compacted communications systems, global travel, whether in terms of direct experience or in virtual terms became a much more common experience adding immensely to the store of human knowledge and the sharing of different anthropological backgrounds and cultures. Everybody became potentially 'connected' in a way that could never have been conceived of thirty years previously and the development of social media and its offshoots have changed forever the ways in which humanity both sees itself and how it communicates. Despite its many teething problems, the almost surreptitious arrival of artificial intelligence in our collective midst as symbolised by the internet has enabled and empowered people from every nation to interact with each other in a way that defies conventional borders. As a result of this the collective ideas of justice and law went through massive reformation and change with a much greater emphasis on community and environmental rights.

As the information exchange began to become a permanent feature in society, the awareness of the need for better education became both obvious and paramount. Pluto passing through Sagittarius helped change and transform global attitudes towards education. One way of seeing this, albeit influenced by the Aquarian influence of Uranus, was the acknowledgement that education is a basic human right and that every child in the world was entitled to a scholarly education at least to some degree. Alternatively, the opposite perspective can also be seen in political attitudes towards education during this transit, as demonstrated by the commercialisation of higher education and the introduction of high fees for specific teachings often sponsored or funded by commercial organisations with an interest in recruiting the products of those teachings. Pluto's capacity for going to extremes can be seen here at the end of its time in Sagittarius with top universities having tripled their fees within a decade whilst at the same time philanthropic entrepreneurs were handing out free solar powered laptops to remote villages in Africa.

It is around religion that Pluto in Sagittarius has been at its most virulent and powerful. At the start of its transit many astrologers were predicting that Pluto would bring its transformative and eliminative energies into the field of religion worldwide with potentially terminal effect. Looking back, church attendances planet wide and, in all religions, have fallen steadily in the last twenty years despite an ever increasing population. Pluto's legacy here is not so much the elimination of religious attitudes but the transformation of them, especially when it comes to the individual defining for themselves what their relationship with the Divine or divinity is. However, what nobody expected but astrologers should have predicted was that Pluto's capacity for extremism would find a happy niche in the religious side of Sagittarius, bringing with it all manner of fundamentalism, religious extremism and inflexibility. This is best seen through the Pluto/Saturn opposition of 2001 and the corresponding bombing of New York by fundamentalists which served as a trigger point for the second Gulf war. (Writing in the national newspaper The Daily Mirror, on August 6th 2001, I wrote *Saturn in Gemini (2001-03) is telling us to restructure our systems of communication, whilst Pluto in Sagittarius (1995-2008) is transforming our attitudes towards truth, philosophy and religion.*

The opposition of these planets occurs every 35 years, from last night until May 2002. During this time, intensification, and hopefully, resolution of religious conflict worldwide (Israel, N. Ireland, Afghanistan etc.) can be expected whilst extremism will rise in the short term. The opposition hits the USA horoscope powerfully, and immense changes in American political, financial and even constitutional circles are more than possible, even probable. Closer to home, "secrets and lies" will be exposed, with individuals demanding far greater accountability, commitment and truth across the board, both personally and professionally. It's time to revolutionise our concepts about honesty, religion and communication. Don't we all deserve a better future?).

It became apparent as Pluto approached the end of Sagittarius that as the numbers of religious devotees diminished in the face of emerging technology and individual self-determination so the capacity for extremism in the remnants became increasingly volatile and potential, leading to many of the troubles associated with Pluto in the next sign of Capricorn. It can certainly be said that Pluto in Sagittarius transformed forever the ways in which we collectively and individually see God.

Pluto in Capricorn 2008–2024

Capricorn deals with structures, especially collective ones such as governments and other similar large organisations. Pluto deals with transformation at all levels both personally and globally. The combination of these two energies could easily bring a collective rebirth in ideas of governance and it can just as easily bring nihilistic opposition to all changes at any level. Most astrologers agree that Pluto in Capricorn is a favourable influence broadly speaking, in that it will be seen as positively changing and regenerating the ways in which we live together in our social and economic groups.

When looking at the comparatively recent concentrated planetary activity in Capricorn it can be seen how the power bases of world politics have changed forever in the last thirty years. The movement of Saturn and Pluto together into Scorpio in 1982/3 presaged a decade of unimaginable change, compressing and intensifying the common feeling of dissatisfaction in the world and accelerating the urge for transformation. This manifested in the late eighties with the advent of the technological revolution and the end of the old power blocs as symbolised by both the Saturn/Uranus and the Saturn/

Neptune conjunctions in Capricorn, within a year of each other. A few years later in 1994/5 just as Pluto left Scorpio, the Uranus/Neptune conjunction in Capricorn was at its height and the monoliths of power were either being forcibly transformed and changed or else they just slipped away, like sand and water in the tides. The transits of Saturn, Uranus and Neptune through Capricorn in the late 1980's and the early 1990's changed the ways in which the world was run whether politically, economically or militarily and gave the world a good shot at making things work before the time of examination came in with Pluto entering Capricorn in 2008.

Saturn, ruling structure and boundaries and Uranus, ruling chaos and revolution, moved into Capricorn together in February 1988. In early 2008 Pluto passed at the same degree, scrutinising everything done by that conjunction in a way that was both intense and merciless. Saturn and Uranus together tried to rewrite the rules of economics in 1988 and Pluto responded thirty years later in 2008 by symbolically initiating the biggest financial crash since the late 1920's. Saturn with its discipline and order and Neptune with its capacity for dissolution and imagination came together in 1989 at eleven and twelve degrees of Capricorn and in ways this aspect is seen as the initiator of the internet. Pluto is passing over these degrees during 2013 and 2014 as can be seen in the exposure of celebrity sex offenders, the attempted control of the internet and the resultant development of 'darknets' where drugs, arms and paedophilia is traded daily. This is against the increasingly obvious hypocrisy and misogyny of most mainstream media canvassing against smut whilst using it to sell their wares. Pluto will pass over the degree of the 1994 Uranus/Neptune conjunction in 2018 and 2019 which should theoretically bring conclusion to the ongoing social experiment that seems to have involuntarily developed since the late 1980's. The times of 2018 and 2019 will also see the conjunction of Saturn and Pluto together in Capricorn. Astrologically speaking it might be said that the start of the recent evolutionary surge was marked by the conjunction of Saturn with Pluto at the start of Scorpio, Pluto's sign. If that were to be so it could equally be said that the conjunction of Saturn with Pluto in Capricorn, Saturn's sign, will be the end of this process.

The overriding astrological influence during Pluto's transit through Capricorn is clearly the square between Pluto and Uranus repeating to a considerable extent the patterning of the last time this happened in 1929-32 and with similar but different developments. Eighty five years ago Pluto was in Cancer and Uranus in Aries, suggestive of conflict between individuals and the needs of the family and tribe. Nowadays with Pluto in Capricorn and Uranus in Aries the conflict is more between the needs of the individual (human rights) and the needs of the corporate or nation state.

With Pluto not yet halfway through Capricorn at the time of writing it is too early to say what the influences of this transit will be long term both on individuals and collectives. What can be said safely is that old ideas of politics and governance are clearly being seen as archaic and redundant and that innovative ideas of representation, governance and individual responsibility are beginning to take hold. It is these ideas that hopefully will enable humanity to use the power of the upcoming Saturn/Pluto conjunction in 2018 and 2019 to launch ourselves in a collectively entirely different direction. The alternative does not bear thinking about...

6

Pluto in the houses

In the following section, the nature of each of the individual twelve zodiac houses is summarised before presenting an in-depth description of the influence of Pluto at its best, in its neutral state and its most challenging in each house.

Pluto in the first house

The first house is commonly experienced as being the area of the horoscope that defines the relationship that one has with oneself. It is known as the house of identity and as such deals with everything that relates and pertains to issues of individuality, self-development, self-acceptance and personal space, as well as the lack of these things. Related to dynamic and fiery Aries, Pluto here is astrologically not challenged but should not either be considered a lightweight as it brings a sense of both depth and gravity into ideas of identity and self.

A favourably aspected Pluto in the first house suggests that the transformative urge is strong and that the individual will go through a number of firsthand experiences designed to test their strength of character. At the same time, this breeds and infuses a sense of personal invulnerability and stamina that becomes steadily both stronger and more obvious as the person ages and evolves. It gives the willingness to go the extra mile, to be able to stand up for oneself and to come across to the world as someone who is strong and consistent in their output and who presents a kind of steely eyed determination, powerful gaze and a firm jaw. There can be an almost innate tendency to see life as a struggle that needs to be 'battled' and overcome, as this is the only guaranteed way to be sure of oneself, or to compensate for any real or imagined vulnerability. It can and normally does signify a strong will power, a powerful concentration and a degree of emotional determination that can be almost unstoppable. Pluto here is likely to have a firmly established set of personal values, as well as the capacity to express them to the best of one's ability and is often experienced by others as being ultra-resourceful and structured in a way that tolerates no interference. It is not that concerned about public image or other peoples' opinions, instead preferring to concentrate on the maintaining of a degree of both personal dignity and external integrity. At the same time, many with this position show an almost fanatical desire to be an agent of change for others. It is as though their own personal transformation can only be achieved through the catalysation of other people, sometimes to the point of obtrusiveness. Furthermore, there can be a penetratingly deep understanding of human dynamics, but often this is kept to oneself.

When in a neutral space, Pluto in the first house can come across as almost ruthless in its application to life. It is as though there is an unconscious compulsion driving the individual towards something indiscernible in the future and that they must constantly strive, to extremes, for the potential reward to be worthwhile. There will be the archetypal Plutonian obsession with mysteries and secrets and the need to be preoccupied or focussed on something for most if not all the time. When asked difficult or personally invasive questions, individuals with Pluto in the first house are likely to unleash an intense gaze, making the questioner more than a little unsure of both themselves and of what they are asking. A sense of purpose is always evident, even if they do not know what that purpose is. There is something very strident about this position that at times can be almost eliminative towards oneself and can lead to occasional periods of purging, cleansing and detoxing. The imagery of the first house Pluto person who occasionally retreats into the dark, shadowy confines of their cave to undergo periodic recuperation and transformation has an almost shamanistic feel to it and they can be very protective of their privacy. Pluto in the first house people can desire to spend their time alone, although the universe rarely lets this happen. There is a need to avoid puritanical attitudes towards oneself or to demand too much of others lest alienation occurs. Cooperation can sometimes be just that little step too far for these rugged individualists of the zodiac. These are the people who dress to impress, often in black with a touch of crimson, a kind of goth/vampire chic that says, 'mess with me at your peril.'

A challenging Pluto in the first house can have a fanatical and potentially compulsive attitude towards personal transformation, often going through periods of almost phobic intensity (although this is more common in those under forty than in later years). In some cases, there can be a destructive element, manifesting rarely in cases of self-denigration or self-harm. Commonly, there can be a rejection complex during the first half of life and an element of alienation, leading to a lack of self-esteem, embittered resentment, or both. There will always be an element of extremism present, although the more mature eventually learn how to both manage and channel this energy into incredible accomplishments. These are the people who are often said to burn others out, primarily because their level of personal involvement in whatever they are interactively engaged with will always be optimum, which the rest of the world will often have trouble keeping up with or else find intimidating. Every so often a period of crisis or trauma – or sometimes both – can occur, which whilst extremely challenging for the duration nevertheless brings along with its difficulties the required energy and determination to overcome those challenges, regardless of the cost. This can be the person who will go all out to achieve their goals and will not allow anyone or anything to stand in their way no matter what. A difficult first house position of Pluto will often have an obsessive component to its nature, which can only be transformed into something more positive by metaphorically and sometimes literally going through the torment represented by the fires of hell. As a client with Pluto in the 1stt house wrote, *'It's like this deep urge for transformation can happen both consciously and unconsciously – either I move into the fire willingly, because I crave the intensity and insanity of it all, or it happens anyway without my consent. Some part of me wants to transform, and transform it will, I have absolutely no say in it, I just have to go with the flow and enjoy the grilling.'* Pluto in the first house people are more self-aware than most and they wrote the manual on self-transformation and self-identification; they know themselves, warts and all. Remember, Pluto is Hades by another name and when going through the darkness of their own personal underworld, these power obsessed individuals are sometimes best left alone. Every so often, a little purging harms no-one and it does keep oneself both clean and sharp.

Pluto in the second house

The second house, normally associated with Taurus, is commonly accepted as being the house that pertains to issues of value, usually but not necessarily material ones. It describes where one finds value in oneself, in the outside world and what it is both in the material world and in terms of human behaviour that is considered worthy. Pluto is often seen as the agent of transformation from one state of awareness to another, sometimes from lower awareness to higher, at other times the opposite. However, when it comes to material values, Pluto in the second house assumes an attitude of 'you cannot take it with you,' hence this position's ongoing lifetime experiences of different types of value and worth. It should be remembered that astrologers consider Pluto to be at its strongest in Scorpio, the eighth sign, relating to the eighth house and that as a result Pluto is in its detriment in the second house.

When Pluto in the second house is under positive aspect, the individual will normally exhibit a commonsensical theme around the value systems in their life, knowing that their needs will always be met but that they may have to work at making their wants or even their desires come true. There will normally be a grounded and practical approach to the day by day lifestyle, often indicated in the first forty years of life by the desire to have beautiful things, people and environments in one's surroundings and to not be 'without.' As the years pass, so the value systems transform from that of quantity to that of quality and whilst the number of materials or possessions may decrease, the refinement and thus the pleasure derived from these things will steadily increase as one ages, to the point in certain fields of considering oneself a connoisseur. At the end of the day most of these people eventually realise that money is for spending and that there is more pleasure gained from generosity and benevolence and the spreading of resources around than there is from scrimping or hoarding. There is also the ongoing realisation that wealth is not just about money, possessions or other tangible assets; it is as much to do with one's own sense of inner security and the way that one finds value in and with oneself. The healthier the relationship one has with oneself is, the more centred and grounded the person's values becomes as time passes and the better the overall quality of the things, relationships, resources and materials in one's life.

When viewed from a neutral perspective, the purpose of Pluto in the second house is that of the transformation and regeneration of value. This can be the position of the bull in the china shop where the desired objective is focussed upon, the neck and head are lowered and anything that gets in the way had best watch out because the individual is coming through! Yet there is also the desire for increased sophistication as one ages and whilst the individual can sometimes regard attachment to anything or anyone with a degree of impersonal bemusement, their basic philosophy becomes that of either the best or nothing, although their experience and description of what that 'best' consists of changes and is refined over the years and decades. Because of Pluto's relative unease in the second house, there can be a kind of subterranean impulse around the level of personal control in one's life. As a client stated, '*I recognise the anachronistic in my patterns but feel clueless as they are shadowy.*' There is a need to recognise within oneself the nature of possession and attachment. Pluto in the second house will happily give away anything – but woe betide anyone who tries to take it from them without asking. There are clear boundaries about what belongs to the person and what does not. These are the people who can 'take it or leave it,' who can metaphorically transcend their attachment to the material world. In time, they learn to be free of attachment and by using their own internal resources they can develop a steady and consistent sense of personal self-worth, although even with that transcendence of value there will still be no separation from the material world.

When under a difficult aspect, Pluto in the second house can represent the most unsubtle of energies. In the worst cases, it can result in extreme jealousy, overt possessiveness of things, money and people and a phobia of being without. It can foster resentment towards other or others for what is seen as their better fortune, although in truth this reflects one's own insecurity about oneself. It is as if the individual can never have enough and that their purse or pockets will never be full no matter how much they have. Again, this attitude or feeling of poverty no matter how physically wealthy points to a lack of internal value of oneself. There can sometimes be an unconscious fear of abandonment, often rooted in a childhood spent without much in terms of physical or material comfort and hugs and cuddles, often both. What can be seen as resilience and steadfastness when it comes to maintaining a chosen lifestyle can easily turn into dogmatic stubbornness if not careful, which in turn generates a refusal to move with the times. This can result in anachronistic patterns developing where one becomes knowingly stuck in outdated value systems and yet at the same time fearful of change to an almost paralysing degree. It eventually can lead to the Pluto in the second house individual demanding that others change to suit them, thus attracting the more manipulative or weak energies instead of the potentially joyous and equally based energies that most good relationships work on. What good does having all the gold in the world do if there is no-one else to share it with? This can be a sometimes callous and survivalist position, often with the ends justifying the means, but as one evolves so hopefully the need for simply having so much dissipates. Constantly being in rigid and inflexible control of one's resources can often lead to a possessive nature and there may be times of irrationally compulsive spending. Nevertheless, this position will constantly challenge the individual to upgrade and update their value system as the times change, or else run the risk of becoming stuck in the past.

Pluto in the third house

The third house, with its Geminian nature based on communication of all types, can be a very fertile breeding ground for Pluto. Here the power of the mind, the spoken word and the communication systems of both old and new that operate between people are emphasised and one's persuasive skills can often be called into use in ways that are quite subtle in their application. The third house is also concerned with one's immediate environment and the relationships one has with siblings and/or close neighbours and Pluto here can bring the desire for control over one's surroundings in a way that needs to be measured and respectful of others' space.

If Pluto in the third house is in receipt of favourable aspects, then different skillsets are likely to be present. There will be an insatiable curiosity and a powerful and penetrating mind, where the individual will possess strong opinions and attitudes on different matters and will not hesitate to let them be known should the need arise. The voice may have a degree of projectivity about it that almost compels the recipient to not only hear but to actively listen. Pluto in the third house brings with it the capacity for inspiration, primarily by constantly refreshing and updating one's mental circuitry, as well as being up to date with emerging contemporary communication systems. There will often be a kind of resilience that produces both a mental and verbal consistency, evident in the ways that the person deals with other people both at the individual and at the group level. These Plutonian powered individuals will go to incredibly thorough lengths to ensure that people understand what they mean and that their ideas are being listened to. There can be a fraternal relationship with some of the people around oneself and often these natives end up feeling that their true family is not necessarily that of flesh and blood, but more those that espouse love and friendship without any pre-set conditions or rules. Pluto in the third house people can be obsessively involved in ongoing social media to an extent that it can consume them, at least at the daily level. These are the people who like to know where everything is in their neighbourhood and when it is all happening, as well as when to expect their loved ones home for dinner. It is not that they are control freaks, but having a semblance of routine helps calm their restless mind and puts them into a 'chill zone' where they can almost mindlessly get on with the daily business whilst at the same time at the subliminal and psychological level they are working out possible answers to some of the greatest problems in life.

When Pluto is not significantly aspected in this house, or when it does not come under scrutiny or pressure, it can be one of the most innovative thinkers in the zodiac, knowing full well that knowledge is power and that they will never stop learning. They are not attracted to superficialities, instead being drawn by the deeper mysteries of life, but there will always be a degree of intensity about the mind. This is best used and managed by finding something deep for it to do; hence these people's occupations often involve some type of detective work or research, whether academic, magical, mathematical, investigative or otherwise. They are imperious when it comes to finding out things and uncovering buried truths, with a scarily accurate ability to spot someone lying the second they open their mouth. Pluto in the third house is incredibly good at ferreting out people's motives. They will often go through periods of vocal abstinence, only to then pontificate at length about something and not be able to shut up. Yet amid this budgerigar-like outpouring there will also be one or two kernels of pure wisdom and if only they could be refined out of the mix of superficial chit chat, this person would then find other people paying them a lot more attention. They like to think that they are in complete control of their nervous system and that facial tics are for other people. They undoubtedly take in every word, even if they do not superficially react, instead giving the indifferent poker face and they do remember, even if it takes years for them to say so. It might also be said, as a client with Pluto in the third house delightfully states, that '*this Pluto position yearns for a more light-hearted approach to life from time to time whilst knowing for them that it is not truly possible.*'

When Pluto in the third house comes under a difficult aspect, there can be extremes of expression. The individual can be embarrassingly shy, bordering on the timid. Alternatively, they can be bombastic, loving the sound of their own voice to the point of not letting anyone else have a say or even an opinion, guaranteed to lose them friends. There will be trust issues relating to the duality of life and diversity of attitude and there may be a tendency to put oneself or others down in terms of output value or intelligence. It is quite common for siblings with this position to grow up apart from each other, or for there to be a type of quiet antagonism between them often related to issues concerning trust and transparency. The sensible person with this position learns from an early age that if someone will lie to them once, they will do it again and again, so an eliminative attitude towards deceitful people is a necessity in order for these people to work out whom they can really trust, although this can sometimes take many years. This position becomes far less challenging once the individual realises that in order to know the truth, they first of all have to be the truth in order to recognise it and that only honest and straightforward people are going to be a part of their future. The more unevolved types with position may in themselves be sometimes duplicitous, not willing to look at their deeper sides lest there be something they would rather not see. It is not so much that they are scared of anything in particular as much as they are scared of what might be, a kind of fear of being afraid, often leading to a sharp tongue directed or projected towards others as a placebo for the alternative of looking at oneself, although the opposite and equally valid way of seeing this is introspection played out via the world stage, where the individual has a role of being almost the passive observer.

Pluto in the fourth house

The fourth house, located at the base of the chart, is the area of the horoscope that governs affairs of the home, roots and foundations, whether family or emotional. This covers a multitude of different areas, loosely coming under headings of emotional and residential security and stability, family consistency and parent/child relationships. The base of the horoscope supports and maintains the rest of the chart, leading to the identification of the fourth house with the main nurturing influence when young, normally the mother. Pluto in this house will bring an element of intensity into some of the above mentioned and cannot be ignored without risking a degree of rot and decay developing in one's own personal underworld. Pluto here is also strongly associated with the 'death and rebirth' experience, where the theme of ongoing regeneration through endings and new beginnings is continually emphasised in many separate ways.

With a favourably aspected Pluto in the fourth house comes the ability to be seen as the 'strong one' in family circles, the one who does not break and who holds things together when everyone else is losing the plot. There can be a 'my home is my castle' attitude, where once within the front door there is a quite different lifestyle to that manifested in the outside world. Pluto's prime interest here is that of family security, so people with this natal position should strive for a home lifestyle of tranquillity based on everyone in the family home getting on with little if any dissent. It is common for these people to assume the main nurturing and provisional role within the family regardless of gender and the establishment and healthy running of the family home is in ways the pinnacle of success for these security conscious home builders. The relationships with women within the family may have a measure of intensity about them, regardless of one's own gender, at times to the point of feeling overwhelmed. There is no major cause for concern here, merely a willingness to uncover family secrets and bring them into the open rather than leaving them to fester in a deniable pit of neglect and shame. There may be the desire to uncover family history, even in the face of opposition, on the grounds that things are better dealt with out in the open rather than subversively. This position enables the individual to reach out across different generations of family and to assume the role of 'the wise one,' who mediates and brings differing sides together.

A passive or more neutrally placed Pluto will bring an acceptance of all things both nurturing and feminine and an openness to the more sensitive sides of life, especially within the confines of the family home. There will be an awareness of all diverse types of psychological nuances ongoing within the home, family and immediate environment, whether blatant and deliberate or innocuous and unintentional. As the individual ages, their desire for emotional self-sufficiency becomes more important, hopefully at the same time without building towers of isolation. It is a transformation of foundation that is being asked of the individual here, to change their inner security into something more solid and reflect this into the outside world. They will venture out into the world and even let the world into their home, but only under their terms. There is a need for the individual with this position to be honest, transparent and clear with themselves about their childhood, without being simultaneously judgemental about themselves or others. Pluto here often brings with it a willingness to go that extra mile to deal with the past, knowing that only by doing so properly can they facilitate a future allowed to develop without baggage or hindrance. A sensible person with this position will make allowances for the occasional emotional upheavals that inevitably erupt around home and family, knowing that it is better to get the poison out to where it can be dealt with rather than allow it to be suppressed into a place where it festers and then becomes really difficult to manage.

Challenging aspects to Pluto in the fourth house indicate a degree of dysfunctionality somewhere within the family structure, occasionally to a level that can border on the extreme or even abusive, although this is less likely to be physical, instead bordering on the mental and emotional. There may be a degree of emotional suppression evident during childhood, where the individual finds it hard or even impossible to express themselves without fear of criticism. It can create difficult relationship patterns with what is likely to be seen as a dominating or controlling parent and once an adult, there may be the need for the native to live more than a reasonable travelling distance from the family home in order to find a degree of balance in their own personal life without undue influence from their past. It sometimes helps if people with this position try to appreciate what their parents' childhood would have been like, there finding some type of reason or justification for their own childhood experiences. And sometimes it is not just enough to forgive one's parents or grandparents, it is necessary first to forgive oneself and to deliberately and consciously choose not to allow domineering patterns of influence from one's childhood to influence their adulthood, especially the relationship one has with one's own children. By not dealing with childhood traumas, the potential for these difficult circumstances to be perpetuated further down the family chain is strong, getting steadily harder to deal with as the generations pass. It is important to absolve oneself of guilt surrounding the relationship with the parents – it is enough to know that you did your best, which after all is all that is realistically being asked of anyone. With a difficulty aspected Pluto in the fourth house, it is best if the individual and their parents become friends as they age, rather than perpetuating a dysfunctional parent/child relationship.

Pluto in the fifth house

The fifth house is the house connected with the creative principle and sometimes the most common example of creativity is experienced through the procreative urge of having children. The fifth house is also the area connected with the more romantic and sometimes transient side of love, the ability to have fun and to be childlike as opposed to childish. It is where one can be overt and demonstrative without worrying too much about looking the fool. Pluto here brings an element of depth into the more light-hearted sides of life, but in a way that encourages confidence in oneself through play and the stretching of one's boundaries through creative development. It brings the native into contact with the concept of 'ego' and the challenge to either be consumed by it or to transcend it – or at least to make the attempt – is a recurring theme in life.

When Pluto in the fifth is well placed or in receipt of beneficial aspects, there can be a depth of creative potential that truly astounds those around them. It is as though these people have a direct line to pure creativity that they can occasionally access which is somehow denied to other lesser mortals in the rest of the population. Their libido becomes steadily more refined as they age, and they learn that the quality of exquisite sensuality they can steadily access far outweighs the potential of low level sexuality. There can be a sense of achievement that gets steadily stronger as one ages and witnesses the fruits of one's labour and this can translate into a really justifiable pride where one is proud of oneself for having stuck at it, knowing that only by dogmatic and perseverant work over a period of time does the truly worthwhile and valid gradually emerge out of the mix. This pride can be most obviously demonstrated when the relationship of the fifth house Pluto person with their children is considered. The fifth house is related to Leo and the story goes that you can tread on a lion's tail but if you tread on their children then you are dead. This is the lion's pride and when translated to the fifth house it gives an almost fanatical determination to provide for one's children, even to the point of going without oneself in order that they may benefit. Yet when the children leave home, the need to rediscover one's creative urge and potential becomes heightened. As the Pluto in the fifth house personality evolves and develops over the decades, the quality of one's creative output becomes more important than the quantity. At the most basic of levels this is the individual who needs to feel free to always express themselves, whilst still retaining an element of the innocence and the wonder of childhood.

From a neutral perspective, this position gives the individual both stamina and durability without being ostentatious. By living a life of experience tinged with conscious knowledge, this position in time becomes the wise one with an innocence or simplicity about them that becomes steadily more believable to others as time goes on. Although these people are not given to speculation or gambling, other people can never be quite that sure whether the fifth house Pluto person is bluffing or not. Rarely do these superficially playful people take risks: but when they do, they normally win simply because it is do or die with them. They will go to the edge and beyond to get their way, so only play cards with them if you are sure of your hand. When they do finally decide to do something specific, then Pluto in the fifth house will act in an almost clinical way that really is all or nothing. As a client explains, '*there can be an almost obsessive or compulsive search for depth and meaning in the context of personal creativity, the desire to wrench something twisted, dark and beautiful out of the sea of consciousness and then present it to the world.*' It is that attitude that brings not so much luck as fortune; rarely do they have to retreat into their cave to lick their wounds. It may be that their life revolves around children in a large way, bigger than just parenting. They may work with education, neonatal care or they may particularly be drawn to working with children with specific challenges and needs. But at the end of the day, their energy is best used in doing something special rather than just being someone special and making their creative output the vehicle for their and others personal transformation. As another client put it '*creativity seems to be more accessible when self-discipline is exercised via willpower.*'

When under a challenging aspect, Pluto in the fifth house can show different forms of a central theme of staying forever in early childhood, generally under eight years. This can be the 'little miss' or the 'little lord,' always needful of being on show and quite willing to throw an on the spot tantrum if they are not the centre of attention. When adult, it is common for there to be a degree of unconscious jealousy towards their children, because suddenly, they are not in the spotlight anymore and children's needs must come first. Rarely, this can be the arrogant and conceited parent who pushes their child in the hope that the child can be what the parent aspired to be but failed. This obviously creates major problems further down the line, with both the parent and the child feeling disappointed in themselves and the other, so overbearing or pompous parenting should be avoided at all costs. Whilst pride in oneself and one's valid achievements is a laudable attribute, the other side of the same coin is that of arrogance and conceit, sometimes quite common with this aspect. In certain cases, it can indicate difficulty in conceiving or giving birth, or of being (in)fertile. Alternatively, the individual themselves may have been adopted, or have experienced some other type of anomaly or unique experience during childhood. Until these individuals have children or find other similar types of all-consuming creative projects, they may tend to take their relationships with an all or nothing attitude, yes/no, black/white in their apparent indifference towards emotional content and attachment. However, children and/or creative output really do change everything and can act as a vehicle for the individual's personal transformation through the conduit of the creative output in question in a way that is distinctly profound, although this has to be freeform and unconditional. Any attempts to mould the world or others in one's own image will most certainly backfire.

Pluto in the sixth house

The sixth house, relating to Virgo, is the engine room of one's lifestyle. It governs health as in body maintenance, exercise, nutrition and wellbeing and has a powerful connection with the idea of work in terms of duty or responsibility towards those less fortunate than oneself and/or working on oneself as opposed to monetary gain. Often these people work in either the allopathic or the naturopathic field, in a service capacity or in some other form of beneficial public work. Pluto here is seen as quite comfortable in the sixth house, bringing a sense of gravity and dignity into all the functional sides to life.

In a favourable light, the sixth house is one of the best places for Pluto to live in. If there are beneficial aspects to Pluto in this house, the individual will have a sense of thoroughness about them that will calm others and make them reassured that things are in safe and capable hands. There will be a willingness to go to the bottom of things and the idea of getting one's hands dirty, either metaphorically or literally, holds no fear of anything because of Pluto's desire for unearthing things and the sixth house's capacity for effectiveness and efficiency. There is a forensic ability that delights in stripping everything down to basics before cleaning and reassembling and an almost obsessive attitude towards health and particularly hygiene. One client, on hearing that she had this position, stated that she now understood why her husband said that every microbe in the house was terrified to show its face whenever she was around. This position gives a diligent and hardworking approach to getting things done. Pluto likes bringing things into the light or burying them forever and in both cases the sixth house attributes of effectiveness and functionality appeals to Pluto's clinical way of doing things. Strong aspects can indicate real skill at delicate procedures, or the ability to really unravel complicated stories. There is always an aspiration to do better, to uncover more and refine the processes of purification. Here lies the best lesson of the sixth house – whilst in human form, you are never going to always get it right or be perfect. Doing your best is all that is being asked and the favourable influences of Pluto in this position will aid and positively influence you in this respect, even if you are sometimes a hard taskmaster on yourself.

From a neutral perspective, Pluto in the sixth house is comfortable. There will normally be a workaholic attitude and it is important to these people to have a degree of control over their immediate working environment, although over the course of a lifetime there is a transformation in routines that brings a greater degree of flexibility. This is the person who is easy with the ideas of detox, cleansing, purifying and occasionally purging oneself, all good Plutonian words. This is the person who if they are going to clean the kitchen or the bathroom will do it thoroughly, terrifying every bacterium within a mile from coming near. Pluto in the sixth house will always wash the salad and vegetables properly before serving them, they can be fastidious but in a sensible way in all issues concerning foodstuffs. In most cases, they will only relax once the washing up is done, although another client with this position, acknowledging their own capacity for obsession, states *it took me almost three years to let myself go to bed without doing the washing up, but I made myself go through the process so that I had choice in the matter*. There is a quiet and understated resilience about these individuals that has certain standards and is willing to put up with the banter and occasional criticism to maintain them. Pluto likes to constantly repair and upgrade and will go into the bowels of the problem if necessary and even then, they do not mind getting dirty if the ends justify the means and if there is a hot shower at the end of it. The transformative urge here is directed towards keeping everything flowing and not allowing blockages to form, using this as a metaphor for all areas of one's life.

In difficult or challenging cases, Pluto in the sixth house can represent a form of eternal suffering, the unrequited desire of separation in some form or another. Feelings of alienation are not uncommon, along with memories of neglect, or even in some cases abandonment. This can be the position of the hypochondriac, convincing themselves that they are not well – which obviously enhances that very same possibility! Alternatively, it can be the person who constantly seems to sabotage oneself, who buys into the guilt syndrome often due to negative reinforcement over periods of time from outside of oneself. Certainly, any potential signs of worry or fretting can at times become obsessive and there is a need to almost stalk oneself regarding this, sometimes deliberately choosing not to be so focussed or concentrated, at least for a time. There is a need to recognise and work with the more compulsive side of one's nature, to allow it expression through some type of channelled and managed interface rather than trying to eliminate it. There is also the need to have a steady and consistent approach to nutrition and diet, because if the body is not working then everything else is vulnerable. These people sometimes become so obsessed with their work that they forget to feed themselves. Pluto in the sixth house individuals need to remember that they live in a body that needs maintenance and every so often they purge themselves not only physically but mentally as well. This lessens the potential for becoming so unidirectional at work and self-judgemental in lifestyle that they can permanently lose touch with those in their community.

Pluto in the seventh house

The seventh house of relationships, akin to the sign Libra, is at a fundamental level about the interactions the person has with others at the one to one level, whether that other is parent, child, social, friend, professional or personal and intimate. It is about the way that individuals share space and energy with each other, where the boundaries are, what is acceptable and what is not. Pluto here can take its time in working with these energies, needing to be convinced of the validity of others intentions and worth before commitment, but once this has been given it brings the potential for mutually transformative and uplifting relationships.

When there are positive aspects to Pluto in the seventh house, the individual will often find themselves as the 'strong one' in the relationship and that over time people become used to leaning on them for support or advice, although hopefully not to the point of dependency. The better their relationships with others, the better their relationship with themselves and vice versa. In general, when they commit, they commit for life. No-one puts as much effort or works so hard at establishing and rebuilding their relationships as do people with Pluto in the seventh house and as a result over an extended period their relationships become the vehicle for their own personal transformation. These are the people who will make great willing sacrifices for their partner because they know that the true secret of synergy is when two and two equals five or that the combined output of two people working as a team is greater than the two individual outputs added together. If their motives for being in a relationship are as clean, sincere and pure as possible, they are practically guaranteed a quality of experience within the confines of personal interaction that other people can only aspire to. Occasionally, Pluto in the seventh house people may be drawn towards others who espouse the more negative sides of Pluto, including jealousy and manipulation to 'cure' or 'heal' these other people. This tendency should be avoided at all costs, on the grounds that you can take a horse to water, but you cannot make it drink. For transformation to occur in others they first must want to change and imposing it on the unwilling is never going to work.

From a more neutral perspective, this is the position of the counsellor, the referee, the adjudicator and the intermediary, bringing opposites together and finding a middle ground that is at least acceptable to all. Pluto in the seventh house can be altruistic in its attitudes towards other people's problems, in that it is not judgemental in most cases, preferring instead to make informed decisions from a dispassionate perspective whilst aspiring to the best outcome. However, in the rare cases where specific and incisive action becomes necessary, Pluto will not hesitate to act in a way that tolerates no disagreement, and its actions then will be irrevocable and final. Ideally, individuals come together for common purpose and mutual appreciation and in these scenarios Pluto acts as a kind of subconscious glue, bringing an element of guaranteed reliability to the interaction. Pluto will encourage the individuals in the relationship to be thinking of their partner as much as themselves, thus fostering and nurturing the relationship to a level not normally conceivable, let alone achievable. Operating from a position of balanced and shared power, Pluto in the seventh house normally adds depth and strength to any working interaction between two equal individuals operating in a form of partnership or team. For the individual with this position, they will find over the course of a lifetime that their close and personal relationships become the primary field for personal transformation and rebirth. This is why so many of these people become some type of therapist or counsellor, because sometimes only by working with others at the one to one level can they simultaneously facilitate their own personal transformation.

It is when Pluto in the seventh house receives difficult aspects that problems can occur. Relationships can prosper and grow, but only if the individual surrenders to the inevitable personal changes required to ensure that the relationship works. There can be an almost fanatical subconscious compulsion to have some kind of inappropriate influence or power in the relationship, which if expressed overtly can manifest as direct control and domination issues. If expressed subversively this can come across as insidious manifesting in the development of increasingly manipulative patterns designed to undermine the influence of others and promote the Pluto individual into a position of power. This is often done in a way that is seen in retrospect as being coercive, a vastly underused Plutonian word. Often, an individual with this position will choose to go through prolonged periods of life alone, working on the relationship that they have with oneself and bringing that to the highest order before venturing out in the harsh world of personal interactions. When younger, the people they get involved with often function as mirrors for the individual's own internal issues. When older, they may become more emotionally possessive of their partners, fearing abandonment and trying any way possible to ensure this does not happen. The more honest about their fears, both to themselves and their partner, the better the long term outcome. Conversely, the more underhanded or fearful one's expression within a relationship is, the more unhappiness and loneliness is guaranteed. Sometimes, the only way to really find your own power through relationship patterns is to consciously surrender that lust or desire for power and trust your significant other with it, freeing you of the urge for control and liberating you into true teamwork – sometimes, two and two do make five, with synergy being the ultimate Holy Grail.

Pluto in the eighth house

The eighth house relates to Scorpio, which is quite clearly Pluto's domain. Older translations of this area of the chart suggest that this is the area most connected with the great imponderables of existence – life, sex, power and death. Modernly, it is now understood as being concerned with self-empowerment, one's psychological states, how one deals with fear and self-acceptance and how other people's resources and values affect the individual's life. Pluto here brings an element of gravity and depth which cannot be denied by the individual and should not be trifled with by others. It brings an evolving understanding of the true nature of power.

When Pluto in the eighth house is under good aspect, it is potentially at the peak of its power. Here can be found the aspiring shape shifter, constantly seeking to cleanse, purify and refine oneself in an alchemical or shamanistic way. This is the caterpillar transforming into the butterfly, going through a metamorphosis that allegorically brings a more refined, visionary and beautiful perspective. This can also be seen as the individual periodically shedding their skin snakelike, whereby every so often they go through some type of voluntary detox that removes a lot of metaphorical excess dead weight. This is the invulnerable one who goes into the dark willingly, knowing that darkness is only the absence of light and there is nothing really to fear. This is the person who holds no fear of dealing with substantial amounts of money or authority, either their own or that belonging to others, because these people have a deeper understanding of the nature of value and resources than most and hold little attachment to that which can merely be bought. This is the position of the phoenix rising from the ashes, refining and purifying oneself on a constant mission of regeneration and transformation into something stronger and full of power. The wisest of all with this position understands that they are powerless and that the power in them is not theirs; instead, they are just acting as a conduit for the power and expressing it in a way that is seen to be ethical, transparent and for the benefit of all. However, sometimes even with the best of aspects and intentions the sheer power of Pluto in the eighth house can sometimes push the individual into necessary solitude. As a client eloquently stated; *'On the one hand there is a certain pride in sensing being a 'chosen' individual, whilst on the other, it can give rise to a subconscious reaction in individuals, sometimes to the point of aggression, even when their conscious minds can find no reason for their aversion. People generally do not like to sense greater power in others – (even if that power comes through rather than is generated by), perceiving it as a threat, and self-awareness of this 'gift' cannot always ameliorate the situation, since it is, by definition, uncontrollable, and therefore it can be necessary to withdraw if possible'.*

When in a neutral aspect, Pluto in the eighth house will bring with it the willingness to go to the very bottom of whatever it is that needs dealing with and then whilst they are at that very base of the matter, they will get the scouring pads out and really scrape away at all of the roots of any metaphorical poison. The concept of purging and cleansing at the most basic of levels holds no fear for these people, on the grounds that if they are going to do anything, they are going to do it properly or not at all. Pluto in the eighth house gives more than a passing interest in the concept of life before birth and life after death, regardless of religious persuasion. The problem can be that the emotional experience can be so intense that the individual feels that they must control it, instead of learning to just flow with it. An inhibited Pluto in the eighth house will always insist on knowing exactly what the schedule is, when the breaks are and what the outcome will be in order to not panic about what might be. At the same time, there can be a basic approach to elimination that can be scary to lesser mortals who do not understand that ruthlessness is neither good nor bad, just an occasionally necessary rule of engagement. These are the people who if ill will go to bed for two days with the lights out, lots of blankets, garlic, chilli and ginger and just sweat for two days and then suddenly they are better. Lurking in the back of the mind is the notion that they could be trying just a little harder, but this only inspires and spurs them on to greater achievements. The nature of the eighth house is to strive, never willingly being satisfied with ongoing situations and instead looking to refine and purify, if necessary by doing things the hard way.

Under challenging aspect, Pluto in the eighth house can be a difficult energy to manage. There can be, when young, the fear of being without: without money, without love or friends, which in turn can generate almost phobic attitudes towards possessing things or people. Because the nature of the eighth house is that of the more hidden or occluded sides of life, the rational and analytical side of explaining problems does not work here. Instead, there is a need to be aware of the potential for obsessive or compulsive behavioural patterns, which if not acknowledged and worked with will invariably lead to periods of crisis and/or trauma brought about by the build-up of unacknowledged or repressed pressure and stress, like a boil rising to the surface to be dealt with. There is a need to almost stalk oneself at times, to allow the transformative urge to pass unhindered through one's life. Pluto in the eighth house can have the desire to have total and exact control over one's circumstances in life. This obviously clashes with the free will aspect of other people's lives; sometimes erupting in titanic power struggles which inevitably end in failure unless there is a total honesty with oneself and other(s) about motive and reasons. And this is most obvious when it comes to sex as once these people learn to trust both their partner and themselves in the bedroom; they make the most consummate lovers. However, the road to that trust is littered with tempting diversions and easy distractions and by not facing and dealing with the shadowy side of oneself; one only attracts the same shadowy energy from others in a way that simply cannot be ignored.

Pluto in the ninth house

The ninth house, with its Sagittarian influence, is the area of one's chart where personal belief systems, philosophies, attitudes and opinions are formed. It governs the usage of the higher mind, often manifested through either extensive foreign travel and/or higher education. Pluto in this house brings with it the potential for a devout and almost pious attitude to life but can just as equally represent the fundamentalist in all of us. Pluto here will uncover the truth regardless of content and that truth, no matter how painful or harsh, must be not only revealed but lived.

When Pluto is beneficially aspected in the ninth house, there will be an ongoing and almost insatiable desire to constantly expand and stretch the higher mind through direct experience. These are the people who will explore several types of environments by going native fast and easily insinuating themselves into local culture. They will explore a myriad of different anthropological experiences and dip their finger into many different religious and theological options, eventually deriving from all their study and experiences a philosophy and relationship with the universe and the Divine that is for them and them alone. They are constantly looking for deeper or hidden meaning in everything and everyone that they encounter, something that perpetuates throughout life. Often as they age, Pluto in the ninth house people turn to higher education, not to learn anything new but instead to learn how to put what they already know into a more structured and cohesive format. These are the people who can not only see the big picture, they can also grasp the intrinsic meaning behind it as well and so have an automatic advantage when it comes to making the right decision in most cases. Because of this, there is often an unusual talent for working with words in forms such as bookbinding, printing, publishing or other forms of media, in some way always getting data and information out to the larger audience. They can not only see the big picture but to live it and make it a reality, yet without ignoring any of the details.

When Pluto in the ninth house is in a neutral position, there will always be a kind of detached bemusement at the world, tinged with an element of eternal optimism and an underlying faith – not in anyone or anything, but just faith in itself. This will be the person who can really get the underlying philosophy of a subject or understand the fine and subtle nuances of the law. Pluto in the ninth house people will argue about a minute point indefinitely if they believe in it that passionately. To these people, there is no higher pleasure than measured debate and even friendly argument, because this stimulates the higher mind and compels the person to re-examine all their beliefs in the face of constantly changing and challenging information. In some cases, there may be a deliberate atheistic tendency, preferring to strive for the development of the collective human mind as the holy grail as opposed to some form of vague 'higher power.' There can be the occasional tendency to look smug when their long held and cherished philosophies are proven right, but they do work at developing them and rarely can people with Pluto in the ninth house have their philosophies undermined. These are the individuals who aspire to walk their talk to an ever refined quality of degree and seem as though they are constantly searching for ever more profound experience and realisations on their journey through life. At the end of the day, these are the people who recognise that it is not the destination that is the purpose of the journey, but the act of 'being on the road' as a metaphor for self-development.

However, if Pluto in the ninth house is challenged by aspect, various versions of fundamentalism can be seen. At one end of the spectrum lies the narrow minded, religious, political or economic zealot who has no time for anyone who does not ascribe to their way of thinking and at the other end lies the 'happy clappy' type of individual whose glass is always more than half full to a sickeningly sugary degree and who try to convert by seduction as much as dogma. Pluto in the ninth house, when under challenge, can have little tolerance for other people's opinions in many cases and alongside that there can also be an extreme attachment to one's own ideas, which are clung to religiously even when proven wrong. When partnered, it may well be that there can be outstanding and unsolvable philosophical differences between the individual and the partner's parents. This can also be the position of the aesthete, the archetypal hermit who retreats into their metaphorical cave to contemplate the mysteries of existence, preferring solitude to the company of the 'impure' or the 'unclean.' There will be little patience with what is perceived as social injustice and the individual with Pluto in difficult aspect in the ninth house may occasionally think of themselves as acting on behalf of a higher power and being above the law, which if put into action invariably leads to a fall from grace and other associated problems. Hypocrisy is another form of behaviour that is particularly distasteful and the person with a challenged ninth house Pluto needs to follow their own advice and live their life according to their personal truths lest others pull them up on their discrepancies. This is the person who may delight in popping other's bubbles in ways that are nowhere near subtle, tactful or diplomatic – but they can be relied on to be direct, blunt, honest and to the point.

Pluto in the tenth house

The tenth house, relating to Capricorn, is primarily associated with one's outside world interactions at the public and professional level. It rules the job, work and vocation, public image, profile and status, as well as having a great deal to do with the ways that one manages relationships with all forms of authority, whether father, god, teacher or employer. Pluto's relationship with the tenth house is that of power manifestation at all external levels ranging from competition to synergy.

When Pluto in the tenth house is positively aspected, it normally denotes an assured confidence about projecting oneself into and onto the outside world as being a person of substance. There will be the willingness to take on pressurised situations requiring tough decisions and if necessary the wielding of authority, whether that is at the head of a corporate company or by simply working for oneself. This position can have a magnetic effect upon others in the professional domain and certainly has good leadership material. There exists an easy understanding about the fundamental natures of structures of all unusual types, suggesting that these people know when to bend and when to stand firm and their ability to inspire confidence in themselves does wonders for the public image and the way that their peers see them. There can be an almost forensic-like ability to find the underlying cause of things and uproot wherever necessary and others in their professional environment may at times see them as ruthless, doing whatever it takes to get the required results. Tenth house Pluto people know that success is not necessarily based on riches or fame in this position, it is more concerned with the internal feeling of having simply done one's very best and if the desired results do not come, then it is not for the want of effort or trying. Nevertheless, by steady and constant application this individual makes a meaningful contribution to society in some shape or form, normally through the workplace or other forms of public interaction. This is the person who can inspire others by their own efforts, leading by example and making solid headway with the tides of life.

From a more neutral perspective, Pluto in the tenth house is seen as a troubleshooter, brought into companies or organisations as the ferret and if necessary the hatchet man, using its ability to maximise potential output whilst streamlining and refining input to an effective but base minimum. Pluto here prides itself on words like efficiency and effectiveness and will do whatever is needed to get results. It can sometimes lose touch with its environment, occasionally resulting in inadvertently treading on other people's toes or riding roughshod over other people's feelings, getting so caught up in the focus and passion of the matter at hand that it genuinely is not aware of its less tactful side. At times, Pluto in the tenth house individuals are best off working alone, simply because they have such a strong drive and dominating willpower that when they are on a charge they can quite easily burn out everyone else around them. Every so often they may just throw their career up in the air and start again elsewhere, because sometimes occasional upheavals and transformations are felt to be necessary in order for them to feel that they are still making their mark and extending their influence on the world, even if it takes a metaphorical death and rebirth in order to do so. Pluto in the tenth house people are the most persistent in the zodiac and have incredible staying power, if they feel good about what they are doing and believe in their actions. If a job is worth doing, it is worth doing well and these professional powerhouses can apply stamina, zeal, enthusiasm and rigorous self-discipline in the quest for both personal and professional achievement in a dogmatic and perseverant way that effectively guarantees long term success.

'Nothing comes for free' is the banner sometimes seen underneath the tenth house Pluto flag and when it is under a difficult aspect then Pluto here has some hard lessons to learn about value, worth and status. It is all very well being rich, famous or successful, but what about the loneliness? No matter how hard one works, or how much one has or earns, there is one currency that cannot be bought, only earned and that is respect, both internal and external. These are the people who will drive both themselves and others into the ground in pursuit of something ultimately not quite worth it, almost as if they are under the influence of some unconscious compulsive behaviour pattern, possibly rooted in childhood and the relationship with older male role model imagery and the supposed search for approval or acceptance from that male role model. Certainly, parental conditioning has a bigger influence concerning career in this house position of Pluto than in any other and if there is an obsessive intensity in the approach to work, then perhaps a new approach to understanding the potentially extreme influences of childhood is required. What these people eventually realise is that it is not the outcome or result that is desired, but instead the knowledge gained whilst on the path. They may occasionally attract opposition within their professional sphere and in that scenario, there is a glaring need to ensure that everything is completely transparent and accountable so that if necessary, they can hold their hands up and say that their back is covered. Those that live by the sword normally die by the sword and whilst this individual can rise to the very top of their respective tree, the only guaranteed safe way to do this in a long term and sustainable way is by keeping everything clean and open.

Pluto in the eleventh house

The Aquarian influenced eleventh house is primarily that area of the chart concerning group, community, humanitarian affairs, common goals and the larger social world including one's friendships, acquaintances and associates. Pluto introduces a dynamic into this area that is certainly not light-hearted, suggestive of a deep rooted desire or passion for transformation of community life and for one's position within that community to be in a role of influence.

In a favourable light, Pluto in the eleventh house brings with it the willingness and the ability to be the facilitator, organiser or coordinator of the group dynamic, whether at the social, family or professional level. Pluto here will take on all the minute details that go into the making and working of a group endeavour and it will be done painstakingly and correctly, taking the appropriate amount of time necessary to do things properly. Pluto here brings with it the quality of being a resolute and dependable friend under the most trying or difficult of circumstances and to these people it really does seem as if their true family is not just that of flesh and blood but also those who unconditionally love and support them on their pathways through life. It is the unconditional support and love that one gets from a community that truly represents one's real family or tribe in this context. In return for this unconditional acceptance into community, the eleventh house Pluto person, without compromising their sense of individuality, will grow into the role of detached humanitarian whilst retaining a complete and utter loyalty and support to those who have been there for them in the past. These are the large scale and long term instigators of social change, both at the personal and collective level, who believe that they (sometimes single handedly!) can change the future in a better way for everybody. They are the futurists of today, seeing the large-scale changes needed for a sustainable and vibrant global community, although sometimes the future can seem so important that the lessons of the past or the needs of the present can sometimes be neglected.

With a neutral eleventh house position, Pluto is likely to find itself in the position of organiser of one's world in a way that is as much formal as it is social, which satisfies their need to feel a part of the greater community. Over the years they may take on increased responsibility for people within their community, bringing these people through into a role where they feel valued and wanted, as well as benefiting the larger community through their social efforts. There will certainly be a strong reformist streak which is always trying to bring a greater degree of equality into the community at large, based on the sure internal knowledge that what goes round comes round and the more one helps others the more one gets helped. Even the best of friendships will go through occasional periods of test, challenge and reformation, designed to keep one's community fertile and vibrant as opposed to sterile and boring and none of these friendships will be conventional or orthodox. Lightweight people need not apply, as most if not all of Pluto in the eleventh house people's community will have a profoundness about them that borders on the mystical and metaphysical. There will be a magnetic attraction towards the more hidden sides of life within the framework and context of community and the eleventh house Pluto person will dig deep to uncover everything, surfacing every so often with the demand for room to breathe and to exchange discoveries with one's contemporaries and peers before once again diving into the underbelly of the beast to bring more things to the surface. As the individual with this position ages and matures, so the quality of friendship and community in life becomes increasingly refined, purified, cleansed and transformed into something valid and meaningful in modern community terms.

If Pluto in the eleventh house comes under a difficult or challenging aspect, then friendships and community associations are likely to be a battleground for control or dominance. These people could easily become overbearing or pompous when dealing with their friends or contemporaries, or they could just as easily attract these qualities from others around them. The best and the worst friendships will have an intensity about them that is both evident and powerful and there will be times where these people seem to bring out the worst in others, even to the point where it seems that others are trying to stop or block situations regardless of whether or not there is any apparent or logical reason for this. It can arouse an almost pathological opposition from others within groups who may see the eleventh house Pluto person as getting out of control or becoming too dictatorial. Some people with this position find their role within any type of community just too much like demanding work and prefer the lifestyle of social abstinence, often becoming quite solitary for a time. If taken to an extreme, this can occasionally be seen as a phobia or paranoia of crowds or being in a tightly controlled or constricted space – claustrophobia. There may also be an almost fundamentalist like attitude towards being an individual within the larger society, expressing one's own uniqueness in any way deemed necessary regardless of convention or expectation and whilst one is willing to spend one's life in and with community, there will always be the ability to rely solely on oneself when necessary and an almost survivalist attitude can prevail at times, plus the occasional need to make one's mark no matter what.

Pluto in the twelfth house

The twelfth house represents everything that you cannot think about – it governs the unconscious, the subconscious, the psychological, the transpersonal and sometimes the pathological as well. It is the area of dream, intuition, second sight, sixth sense, third thoughts. It is an extremely sensitive position, creating saints, sinners and heroes as well as the more pathological role of victims and martyrs. Pluto here brings one's unconscious to the surface via a number of different routes, not all immediately apparent or obvious; it is just a question of whether that journey is done willingly or kicking and screaming.

When Pluto in the twelfth house receives healthy aspects, the individual will find that they naturally and organically blend into most situations developing around them with a great deal of comfort and ease. Rarely do they initiate or take the lead, preferring instead to merge into the background, quite comfortable to stay behind the scenes and allowing others to take the limelight. This is the person who knows how to be alone in a room full of people, who can just switch off from their immediate surroundings and go into a kind of detached space where they populate their own little world, private and unique to them. They can abstain from social interaction with complete comfort, not needing the superficiality of lightweight contact. Here in the twelfth house Pluto people feel that they can safely discharge before coming back to the 'real' world for more sensations. These can be the greatest artists on the block if they allow themselves to just flow and dream/intuit, without trying to rationalise or understand the processes that empower their creativity. With the management and subtle guidance of positive and well-meant intent, these people can evolve into being skilled practitioners of the more subtle and esoteric arts, learning not so much by being taught but by osmosis and assimilation of skills through direct repeated exposure.

Learning by direct experience beats being taught every day of the week for these sensation junkies and their ability to call on their limitless resources to keep going, especially when under pressure, knows no bounds.

When Pluto in the twelfth house is in a neutral position, there will normally be an 'if it's working don't fix it' type of attitude to much of everyday existence; these people seem to just glide through life with little if anything sticking to them, as if they are Teflon coated. They sometimes have an unusual relationship with time, in that if they do not deliberately try, they can somehow always be in the right place at the right time, almost by magic! They have an innate understanding of the ways of the world and if they can retain a degree of detached humour about the whole charade, they are never going to let themselves be absorbed or consumed by the facade of the apparent real world. As a client with a 12th house Pluto reveals: *'what seems solid and obvious to most others is not that way to us. Example: It may look like a couple holding hands is happy, but we understand by other tells (grip of hands, sidelong glances, set of mouth, etc) that this may not be the case at all.'* Having said all that, these are not people who are well versed at forming or gaining attachments and the idea of possessing anyone or anything or being possessed or owned can be quite perverse. They sometimes come across as psychic, often to their bemusement, because they just do not get how deeply intuitive they are and if they did, they would fear themselves. Other people's jaws, however, regularly hit the floor regarding the twelfth house Pluto person's precise utterances. There is always the willingness and the ability to be able to deal with the dying process in all its manifestations, secure in the unconscious certainty that death is only a transition from one state of being into another.

When under a challenging aspect, Pluto in the twelfth house people can easily find themselves living in a world of their own making, to the point where their fears and fantasies can sometimes become real, at least to them. This is unfortunately common in the charts of people who self-harm, even if only in mild forms such as piercings or tattoos and it can also be found in the charts of individuals who seem to be having constant power struggles with themselves and/or others that are hard to specify as to their origin. There is a need to find stillness, peace and inner comfort with this position, something unlikely to be found in environments of pressure or concentrated intensity, so regular visits to nature or to the seaside are recommended. If their lifestyle becomes too frenetic, they can become disassociated from their intuitive path, leading to occasional periods of depression or of feeling lost, or just burnt out. Alternatively, they may find themselves constantly in the role of the scapegoat, being powerless in the face of insurmountable odds, often leading to feelings of either escapism or worse, anger fuelled by sullen resentment. With a difficult Pluto in the twelfth house, there is the need to go into the dark side of oneself occasionally, just to reassure oneself that there is nothing there to be scared of and to embrace a steadily evolving spiritual approach to life based increasingly less on materialism and steadily more on being comfortable with and in oneself, regardless of the input from others.

7

Pluto by aspect

The aspects to Pluto from other astrological points within the horoscope show two ways of perception when it comes to understanding the meaning of the aspect in question. When viewed from the perspective of the aspected planet, then it will be seen how the deeply attractive and occasionally subversive side of Pluto can weigh strongly here and bring a greater element of intensity along with the capacity for transformation in some shape or form. When viewed from Pluto's viewpoint, he brings a no-nonsense approach to most interactions, preferring to know what works and what does not in clear terms rather than fumble around in the dark, and he will always bring the willingness to go to the bottom of things and bring the hidden to the surface. Depending on the aspect, that process may not be subtle.

Conjunctions to Pluto

A conjunction occurs when two planets occupy the same degree of longitude when viewed from the Earth. Occasionally with the Sun and the Moon the conjunction is not only in longitude but also in latitude, resulting in an eclipse. The conjunction links two planetary energies into one point of concentration in the horoscope in a way that brings a laser-like attention onto the point of the conjunction and the area of the individual horoscope that it is in. Whilst obviously the sign and the house of the zodiac that the conjunction is in will have a major influence on the external manifestation of the conjunction's influence into and onto the outside world, it will not dictate how the force or power of the conjunction will manifest. This is directly down to the combined nature of the astrological points being conjoined, and how well they mate. A conjunction forces two sometimes vastly diverse types of energy into an interaction and a form of teamwork that can be the result of need as much as desire or willingness.

When one of these planetary influences in the conjunction is Pluto, a different dimension is added to the equation. Pluto will bring an element of depth, resourcefulness, intrigue and sometimes the compulsive and obsessive into the equation, and much depends on the nature of the other planet(s) in the conjunction as to how Pluto's influence will develop. It is certain that the presence of Pluto in any type of conjunction will indicate that the person will not be a lightweight and that they will always have a keen insight into the true nature of what is going on. If used wisely, this can bring the greatest potential for transformation possible, both for oneself and into the world. The following observations are born of thirty five years of astrological experience, and by necessity are only one person's view but can be taken as a dependable guide to conjunctions with Pluto.

Sun conjunct Pluto

At its core level Pluto potentially destroys and eliminates, transforms and regenerates everything that comes in its pathway and that includes the Sun and its accompanying sense of identity. The Sun represents one's sense of uniqueness, individuality and personal identity. It is who you are regardless of the input from other people, situations or environments. To have the Sun and Pluto in the same place will bring a degree of transformative energy into the core identity in a way that is so powerful that it cannot be ignored without denying oneself or one's sense of intense depth of identity and individuality.

Anybody with a Sun/Pluto conjunction in their chart is going to be no stranger to various levels of intensity in their life and this can often manifest as a kind of 'do or die' attitude sometimes bordering on extremes. The individual may exhibit an almost nihilistic and uncaring attitude towards life, only to suddenly turn it around and become incredibly enthusiastic about and dedicated towards an outcome that allows no interference or wavering from their path. This can be seen by others as having a quality of obsession about it that will not allow deviation or change in any form from the objective, which is to maintain focus and concentration on the desired outcome no matter what the potential distractions. This energy can also be seen at times by others as not only being obsessive but also compulsive, where the individual is acting and behaving in ways that are not being consciously thought about but are instead a reaction to some deep inner, almost primal urge that drives the person forward in ways that could in certain situations or environments be ultimately quite self-destructive. These are the people who sometimes truly do not know when to stop, even when they know that they are wrong and that the eventual outcome of their actions will not bring the desired result. This fanatical capacity can often be their undoing and the Sun/ Pluto conjunction person will at various times in their life exhibit a degree of extremism that hopefully after years of personal struggle will ameliorate as they naturally move towards middle ground. This is accompanied by the realisation that they are not an island and that despite their almost militant attitude towards life they need others around them to balance themselves and bring an element of lightness into their lives.

There will always be an element of ruthlessness present, although this primarily manifests towards oneself rather than being projected onto others. The nature of Pluto with the Sun will bring an ongoing almost permanent desire for purging, detoxing and cleansing of oneself at the emotional, mental and psychological levels as much as if not more so than at the physical. These are the people who when ill will retreat into their own personal cave and sweat illness out rather than take pills and potions, knowing secretly that they have the power within themselves to eliminate any internal form of poison or toxin. This form of purging of oneself is not limited to the physical. Sun conjunct Pluto people are the ones who will delve deeply into the dark crevices of their own mind, hopefully uprooting and cleansing all the hidden shadows that they find there. The alternative to this is living in a type of self-denial, which leads to a vacuous and superficial life with no depth along with a pathological fear of the unknown and the unknowable. This self-purging can also manifest at the emotional level, often through the individual's personal relationship patterns, which is why these people will either attract others like themselves in terms of personal depth and intensity or they will remain alone, choosing to keep their privacy inviolate. People with the Sun conjunct Pluto will have a strong survival mechanism hardwired into their mainframe which can sometimes emerge into the outside world as the apparent capacity for elimination, harshness and ruthlessness. This is because their need for personal security is so strong that they find it hard to rely or depend on other or others, because working with others can be seen as weakening their power in situations. These people often prefer their own company rather than taking a chance on trusting others until they have known them a long time.

It is these people's desire for absolutes that mark them as being different than most. Sun conjunct Pluto people can deal with the worst of trauma and crisis, they can handle both their and others' dark sides and they are no stranger to paranoia and phobia. However, if you want to keep their trust and friendship, then there is one simple but critical golden rule and that is to always, but always tell them the truth no matter how hard or difficult it may be. These people can manage problems, but they cannot and will not deal with lies or similar forms of deceit and whilst this is a general rule of thumb across the board it is especially true in the bedroom. Sexual congress is such a personal and intimate thing with these people, often leading to fears of betrayal and disappointment, that many of them will go through life with lengthy periods of abstinence preferring to keep their energies to themselves rather than take chances on opening to or trusting others. The sharing of one's most intimate and personal sides with another could be seen as the surrendering of one's individuality and if that degree of intimacy is in any way compromised or (even worse) betrayed, then these individuals will shut up shop forever and a day. These are the people who never forget and sometimes also never forgive, although in the latter case they can also bring the capacity for bearing grudges that will wear them down, lower their vibration and make them serious and even grave. Yet there also, in the Stygian depths of the Hadean experience, exists the capacity for a dark humour that can bring the most visceral and twisted side of one's nature into the light through the ability to find humour no matter how challenging the circumstances, wrenching the pathos and the irony into the world in a way that be seen as somewhat caustic, sharply accurate and outrageously funny in a weird and slightly disturbing way. This dark humour is often based around the more primal and basic of experiences and sex and death are equal and opposite in these people's eyes. The Sun conjunct Pluto individual will either have a pathological fear of death or else will see it as merely a transition from one state of consciousness to another, whilst sex creating life will be seen as one of the conduits of that transformation.

This aspect brings with it a degree of stamina and drive unmatched by any other aspect and it is indeed the strongest 'do or die' aspect in astrology. There will always be an unstoppable and indomitable willpower present as well as an unswerving determination to succeed no matter what the cost or how long it takes. There will also be a persistent drive for personal power present that if used correctly can bring a quasi-shamanistic ability to bring regeneration and transformation not only into these individual's lives, but also into the lives of those others around them. However, when used incorrectly, this power can also corrupt and poison the individual so that they seem out of control, almost possessed and naturally repugnant to many others because of some dimly perceived sense of detritus or other form of unhealthy disorder. Sometimes, it may seem that moderation and compromise are a strange land in which the 'all or nothing' attitude dominates and thus where they find themselves once again alone, in which case the need to find and unearth the aforementioned dark humour becomes paramount. The less evolved with this conjunction will seek to become powerful in a dominating or controlling way, both in their own lives and in the lives of others, whilst the sensible know that they are full of power, that they are the conduit for power to flow through them and that they are the steward of that power, not the owner.

The Sun conjunct Pluto individual will, once they have grown out of their own fear, become a person to whom words like strength, drive, nobility and precision become second nature and then they really can metaphorically move mountains. In terms of raw power, this is the single strongest aspect in astrology, but it does not on its own say how that power will be used, just that it exists. The definition of how that power is used is best described by the zodiacal sign house and aspects to other planets that this conjunction makes.

Moon conjunct Pluto

The Moon is all about one's feelings and emotions, the habit patterns, routines and day to day activities of one's life. The Moon represents the basic personality as opposed to the Sun's sense of individuality. Pluto has an affinity with the Moon at a number of symbolic diverse levels, all of which are rooted at least primarily in mythology, where dark Pluto (Hades) abducted and impregnated Persephone only allowing her to return into the light in cyclical and regular rhythms before once again returning to the dark, nurturing underworld.

The identification and quality of emotional nurturing (or absence of it) when young will inevitably have a powerful effect on adult life, as well as the quality and depth of feeling that goes with it. There can be a strong potential for an addictive emotional habituation that strongly drives these people both towards and away from intense emotional encounters, primarily with women, often experienced as the push me/pull you phenomenon. The Moon/Pluto conjunction is an aspect common in the charts of individuals who have had powerful relationships with female role model imagery, normally the mother and often in a not very transparent or pleasant way. It may be that the individual was raised by the grandmother, an aunt or older sister, or else was adopted, fostered or raised in different and challenging family circumstances. It could be that the mother over-identifies with the child, making them the bearer of the mother's unrealised dreams and that the childhood experience was about smothering as much as if not more so than mothering, with the feminine authority being over powerful or domineering. There can sometimes be the feeling of emotional abandonment associated with childhood, or at least an element of emotional neglect. The extremism of Pluto is clearly seen here, ranging from the controlling, manipulating and dominating, overly protective and smothering to the neglected, abandoned and emotionally isolated. Yet the Moon with its phases of light and dark can relate to Pluto in more favourable ways as they both exist at least partially on a diet of raw emotion, passion and dark feeling. As the individual with the Moon conjunct Pluto ages, so the gradual realisation develops that there is simply no other way than to go into one's own internally private dark spaces and confront the shadow. It is either that or constantly live in that sense of trepidation where demons are constantly knocking on the door and that the sword of Damocles could drop at any time. It is surprising how people with this aspect end up looking after or at least tending their mother in her old age, as a duty as much as a pleasure. The Moon conjunct Pluto is the single most repetitive aspect in generational astrology in that it is found in consecutive generations of females who being unable to deal with the raw emotional intensity of their life seem to shunt it along further on down the line to the next generation until eventually one brave soul decides to deal with things, once and for all. Only by going into these Hadean caverns is it found that the fear of what might be is always much bigger than the fear of what is. The Moon/Pluto conjunction can be given to brief periods of acute emotional terror and the sooner this is acknowledged, accepted and worked with, the quicker the long term emotional integration. It is this personal integration at the emotional level that enables these people more than almost any other astrological aspect to understand the fears that motivate other people's responses. This is a good reason why so many people with the Moon conjunct Pluto end up in professional situations caring for others less fortunate than themselves in some way where their deep and penetrating psychological insight is best used to benefit others at least as much as themselves.

Like and sometimes synonymous with the relationship with feminine role model imagery is the willingness or not to deal with guilt (whether received or projected). Patterns imposed at an early age can be embedded permanently, resulting in feelings of unworthiness. The most common manifestation of this is the 'you should' phenomena, often prefaced with 'if you love me...' Upon hearing the 'you should' words, the Moon/Pluto conjunction person will hopefully immediately head for the exit as this type of (albeit often unintentional or unconscious) emotional manipulation is unfortunately all too common and these people have enough guilt on their own plate without having others add to it, even inadvertently. It can be easy to understand what it is that makes people around oneself use these patterns and forgiveness of others is allegedly a virtue, especially when they are acting or behaving in unconscious ways. However, the hardship here comes when the individual is asked to forgive oneself and this is only the first step to becoming a guilt free zone. On the one hand, betrayal and deceit (especially of one's feelings and emotions) are the single biggest crimes imaginable to these people, yet on the other hand they can come across as cold, calculating and ruthless when necessary. The survival instinct is almost animalistic, very deep, primal and darkly strong with this position.

The Moon/Pluto conjunction can symbolise the adult emotional games that are played day in and day out by people within networks such as work environments, families, relationships and close friendships. These games can be constant and ongoing to the point where they become a theme of day to day life, almost invisible unless specifically looked for or stalked. Yet it is these patterns which over a period insinuate themselves into life so much so that before one knows it, they have become an insidious part of identity and the individual becomes the person that they have always feared being. The emotional power struggles that occur with other and others are all representations and external manifestations of the ongoing internal power struggle one has with oneself at the emotional level. Until the process of self-acceptance has been fully integrated and assimilated, there can always be the potential for self-loathing and/or the attracting of draining or otherwise negative emotional energy from others. The potential here for emotional extremism can be so strong that occasionally the Moon/Pluto conjunction individual may temporarily tire of life and thoughts of retirement into a monastery or convent, or even the idea of quitting this life altogether can be common with this aspect, more so than any other aspect in astrology. There can be the potential for self-harm, because 'they are never going to be good enough.' Intense jealousy on the one hand can only be matched on the other by a horror of possessions, or the notion of being owned or possessed. The idea of being consumed or absorbed by others can also be a common fear, so much so that the individual with this conjunction must be aware of their own potential for emotional blockage caused by a deep rooted fear of opening to others.

It is their constant closeness and awareness of the death phenomena that can sometimes make these people so psychic. When the Moon is with Neptune, the potential is for intuitiveness and when the Moon is with Uranus the potential is that of being precognitive. However, when the Moon is with Pluto, the energy is that of being psychic, where the individual will sense and see phenomena that other people simply just do not get. The problem with being psychic, as opposed to intuitive or precognitive, is that it cannot just be turned off. It is a permanent feature which brings its own attendant problems. Often these people will tune into the residual energy fields left behind by people who have passed over. Also, it is not surprising that many of these people go on to work as midwives, or in neonatal care or palliative care. It can sometimes seem as though these incredibly sensitive people have taken it on themselves to be the ushers of life both into and out of the current world. It is the very nature of the intensity and extremism of the Moon/Pluto conjunction that makes these people so comfortable and good at dealing with life and death issues. Sometimes, it seems that only by skirting and flirting with death do these people truly feel alive. The awakening process of Moon/Pluto is epitomised in the worlds of a client; *after Pluto nothing is ever the same again. I can remember driving towards my first astrology reading with that thought arising in my mind. I knew I could turn the car around and stay the person I was or carry on and take that first step. It was a long process of discovery and enlightenment and I loved it (and still am). I won't say the process was painful because what went before was the painful bit. Once you start shining the light the only way is freedom.'* There is an understanding of 'dark beauty,' where the individual knows that by going deep into their own metaphorical cave and by going to the depths of their being, they can access their own internal power in a way that makes it clear to them that they are not so much powerful as they are full of power. The acceptance of the need for occasional periods of crisis and trauma in one's life leads to an understanding of how the periodic purging of oneself leads to a better, cleaner and purer lifestyle, leading to true emotional invulnerability.

Many of these people will end up on the psychoanalyst's couch, looking for answers outside of themselves or in their past instead of allowing their natural emotive process full rein in the here and now. It is important that people who know that they have the Moon/Pluto conjunction remember to cultivate a degree of humour directed at oneself, even if that humour is dark or cynical and not to take themselves too seriously lest they forget how to have fun in life and instead become enshrouded in clouds of guilt, normally rooted in the first seven years of life. Old skeletons in the cupboard need to be taken out and dusted down. Real transformation only occurs when the individual stops looking for the answers to life's questions through their relationships with others and instead looks deep within for those same answers. Dark beauty indeed.

Mercury conjunct Pluto

Pluto is the planetary energy that astrologically deals with compulsion and obsession, with periods of crisis and trauma, painful endings and new beginnings as well as the purging, purifying and cleansing that leads to the metaphorical snake shedding its skin, the caterpillar emerging from the butterfly and the phoenix arising from the ashes. Mercury, being the closest planet to the Sun, has the fastest movement of any planet and thus rules all forms of motion. This can be the motion of the mind, with the communication one has at different intellectual levels with oneself. It can be the communication with other, whether by letter, phone, email or by voice and it can be the movement and communication in society through interaction, networking and travel. Because Mercury astrologically is a neutral and objective energy without gender, it can convey and translate the Plutonic message without adding any type of subjective influence. Therefore, the sign and house of the zodiac that the conjunction of Mercury and Pluto appears in will have a powerful effect on the individual's life in terms of setting out the mental and psychological environments that they evolve in and through. And aspects to a Mercury/Pluto conjunction will have a powerful influence on the communication at all levels, especially when it comes to the concentration and/or focus, with the individual often liking to think that they are in control of the conversation or communicative process. At most times, truth comes ahead of comfort in the list of priorities, even if it hurts...

It will always be apparent to others that the Mercury conjunct Pluto individual has a greater focus and concentration, insight and deep psychological perception than most. This can manifest to others in the outside world as well as to oneself as phobia or insecure paranoia when young, but invariably turns into a precise, sharp and effective way of measuring the world at any given moment as well as the ability to arrive at accurate conclusions and go into areas that other people might think of as being 'taboo' with safety and surety when older. The in-depth questioning of one's own mental functionality can manifest externally as intense concentration or single mindedness and the need to leave no stone unturned in one's own psychological self-examination and to constantly be scrutinising oneself is paramount. These are the people who can be relied on to keep secrets to the grave. Certainly the questioning of one's sanity periodically leads to a re-assessment of what sanity really is as one ages and these individuals will have an extremely powerful capacity to cope with the most difficult of mental and verbal aberrations as they get older, which is why so many of them are involved in some type of forensic or research work. Mercury/Pluto on its own does not so much dictate what the mind produces from opinions and attitudes, or dreams and ideas but it does convey these impressions with a strength and conviction that whilst sometimes the intense or extreme or even acerbic, can also enthuse and inspire with a sense of mental self-empowerment. Gary Kasparov, the genius of chess, has this aspect, as does Sylvester Stallone and GW Bush and amongst other things these people are known for their capacity for biting sarcasm of those who disagree with them, a classic Mercury/Pluto tactic.

Individuals with Mercury conjunct Pluto are rarely loud or verbally abrasive and can be quiet in a scarily understated way. As a client stated: *'At times I felt alone as a child, like no one understood things the way I saw them, and I would see and articulate stuff that made family members feel quite uncomfortable.'* Yet when Mercury conjunct Pluto people do speak, normally it is as though the world stops just for a split second to register their message. They carry in their voice the ability to get under the skin of those around them and convey in-depth meaning more than superficial understanding through their communications. These are the people who will use facial characteristics along with voice and tone fluctuation to emphasise their message. The negative side of this can result in vindictiveness or jealousy, sometimes manifesting as verbal or mental spite. At all times, this aspect can manifest as a very powerful and persuasive talent to influence people, hopefully in ethical and morally acceptable ways. This brings with it the skill and ability to enthuse, inspire and stimulate others into delving into their own depths in search of mental peace and self-empowerment. Sometimes this can happen through powerful poetry or literature, or simply through enthusiastic oration, whilst at other times through expressing something that captures the moment perfectly, the ability to say exactly the right thing at exactly the right time, often without even realising that it is happening.

There is an element of the shrewd about these people and they always keep their cards tight to their chest. Also, there will always be a tendency for occasional suspicion, and they take their time before revealing too much of themselves. Mercury conjunct Pluto likes to think that it has complete control of one's life and the realisation that Mercury is only the library that puts words to Pluto's deeper and sometimes darker energies can sometimes manifest as a sharp and penetrative insight into immediate surroundings. This can be to the point where others may wonder at their ability to notice unspoken words, which is why they make such good private detectives, crime or mystery writers, researchers of all types as well as being amateur psychologists on the side. These are the quiet ones in groups who watch and listen more than act, at least until they are sure of their ground. Rarely, there can be a real fear of communication, especially if Mercury is retrograde, with these individuals being acutely aware of how words can both hurt and heal.

Sometimes these are the children who grew up stuttering or with mental or verbal manipulation or power struggles ongoing around them, who learnt how to say just the right things at the right times to keep out of trouble.

The hardest challenge but greatest need of Mercury/Pluto is to be as precise and to the point as possible, lest their communication become exhaustive or exhausting of both themselves and others. There can sometimes be the tendency to look for hidden meanings even when there are none, so there is a need to be as objective as possible. As these people age, the sensible ones deliberately choose the middle ground choosing to negate extremist dogma, theology or other forms of imposed belief systems and thus avoiding the possibility of seeming overbearing or over-righteous, or for that matter phobic or paranoid. Nevertheless, these people make great spokespersons for any cause they have passion for, they can have incredibly strong convictions and can swing public opinion to a greater degree than most when they are on form, Mercury conjunct Pluto being one of the most persuasive aspects of all. Hand in hand with that persuasive power comes the knowledge of conscience and the price exacted when that power is abused or misused. Eventually they all realise in time that what is times of breakdown are times of breakthrough, at least at the mental level. With this position, cynicism can be a negative virtue whilst healthy scepticism will always be a reliable option.

Venus conjunct Pluto

Venus conjunct Pluto in an individual chart brings a deep and dark dimension to the horoscope analysis, being an aspect that compels the individual to face up to and deal with experiences of direct power, especially in situations involving value and the influence of 'other' in one's life. This power can be self-empowerment, where the ability to make and take actions and decisions makes for a no nonsense kind of person with other people quickly knowing where they stand. Or this can be other people attempting to hold some type of manipulative or otherwise inappropriate or unethical influence over the individual with this conjunction, which unfortunately is far too common in today's world. However, the strength of the conjunction makes the realisation of the power flow through one's life inevitable. It is what one does with it and how one reacts to it that counts, not how much one has. A Venus/Pluto conjunction can be an incisive and accurate point of specific intuition and insight with excellent value systems, or it can represent a blunt and misdirected force that can blunder about the place without direction or subtlety.

In the bedroom, Venus conjunct Pluto brings a focused and concentrated power into the sexual and sensual arena, giving a powerfully charged aura and a magnetic and charismatic personality. Sex will never be just light-hearted fun; it must always have an element of depth, mystery and communion with the unknowable about it, almost shamanistic. Pluto conjunct Venus often describes what you really want and desire at the most fundamental of levels. Although most people are secretly quite scared of their own desires, the most powerful of people with this position are strong enough to surrender to the unknown and the unknowable, especially in and with their partners, knowing that they are invulnerable yet able to grow with a partner in ways they could not do alone. These people are willing to explore every taboo and boundary, insisting only on privacy, respect and trust as absolutes – the archetypal 'forgive but never forget' types of individuals. Just do not ever treat them as lightweights because they will not hang around for long if they feel undervalued.

The core meaning of Venus conjunct Pluto is that of transforming the desperation to be loved, wanted and of value and worth to others into something that one finds within oneself first and foremost before looking for it from other or from the outside world. Most people with this position will do anything and everything to find a position in the world where they are held or considered as being of substance and of worth at the material and physical level, although the sensible ones know that the true arbiter and judge of value and worth is through the eyes of oneself, not others. Even evolved people with this position will still have a judgement system, but at the end of the day only the individual can decide for themselves what it is that is really of value and worth to them.

Venus conjunct Pluto will bring ever more deeper and revelatory experiences and understandings which serve to broaden both tastes and knowledge. What the individual does with these understandings is obviously a choice, but the cleaner and more transparent things are kept the easier new situations, events and developments become. Certainly, the more complicated or underhand things get the more the quicksand and treacle thickens. Power brings with it the responsibility to behave in an ethical manner. In day to day operations this aspect has much to do with interpersonal dynamics, in the workplace, on the street, in one's social life and in the family as much as in personal and intimate relationships. People will experience the Venus conjunct Pluto individual as someone not to be trifled with or considered insubstantial. There can be an intensity and resolve that can unnerve the faint hearted and sometimes silence speaks volumes, along with a sense of 'knowing' without any rational reason for that assumption. This will sort the wheat from the chaff and keep the wimps and the vampires at the door but it can also bring isolation to a degree. This is an excellent position for undercover work, research and working in the depths, especially financial ones but the way that these deep urges are manifested will depend on which of the signs and houses of the zodiac are involved, as well as other aspects to the conjunction. What to others may seem compulsive fascination with a particular subject or person is really to the Venus/Pluto conjunction individual an area of concentration, focus and hopefully, successful specialisation which providing one foot is kept on the ground, should become a permanent attribute as time goes on.

As far as eroticism goes, Venus conjunct Pluto likes to think that it wrote both the training manual and all the updates and no-one should try and convince them otherwise without sting proof armour and extreme caution. These are the people who may use sex as a vehicle to a higher level of sensuality where they just drift and dream along in bliss until they must come back down to grim reality when the partner moves or the bladder calls and the return to physical reality can sometimes be a let-down. In truth, this position is more given to the exotically sensual than the erotically sexual; one is the more physical form of the other. These people value their partners for their subtlety, their sensuality and their refined passion as much as and parallel with their raw sex appeal. It is the hint of mystery, the allure and the potentially seductive sides of life that epitomise the elegance of Venus with the mystique, darkness and danger of Pluto. Thus the blending of the two brings a subtle, mysterious and ever so slightly seductive element into the equation, an element that can never be fully satisfied but can be occasionally temporarily sated.

As they age and mature, Venus conjunct Pluto people become more concerned about the quality of life experience as much as if not more so than the quantity. They go for quality experiences, those that they will remember for the rest of their life and their attitude can be all or nothing at times, preferring to splash it all and go for the one memorable time as opposed to many of minor and more mundane occasions. There will always be the desire to peel away and penetrate the different layers of the onion that lie in relationship patterns, both in one's personal domain and in one's interactions with the outside world in all its different shapes and forms. This is done in such a subtly subversive and unconscious way that the recipient does not even realise that they are being probed until it is over, if at all. There is often a charming and seductive manner that beguiles other people into sharing their deepest secrets but in the same moment these at times implacable people are not that good at talking about their own feelings and emotions until they feel safe and confident enough to do so. The way to their heart is through the conscious and willing acceptance of them as they are as well as the constant assurance that they are deemed to be more than good enough. They then make for the most devoted and passionate partner one could ever ask for, resulting in both of you becoming ever happier. This really is the 'warts and all' position and over a period it grows to be one of the most consummate and loving of all aspects, even if it does come to resemble a pair of old, comfortable slippers by the fireside.

Mars conjunct Pluto

Mars conjunct Pluto in an individual horoscope compels the person to face and deal with experiences of direct, in your face power. This can be seen in forms of self-assertiveness where the tendency to take and make actions and decisions leads to clear boundaries being developed with other individuals very quickly. Alternatively, this can also be seen in others trying to disempower by using inappropriate and unethical means often involving manipulation or other forms of subversive control patterns. The power of the Mars/Pluto conjunction makes the realisation of the flow of power through life inevitable and actions will always speak louder than words. A Mars/Pluto conjunction can be an incisive and accurate point of specific timing and event, or it can be a blunt yet powerful force that can blunder about the place in a clumsy and useless way.

In the bedroom this aspect brings a focused and concentrated stamina into the sexual arena. Sex will never be just light-hearted fun, it will always have an element of depth, physicality, strength and power about it, almost shamanistic in its desire to get basic and primal. Pluto conjunct Venus often describes what you really want and desire and Pluto conjunct Mars shows the ways and the levels at which you will operate to make those desires come true. To put it more bluntly, Pluto/Venus is what you want and Pluto/Mars is how you get it. The most powerful of people with Venus or Mars on top of Pluto are those strong enough to surrender to the unknown and the unknowable, to let go to the flow of sensuality and eroticism that can flow when they are partnered with someone who can sense their deep inner flow, knowing that they are invulnerable yet able to grow with partner in a way that they cannot do alone. In the primacy of the bedroom, there can sometimes be a degree of extremism, from the more primal and basic urges of life on the one hand to the epitome of sophistication, occasionally stopping at all points in-between. Mars conjunct Pluto evokes passion and sexuality in its rawest and most basic form, where the instinctual and the primal are as important if not more so than the intuitive and sophisticated and it rarely does things by half measures. It brings lust into the equation either as a tool for self-expression and mutual pleasure or as a tool for control or domination. People with this aspect are advised to keep a quality of transparency about them with their partners, as this cleanly and easily precludes any potential misunderstanding as well as allowing for clearly understood and maintained boundaries.

In day to day operations Pluto conjunct Mars has a lot to do with the physical presence that people bring into their interpersonal dynamics with people in the workplace, on the street, in one's social world and in the family as much as in personal and intimate relationships. People will experience the Mars/Pluto individual as a hard hitter in life, not to be trifled with or dealt with in non-transparent ways and as someone who can deal with the more difficult things in life with a clear cut attitude that gets things done but that also allows for no interference. There will be an intensity to the gaze which can unnerve the faint hearted or those with something to hide and sometimes silence along with a penetrating stare can speak volumes. When Mars, ruling the physical, projective, sexual and assertive nature is in the same place as Pluto, ruling both the more unconscious urges and the psychological well-being, a powerful blend of energy occurs. This fusion of energy cannot be denied, blocked or shelved and must be dealt with and constantly expressed through some type of active physical lifestyle, lest it build up into some type of unwanted explosion. It creates a dogmatic and bloody minded attitude to getting things done and depending on the sign and house of the zodiac that the conjunction is in, this aspect will bring a powerhouse of unstoppable energy into one's life. It does not, however, bring subtlety or tact with it and indeed these qualities may come towards the bottom of the list of attributes. Mars/Pluto is very no nonsense and prefers to deal with yes or no, black or white – it is not really bothered if there is clarity. This combination has a quality of ruthlessness and bloody mindedness about it that can sometimes either appal or attract others (sometimes at the same time!), but normally this quality is shown towards oneself more than it is to other people. Here is the least attractive potential quality of the Mars/Pluto conjunction, the capacity for self-harm or at least self-sabotage, potentially with a dark and brooding 'that will teach them' reasoning, although exactly who the 'them' is will be unclear.

When older and having survived the rigours and examinations of youth, people with Mars and Pluto in the same place become more and more specialised as they age. Here will be found the best surgeons, the greatest scientists and the most visionary architects, those who go the extra mile to get their point across and come across to the world as sharp, effective and efficient. These are the people who cut through the crap scalpel like and deliberately orchestrate their lives in a way that says that they do not have any time to waste on superficialities. Mars conjunct Pluto people's ability to make decisions in an almost forensic way normally precludes them from making mistakes; they have an added edge when looking at problems that eliminates doubt. At the same time, there is a need for them to know when to stop or at least slow down. If they do not take time out to enjoy the company of others, they may rapidly find themselves alone or even lonely, simply because they burn the rest of the world out with their overly sharp focus and concentration and could burn themselves out as well.

There will always be a degree of potential anger with this aspect and parents of children with Mars conjunct Pluto are recommended to introduce the child into some form of martial arts from age seven-eight onwards. This will encourage the child to manage both their physical and their mental/emotional anger in a constructive, disciplined and self-empowered way as opposed to just lashing out, unfortunately sometimes a common feature of Mars/Pluto. If the individual with this aspect is older, then there will still exist the need for a regularly active physical lifestyle that keeps the body from becoming too inflexible or rigid. Pilates or yoga, tai-chi or qigong are always an alternative form of physical energetic expression in a way that deliberately includes self-discipline. At least a few times in life, the Mars conjunct Pluto individual should give in to their raw, primal and almost animalistic energy and go alone to the remote woods, hills, cliffs or beaches and just scream at the top of their voice, because it releases the soul.

Jupiter conjunct Pluto

According to Greek mythology, from which the vast majority of contemporary astrology draws upon for its archetypes, Jupiter and Pluto were brothers, both the sons of Cronos, or Saturn as he is currently known. Saturn, having usurped and castrated his father (Uranus), was fearful that he in turn would be usurped by his children, so to prevent this he devoured each of his children in turn as they were born. However, his wife Rhea became increasingly resentful of this and eventually conspired to deceive Saturn. When Jupiter was born, instead of feeding him to Saturn, she replaced Jupiter with a stone that Saturn ate, thinking that the stone was his son. Jupiter alone of Saturn's children grew up and in time sought to confront his father about his sins and in the ensuing battle slayed his father, thus releasing all the previously devoured children, one of whom was Pluto. In the aftermath of the war between the Gods, the children of Saturn divided the firmament between them. Whilst Jupiter took the overworld, Pluto became Hades and took rulership of the underworld.

When these two planets occupy the same space in the heavens from a geocentric perspective, they are said to be conjunct with each other and it is as though the two brothers are conjoining forces. However, the outcome of that union depends on the house of the zodiac that the conjunction occurs in and to a lesser degree the sign and what aspects there are in the individual horoscope towards it. In all cases, Jupiter will denote the actual area of development whilst Pluto will act in a kind of subversive and behind the scenes manner, empowering the Jupiterian action from a base psychological root. However occasionally the process will be reversed, when Jupiter will shine a light into the Hadean depths of Pluto, illuminating that which has been hidden and bringing it to the surface for dissemination.

Some of Jupiter's attributes are those of hope, optimism and enthusiasm and in this context Pluto will always bring a considerable degree of assistance as well as a sense of depth and resourcefulness into the equation and adding the potential for substance into what might otherwise just be seen as lightweight flippancy. The Jupiter conjunct Pluto individual will always have grandiose ideas, either in terms of their own personal growth patterns or else in terms of what is deemed to be good for the world and they are not normally slow in letting others know what they think or how they feel. Whilst this ability to see the big picture will always impress others, it can also lead to an overinflated sense of one's own importance or position in the world which in turn normally indicates that pride comes before a fall. Preachers are often not the most popular of people, regardless of whether they are right or wrong.

The worst case scenario with this position can be when the individual becomes so caught up in their own importance that they fail to see the relevance of others in their lives, thus isolating and even alienating themselves from the warmth of decent human contact. On the one hand, this ability for self-centred focus can bring an intense concentration on matters in hand to the point where they can be unaware of anyone else's presence, so caught up in what they are doing that they are not aware of how much they are ignoring others. Alternatively, the conjunction of Jupiter and Pluto can emphasise the larger than life side of the individual's nature through being over generous or so caught up in the excitement of helping or being with others' moments that nothing else is important. This is where everything has such a degree of extravagance or big-heartedness about it that anything else outside of the immediate project or person becomes almost irrelevant. These people burn from the inside with such a degree of urgency that they can put all their energy and attention into their ambition, ignoring the needs of the outside world and thus becoming almost fanatical in their desire to get ahead no matter what the cost. They need to remember that the outside world has a right to at least a small part of their attention.

This ability to persevere in their pursuit of their aims and goals is laudable and valiant but needs tempering big time to avoid the potential of fundamentalism. These are the people who can identify so strongly with their beliefs and passions that if they are not careful, they can become zealot-like in their desire to get ahead or to get others to believe in what they do. There can sometimes be the need to convince others. Jupiter conjunct Pluto does bestow the strong potential for gifted leadership ability with the power to inspire but it needs to be managed to avoid the level of control freakery that might otherwise put people off them.

When they feel that they are being ignored or that their talents are not being appreciated enough the Jupiter/Pluto individual can resort in certain situations to becoming overbearing or even pompous in a way that quickly becomes arrogant, again emphasising this aspects' unique ability to become an island in the stream of humanity. If the individual can learn within themselves about the strength of humility, they can not only be a vital and important cog in the larger scheme of things, they can also demonstrate strong leadership ability in a way that inspires others to better themselves. These are the people who aspire to greatness, even (and preferably) if that greatness is only recognised within themselves or within a localised area or group of people. In terms of their position in the outside world, the Jupiter conjunct Pluto person will quickly rise to a position of authority within their chosen sphere of operation, being particularly good at investigation, team management and researching. This is because of their ability to see the big picture as much as if not more so than the smaller details. The extremes of this position may be demonstrated in the professional world through such occupations as mining or deep sea diving (Pluto and the underworld) or becoming an astronaut, pilot or a high rise crane operator (Jupiter and the higher overworld).

Providing they can avoid the potential of becoming bombastic or over the top, Jupiter conjunct Pluto people are the individuals who live life to the full, never doing anything by half measure but at the same time maximising their opportunities to get ahead. At the end of the day and with some age, knowledge and experience these are the people who crave entrance into the domain of the wise (wisdom) and who aspire to the middle ground knowing that extremes are for those insecure people who desperately need to achieve to feel valid.

Saturn conjunct Pluto

Because Pluto does not have a consistent orbital pattern, this conjunction does not occur with regularity, but on average happens every 33-36 years. Obviously, when it does happen, it affects a whole sub generation of people and anyone born within four months on each side of the exact conjunction will come under its influence in one way or another. Even in loose conjunctions, the sheer raw power that this aspect brings cannot be ignored, even in the most moderate of charts.

A look at the mythology can help here. Saturn and Pluto, or Cronus and Hades, are father and son respectively but there is no family love lost between family here. As detailed above in the paternity of Jupiter, Saturn was so fearful of his children that he devoured them all at the time of their birth except for Jupiter who eventually rose against his father and freed his siblings. The fundamental difference between Jupiter and Pluto is demonstrated here in that Pluto spent time and eternity inside the timeless darkness of Saturn whilst Jupiter never knew that form of hell. It may be that Jupiter's position as lord of the overworld is partially down to his never having experienced the darkness of Saturn's imprisonment whilst Pluto's relative comfort with the darkness of Hades could just as easily be attributed to the same reason. In terms of archetypes, Saturn and Pluto will never have an easy interaction as they represent different basic functions. Saturn brings words like structure and boundary into the equation and is uncomfortable with the more formless side of Pluto, whilst Pluto's desire to experience the transpersonal and unconscious sides of life are at odds with Saturn's more restrictive and conservative nature.

When placed in a difficult position, the Saturn/Pluto conjunction can be a powerful but challenging energy – the unstoppable force against the immovable object. This can often be seen in some form of covert and/or manipulative anger or power struggle towards an imposed system of authority. This authority figure can range from the father or grandfather to God via any form of teacher, employer, government official or law officer, the essence being that of superimposed and dominating male force that has an element of control which cannot be fought against. This 'force' can take many different forms. It can be the individual suffering under the yoke of a tyrannical and authoritarian parent (normally the father) or the individual themselves being a dominating and controlling parent. There can be unsolvable issues with siblings, an intransigence where finance is concerned, or an extremist attitude towards health, nutrition and lifestyle. This aspect can manifest in situations of extreme selfishness or selflessness, or where the individual is obsessively attracted to or repulsed by different elements and levels of community, only really finding themselves comfortable in roles in community that bring with them a degree of power. There can also be a sense of deep and dark brooding apparent, something to be conscious of and avoided when recognised. There will always be a fear of being disempowered, or of being powerless in difficult conversations or situations, so occasionally this aspect will feature in the charts of those who explore various levels of sado-masochistic behaviour, whether projective or receptive and there can also sometimes be an element of self-denial as to the levels of depth that one goes to.

At the same time this conjunction holds in it the capacity for unyielding and invulnerable raw power that if channelled in an ethical and appropriate way can lead the individual to great positions of authority, where they will not so much be liked as much as they will be respected. It bestows the capacity for the making and taking of big actions and decisions in a way that goes beyond the range and scope of normal people and gives a durable and uncompromising willingness to stay the course, no matter how hard the route is. These are the people who know that when under the most incredible of pressure, a lump of coal will eventually turn into a diamond but in order for this to happen a great deal of transformation must first of all take place, most notably in the ways that the individual deals with various levels of frustration in their lives. This is fine from a Plutonian perspective, which lives for the constantly refining and upgrading of the transformative experience, but not so hot from Saturn's perspective which prefers everything to stay the same on the grounds that if it's working, don't fix it. Yet even here, Saturn will finally accept the inevitability of change, if he has a say in the ways in which it is done, at least in the material and non-unconscious world.

When viewed from a positive perspective, there are two ways of seeing this aspect. Certainly, there can exist tremendous capacity for physical exertion and tenacity when needed. Pluto conjunct Saturn brings a greater degree of interface between the part of oneself that defines rules and boundaries and the part of oneself that is the un and subconscious, hopefully bringing with it the changing of rigid and inflexible boundaries into something that is made of rubber and elastic, transparent and malleable but unbreakable at the same time. There can be a transformation of attitude towards the apparent carrying of burdens on the part of others and the reasons for doing this. And when viewed the other way, with Saturn conjunct Pluto, there is also the capacity to bring an element of structure and self-discipline into the workings of the unconscious mind, making for a well-adjusted individual that is an effective and more than competent organiser and someone who is not scared to go the extra mile where necessary. To quote the astrologer Deborah Houlding – *'It brings a talent for successfully performing difficult work under trying circumstances.'* This denotes resolve, perseverance and thoroughness in all situations, making the individual with this conjunction someone not to be trifled with.

Pluto conjunct Ascendant

The Ascendant is the point of reference into and onto the outside world from the individual's minute by minute perspective. It is the armour that one puts on as one goes outside of the front door and into the active outside world, the immediate point of reference at the moment by moment level. When Pluto, with its accompanying degree of intensity and intrigue is conjunct the Ascendant, it always colours the impression of the individual into the outside world. Regardless of the methodology or external manifestation, the power of this conjunction will make the individual a force to be reckoned with by others and will not be seen as a lightweight. During the last one hundred years, Pluto has only occupied the astrological signs of Cancer through to Capricorn, meaning that there will be no-one alive today with Pluto conjunct the Ascendant in the signs of Aquarius through to Gemini.

In every case the presence of Pluto rising on the horizon at the moment of birth adds a strong element of deep intensity to the character, making them someone who cannot be ignored but neither can be dealt lightly with. The potentially broody nature of this can come across to others as almost obsessive at times in their refusal to give up, yield or concede, often to the point of their own self sabotage. It can be metaphorically said of this position that they would rather die than surrender or let others hold dominion over them. There can be a compulsive and dogmatic refusal to change course until it is too late and sometimes there can be an apparent anger with the world for some inexplicable reason. They can exhibit a capacity for extremism in their interactions with other or others and once someone has offended them or pushed them just that little bit too far, there is never going to be any way back, they truly are the 'all or nothing individual.' It would appear to the external observer as though this individual aspect brings semi cyclical periods of crisis and trauma, normally sharp but brief, in ways that serve either as signposts for adjustment in the future or as non-negotiable choice points of personal dogma. Pluto conjunct the Ascendant people can attract people who have a powerful influence in their lives, but for long term healthy relationships to flourish this influence must be balanced with the acknowledgement of the need for mutual respect and for that respect to stretch as far as personal boundaries.

Pluto rising brings with it a kind of imprinted pattern that every so often erupts, volcano-like and brings poison to the surface. In most cases this is seen as times of misfortune, trauma or other forms of major loss that imply some type of ending whilst in some others it manifests in the opposite way, that of the person who recognises their psychological intensity and thus regularly goes through a kind of purging of their soul in order to constantly keep cleansed and be able to keep things rolling. There will always be an interest apparent in the ideas of detoxing, purging, purifying and eliminating, as though the person intrinsically knows that their best bet for personal transformation lies in purifying oneself by eliminating as much poison from their lives as possible. Often this will require substantial periods of isolation, abstinence from contact and the taking of one's psychological space regardless of prevailing circumstances. Pluto conjunct the Ascendant individuals steadily grow accustomed to 'living in the dark.' They gradually realise as they mature in both years and experience that darkness is only the opposite of light and that there is nothing to fear. As they age, the phobia and paranoia of youth gives way to an inner awareness and confidence of their ability to go into the dark and operate just as efficiently as in the light. These are the people who as they age become increasingly yes/no, black/white, they can deal with problems but they cannot and will not deal with lies. The biggest danger for these definitive individuals is the shades of grey, the land of indecision between the light and the dark. Many with this position work in either neonatal or palliative care situations, representative of the part of their energy which is constantly on that edge where life is never a certainty.

There is a positive side to this aspect, one that most people either fail to see or else wilfully ignore. Pluto brings incredible power and if used for the right purposes can be a real agent of change in the outside world, as symbolised by the Ascendant and the sign that it is in. Through regular external interactions the individual can steadily transform their lives in a way that is strongly reminiscent of the snake constantly shedding its skin. As the individual ages so the intensity and extremism of their experience decreases and is replaced by a quality of experience that can border on the transcendental. They become the butterfly emerging from the caterpillar, transformed by the quality of their experience into something previously unimaginable. Out of this type of experience, over a number of different situations and times, comes a sense of one's own invulnerability and the recognition that what doesn't kill you makes you stronger and the ultimate transformation and shapeshifting into the highest form of Pluto on the Ascendant. This is the phoenix rising, reborn and purified, exploding in light and rebirthing itself constantly in an ever-increasingly degree of refinement, accuracy and psychological insight, again tempered by the quality of the zodiac sign that the conjunction is in.

In a way that is not quite as powerful as Pluto conjunct the Moon but that is at least as strong if not stronger than Pluto conjunct the Sun, Pluto rising on the Ascendant at the time of birth does bring with it a level of psychic sensitivity that if not acknowledged when older can result in odd unusual occurrences, often involving dreams, hunches, 'second sight' or 'sixth sense' that defy rational explanation.

There will be an uncanny ability to sense phenomena not apparent to others, whether that is in terms of seeing ghosts or spirits, picking up psychic messages or in the main just learning to trust the unconscious and subliminal part of one's system as much as the rational and objective. Pluto conjunct the Ascendant encourages the individual to trust their deep inner gut feelings, but to also be aware of how they can 'dream in' things that are the product of their own imaginings. As a client puts it; *'Proof, or benchmark, for me, is when I receive messages for something I don't want to do, or hear.'* More than almost any other zodiacal position, this aspect brings with it the need to accept that one's perception of the world, the people in it and their actions is going to be different to the norm. Here, the individual will always see the underbelly, the undercurrents and the sordid underworld side of life more easily than others. However, it is the way they live with this realisation that dictates their life in terms of their own psychic ability. Many choose to block it out and ignore it, semi fearful of what they may see or find if they do go there. Others who do face this side of themselves often find themselves becoming agents of transformation in others' lives, whether that is as a catalyst or as a psychological counsellor using techniques that border on shamanism, regardless of the construct.

Every so often, the Pluto conjunct Ascendant individual needs to voluntarily choose to step back out of the world into their own self-imposed exile, to retreat into their cave and to go through an almost ritual self-purging to check that they are still exorcising their inner demons. These demons are not actually theirs but instead have either been taken willingly from others or else inherited or absorbed along the way. The idea of purifying oneself through constant refinement and cleansing in some way is endemic in these people and as they age so they epitomise the transformative rise to an exquisite degree of refinement and purity.

Pluto conjunct Midheaven

The Midheaven has three basic functions as far as astrology goes. There is the archetypal meaning of it as being the significator of authority in ones' life, whether that authority is the father/mother, teacher, employer, state, God in any of its various descriptions or other form of dominant controlling interest in one's life. The Midheaven is also the point in the chart that governs the career, job, work practices and vocation. This can be a routine and mundane job that is done for forty hours a week simply for the money, or it can be a vocation, passion and something that much of one's waking time is put into – or indeed, somewhere in between. Of course, the Midheaven is that part of one's horoscope that deals with public image. If the Sun position represents one's notions of identity, the Moon the sense of personality and the Ascendant governs the armour that is put on as one goes outside the front door, then the Midheaven represents the way that one tries to impress the world as being. It is the projection of oneself by oneself that the outside world sees in terms of first contact. It is the public image, the way the individual is seen at the first meeting. The Midheaven is the profile, the deliberate and conscious persona that is projected, the immediate recognition by others of status and position in the pecking order, one's social standing and to a lesser extent, one's external reputation.

When Pluto is conjunct the Midheaven in a birth chart, the effects are rarely unnoticeable. Pluto carries with it such an intense capacity that when on the Midheaven, it will always be seen as someone not to be trifled or messed with. When dealing with one's ambition, this position can take the individual (and the people around them) to heaven and to hell, sometimes at the same time. The negative side of this conjunction, when dealing with the public image side of the Midheaven, can lead to accusations of tyranny, ruthlessness and an incessant drive for success no matter what the consequences. There can be the tendency to run roughshod over other people's feelings and the apparent inclination towards mercilessness when dealing with competitors in the workplace, which over a period will inevitably lead to the individual becoming ostracised or even isolated by one's professional community. Pluto on the Midheaven sometimes just does not seem to care what others think or feel and that the rest of the world is quite welcome to do what it will if it does not get in the way or conflict with the Pluto/Midheaven persons' pathway forward. Yet on the other hand, Pluto on the Midheaven, depending on other aspects, can be seen as someone who can also both inspire and lead others forward, acting as a lynchpin and fulcrum for everybody else to lean and depend on. It can be seen as the epitome of reliability and dependability, if there is no-one who is trying to shoehorn them into doing something that they do not want to do. Pluto here brings with it the determination, perseverance and downright bloody mindedness to succeed, regardless of whether that success is seen or acknowledged by the outside world. Pluto on the Midheaven is always capable of going to great lengths and if necessary extremes that others simply will not go to get the required results. When it comes to the professional domain, this position brings the willingness and energy to move mountains, providing the incentive is there and that there are no hidden agendas.

When it comes to the more public image side of the Midheaven, Pluto in this position brings with it the desire to make something of oneself, to be successful and to be seen as someone who strives to succeed. There will be the internal wish to be seen as authentic, accompanied by the secret need to be trusted by everyone around them, although this desire for trust is not always reciprocated. Pluto on the Midheaven can come across as secretive, power hungry and intense but alternatively it can also be seen as fiercely loyal, a powerhouse of determination and very, very thorough. Sometimes these people attract a degree of challenge from others towards them without meaning to and if so then this is because that even without realising it they carry such a capacity for endeavour that they can arouse subconscious jealousy in others who simply cannot keep up with them. Whilst this relative opposition is normally so low key that it just rumbles underneath in the background, occasionally it can erupt in a blaze of almost irrational anger either towards the person or from them.

In extreme cases, Pluto on the Midheaven can result in the individual becoming ostracised by their peers to the point that they become almost nihilistic, looking only to live life in a constantly ongoing and evolving pattern of destruction followed by transformative rebirth and making it difficult for others to relate consistently to them. They can feel isolated, regardless of their social and family connections, because they feel that the rest of the world simply does not get where they are coming from. These really are the people whose attitude is that if you are going to do anything worthwhile, then do it properly or not at all. However, if they are dealt with in an honest and transparent way, they will be as fiercely loyal as they can, if necessary to the bitter end and beyond. There is no cause not worth fighting for, no person or philosophy that cannot be defended or argued for and sometimes no justification at all for half measures, in any capacity or situation. Indeed, this is the all or nothing position, at least when it comes to career and profile. These people are more likely than most to engage in careers that take them to the extremes – mining, space exploration, deep sea diving, parapsychology, private detectives, criminal psychologists, investigative reporters, researchers and any other type of career that either brings the depths and the hidden to the surface or that reveals that which has been either concealed or buried.

There is also the relationship with at least one of the parents to be considered. With this position it is likely that one of the parents will either be absent or challenging in some way, often to an extreme. This is a common position in astrology for those individuals who have suffered bereavement of parents at an early age, or are brought up in single parent families, or else adopted, fostered or orphaned. It may be that a parent will try to get the child to become what the parent in question may have been if they had taken their chances and when the child with Pluto on the Midheaven goes their own way, the parent in question may exhibit resentment, jealousy or other forms of manipulative behaviour in an effort to get the child to conform to their wishes. Obviously, this will only serve to push the child away from the family from an early age and parents of children with Pluto on the Midheaven are best advised to encourage their child to develop in their own way with the unconditional support of the family. Any adult with Pluto on the Midheaven would do well to be as completely clear and upfront with their parents as they can, so that at the end of the day they can say to themselves that they did their best regardless of eventual outcomes.

Pluto on the Midheaven individuals cannot avoid facing up to sides of themselves that other people are very good at both concealing and not dealing with. Yet by acknowledging one's deeper and more extreme potentials, the individual not only gets to know themselves better than most others, but they are also capable of getting strong and positive results from their life. This is done simply by living it to the max, even if that is a lonely path, often accompanied only by those who also share that inner restlessness and desire for constant purging, regeneration, transformation and renewal of their apparent mission in life. Their willingness to go through periods of crisis and trauma, primarily through either their older family arrangements or in their career sets them apart from most, although to these individuals the ends normally justify the means and compromise is a land for others. Pluto on the Midheaven can take you to the very top of your tree or the very bottom rung of the ladder, depending on your own willingness to deal with the darker and more hidden sides of life in an open and transparent way. The philosophy here is clear – simplicity works, deal only with honest and upfront people and if you always tell the truth you never have to remember what you said.

Sextiles to Pluto

A sextile is one sixth of a circle, an angle of sixty degrees and is given an orb of influence of some four or five degrees. The sextile is unique in astrology in that it incorporates both the numbers two and three. Three sextiles added together make for an opposition, with all its attendant manifest challenges. But two sextiles added together make for a trine, bringing an element of both pleasure and ease into the equation. The key word for a sextile is that of opportunity. The fact that the opportunity exists is evidence of the more flowing, feminine and fortunate side of this aspect, but the connection with the more masculine and challenging side of astrology also demonstrates that work needs to be done for that opportunity to manifest in a measurable way.

When the planet being sextiled is Pluto, the opportunity is always going to be related to the more subconscious and unconscious sides of life, in that rather than clear cut chances, the likely manifestation is through hunches that always work out. A sextile to Pluto will put the individual in touch with their more transpersonal nature and help them understand both themselves and others in a deeper and more psychologically oriented way than most. It facilitates the steady and gradual emergence and birthing of the metaphorical butterfly from the caterpillar, instead of being dragged from the womb kicking and screaming. A sextile to Pluto enables the individual to deal with the regenerative and transformative process in a more willing and conscious way, thus enabling the ongoing rebirth of life to proceed in a manner that is not so much disruptive and chaotic as it is empowering and favourable. Yet at the same time any aspect to Pluto, no matter how favourable, should not be taken either lightly nor for granted, as Pluto's psychological and in-depth nature will not be taken superficially. Nevertheless, most sextiles to Pluto bring with them the capacity and the willingness for voluntary transformation, like the snake shedding its skin and then moving on, leaving the empty shell behind. A general rule of thumb here is that if one were to put the words opportunity and transformation together along with the nature of the planet or point being sextiled, a clear window of growth and positive change will be revealed that normally always adds something favourable to the influences in the horoscope.

Sun sextile Pluto

The Sun represents one's basic sense of identity and individuality, the part of oneself that is untouchable and inviolate. It is the unique part of one's core being that is separate from anyone or anything else. Pluto when relating to the Sun is that part of one's nature that is called the subconscious or the unconscious, that which governs the autonomic and automatic fight or flight capacity and represents the constantly changing and transforming manifestation of one's life. The sextile aspect, when between these two astrological points, puts the Plutonian depths in touch with the will power of the Sun and introduces the capacity for a great deal of self-awareness across all levels of the spectrum of consciousness and thus pushes the individual with this aspect into positions of natural leadership and dependability. Whatever they do, they know that if it is done with passion and focus, it will be more successful than most. A desire to 'do the right thing' whilst seen as being upstanding and reliable is a trademark of this aspect. These are the types of people who are secret superheroes, wearing masks to protect their identity and going out at night righting wrongs and exposing injustices wherever they find them, it is as if they need an element of both mystery and intrigue to fire them up every so often. As a client states; *'I do like injustices to be exposed and I can be a devil's advocate; I don't purposely need 'an element of both mystery and intrigue' to fire me up but people find me a little intriguing and mysterious. I do love to watch murder mysteries and crime investigation channels,'* whilst another client puts the same feelings in a different way; *'I love going into caves, underground tunnels, labyrinths and going out at night in thick fog.'*

It is this capacity for reliability and durability even when under stress that makes these individuals stand out from others as much as their capacity for intrigue or attracting mystery, it is as though nothing fazes them, they exude confidence in all the tasks they undertake. If the individual has an artistic side to their nature, they may sometimes take on the more controversial, darker or more sexual or taboo subjects rather than the simple and lighter forms of art. It should be remembered that even under the favourable gaze of the Sun, Pluto likes to slip in and out of the light, playing the provocative tease every so often, but generally this is done in a light-hearted way without malice or any form of negativity. Nevertheless, this position leaves no stone unturned and over the years develops a healthy and deep interest in many diverse activities. As another client so eloquently states; *'I've also felt for many years that my life is in stages and I almost know when a stage has come to an end. Not stages as in child, teenager, marriage, home, old age, but more in learning who I am, what I've learnt about life, what can I do with that knowledge, when I've outgrown someone or something etc...'* The transformative urge combines with the individual identity and will power and brings a maturation of confidence that is normally ahead of its peer group and gives a general proclivity to spending time with older or more experienced people.

Moon sextile Pluto

Whereas the Sun represents identity and the sextile to Pluto brings manifestation in measurable ways concerning power management, the Moon is much more connected to the internal and personal side of one's nature. It is that which governs both the emotive states which are often influenced by others and the feelings, seen as more innate and less externally influenced. When this sensitive point is sextiled to Pluto, harmonious transformation is often the result. As a client so succinctly summarised it, '*I am, to put it simply, comfortable in my own skin.*' Pluto really likes working with the more unconscious and subconscious sides of life as symbolised by the feminine, non-logical patterns of the Moon. The imagery here is that of prenatal, embryonic nurturing, nestling, snuggling, being protected and fed by the great dark that is all that there is. It also symbolises that same energy reversed and projected into the world, through a type of unconditional nurturing which in turn acts as the vehicle for the phoenix-like transformation of consciousness into a much more empathic, receptive and intuitive person. Over years of experience this aspect brings sureness into the recognition of one's intuition, one's instinct and the difference between the two. This difference can be loosely summarised as immediate gut feel about two inches below the navel, at the blending point between the human intuition and the animal instinct. In this context, instinct is seen as something we are born with, an innate and basic response, whilst intuition is a product at some level of reason, observation and experience over the years.

When it comes to the projection of this energy into the outside world, the Moon sextile Pluto individual comes across as someone who is resolute in a quiet yet profoundly determined way, with mannerisms that are understated yet carry a hint of both intrigue and caution about them. These are the people who stand just off to one side observing quietly and rarely missing anything, who get the subtle nuances of developments at a glance and who can be relied on to give an accurate and impassive summary of situations at a moment's notice. The apparent willingness to trust the immediacy of the instinctive 'knowing' is what makes these people special in the eyes of others, as though they have been granted some type of mystique that sets them apart from the rest of humanity and their in-depth emotional understanding of others problems and challenges makes them at times both a needed and respected person. There will always be something almost indiscernible that sets these people apart from others, something intangible but that can be caught in the occasional piercing glimpse, sardonic comment or flash of ruthlessness.

Mercury sextile Pluto

Mercury is the only planet in the solar system that is seen as neutral, and genderless. Because of this, its relationship with Pluto is always going to be ambiguous to an extent and will always have deep psychological undertones, regardless of how positive any aspect may be. Mercury's capacity for all communication mediums, whether mental, verbal, electronic or other, gels well with the basic Plutonian urge towards a deeper comprehension of life at all levels. It brings a deep and penetrating mind with a strong analytical bent that is always looking for an inclusive solution to the larger problems of life, whilst at the same time being able to somehow always zero in on the relevant issues and get to the heart of the matter straight away. As a client states; *'Research is something I do for work; marketing research, analysing sales reports, clients and why they do what they do. But I would like to have been an undercover investigator or gumshoe.'* There exists the potential for a strong concentration, often with specific emphasis towards one particular area of study or work. At the same time there is the need to constantly analyse one's motives and be aware of how one's own beliefs can suddenly change one's opinion. Mercury/Pluto is nothing if not flexibly astute and will think nothing of reversing opinion or changing its mind if good reason is found.

There is an element of truth seeker in this aspect and often these people accept careers involving some type of investigative work, especially if it involves deep research. Another client states; *'Whether I have a deeper comprehension of life I'm not sure, but I'm always trying to find it; the why am I here, why does this happen and why doesn't humankind learn from its mistakes.'* Often their opinion is taken seriously, their thought patterns are recognised as being thorough and their ability to draw far reaching conclusions and answers is often unnoticed by others yet is always there in the background. There is a plentiful willpower, with an abundance of curiosity thrown in for good measure and the ability to see the most obscure and evasive sides of life with more clarity than most, leading to a greater and more comprehensive understanding of the subject matter.

Venus sextile Pluto

Venus sextile Pluto gives powerful feelings and perceptions that deepens one's innate and intimate responses to love, people and life in general and brings out any intrinsic artistic talents in ways that both focus on and enhance original creativity.

Venus sextile Pluto individuals have a user-friendly psychological insight into how other people work that makes them easily adaptable, tolerant and flexible towards other people's foibles and idiosyncrasies, although not all of them are aware of it – as a client puts it: *'I wish I could tap into the psychology insight more easily as it only seems to come out when I get emotionally pushed and then it astounds me, like, where did that come from?'* There is a type of superficial geniality that enables these individuals to skate through life without too much sticking to them, but woe betide anyone who mistakes this external bonhomie as being lightweight or flighty. Venus sextile Pluto people have, just below this lightweight surface, an indomitable will power that, simply put, just does not deal with anyone who is less than completely transparent. These people are intrinsically honest with themselves and expect but unfortunately rarely get the same from others. Nevertheless, the opportunistic attitude of the sextile brings a harmonious blend of the Venusian social skill and the Plutonian depth and psychological insight in a way that gives these people a very shrewd and precise observational point from which to view the rest of the world.

The key to success and contentment in relationships with this aspect is through the understanding of people and their motivations. Venus sextile Pluto brings out the potential to see the best in everyone and gives the individual an aura of seeming powerful with a magnetic popularity, as if that individual has a completely non-judgmental magical charm for dealing with people in ways that automatically puts them at their ease. These are the people who on the one hand may find themselves becoming easily attracted by physical appearance and sex appeal, whilst at the same time being just as quickly turned off by superficiality and lack of depth. Venus working in such a favourable way with Pluto brings the capacity to love deeply, passionately and wholeheartedly, to such a degree that sometimes others may find this intensity either extremely attractive or else threatening. When these people choose to become involved with someone else, they can really project themselves into the emerging romance or relationship with limitless energy, although this energy can just as easily be transmuted into other creative or artistic areas of life when they are not involved with anyone or in a relationship where they feel equally treated. There exists a deeply sensual charisma that can have a powerful emotional influence on certain others, especially from the opposite gender and it may be that these innocent people can use their attractiveness to subtly manipulate others without even realising it. The capacity for intimacy is enhanced if there is a 'quid pro quo,' equal shares in both the effort and the reward. The understanding and appreciation of love is instinctive and Venus sextile Pluto is fully prepared to accept the responsibilities of love as well as the joys – if there is a healthy result at the end of the day.

Mars sextile Pluto

Pluto sextile Mars brings a high and often dynamic level of physical vitality. When the capacity for both concentrated physical assertiveness (Mars) and intense and determined impression and expression (Pluto) blends through the opportunistic melding of the sextile, there exists a healthy and positive approach to all forms of physical expression. There will be the willingness to engage in distinct levels of physical interaction through natural and organic ways without inner compulsions or old phobic patterns distorting energy release. This aspect produces a strong will power and forcefulness in style that penetrates to the bottom of the most complex of issues, giving the individual the ability to read people and their motives clearly. There is an expectation of honesty in their dealings with people, preferring to hear the truth even if it hurts rather than be confused by evasion, uncertainty or psychological manipulation. Honesty is one of these people's most highly valued qualities and Mars sextile Pluto people can use this attribute in being very persuasive in the way that they express their opinions, being seen as talking from the heart. There will also be the capacity for a grasp of dramatic presentation with which they can influence others and these individuals certainly do not have any problems with taking calculated chances, on the grounds that it is normally better to try and fail than not to try at all.

Mars sextile Pluto normally brings with it the capacity for a steady, regular and consistent sexual stamina with a perseverant and rolling quality that does not really stop or even slow down until specific objectives have been realised. Whether in the bedroom, in the gym or on the dance floor, there will be an ease in finding and riding that semi-conscious rhythm that just goes with the flow and the beat of the drum, rides the wave and steadily gets higher, clearer and purer as it flows. People with this aspect have a kind of conscious physical assuredness about them that speaks of an innate confidence, they metaphorically carry themselves well. Rarely if ever is there any major dichotomy or personality issue, as their relationship with their physical body coupled with their personal willpower really helps and encourages the assimilation process. Because the sextile is a harmonious aspect bringing both energy and opportunity, there will be decisiveness but no confrontation or conflict when it comes to finding ways of resolving problems. Usually, others will get to know very quickly where Mars sextile Pluto people stand as they are not shy of revealing their viewpoints and they expect the same of others whether that is in the outside world or in the privacy and intimacy of the home and the bedroom. This aspect brings drive, vivacity and a willingness to use their energy in a mutually enhancing beneficial way.

Jupiter sextile Pluto

There is little if anything uncomplimentary that can be said about this aspect. As equal and opposite forces, these two mythological brothers, the largest and the smallest of planets, work well together in a contrasting but complementary way. It is important here to remember that according to the latest understandings of Greek mythology, Jupiter/Zeus took the overworld whilst Pluto/Hades claimed the underworld; both have an equal rulership over their domain. With the sextile between the two, Jupiter shines and directs its light and power into the Plutonian depths in ways that encourage an openness in the individuals' dealings with others, knowing that within that openness also lays an invulnerable ability to override all problems in their way. Jupiter's natural exuberance helps Pluto lighten up, in as much as it ever does so and brings the opportunity for an element of brevity into Pluto's darker side. An element of sarcasm, irony or other harsh form of humour will be present in some form with most people with this aspect. The sextile will bring the opportunity for Jupiter to expand upon Pluto's internal dark knowledge and its psychological foundations and roots in ways that can educate or inspire the world. This aspect is common in the charts of teachers and students of the more philosophical forms of higher education, including theology and religion.

In turn, Pluto brings an element of depth, seriousness and gravity into what can otherwise be seen sometimes as Jupiter's more insubstantial or lightweight nature. It brings an element of forcefulness and intensity into the personal ambition and desire for success, as well as the understanding that their success also needs to be the success of others for it to be worthwhile, because what good is transformation if it does not benefit others besides oneself? When Pluto is in a good mood, as he is seen to be when he is in sextile, his energy is that of helpful transformation mixed with opportunity. When this is directed towards Jupiter, a deep and penetrating insight into the philosophy of religion, law and global order is often both common and strong. This aspect brings enthusiasm unbridled if the matter in hand is something worth getting passionate about. The power with which the Jupiter/Pluto sextile person imbues their chosen theme often makes them a powerful orator, teacher or advocate of some type. There are often global aspirations, normally for the most altruistic and higher minded of reasons. However, even here with the sextile between these two competitive but balanced energies, there will be the need to ensure that boundaries are not exceeded and that wisdom prevails at the end of the day. Jupiter will take you to the highest of highs and Pluto to the lowest of lows, but finally and after decades of practice, the middle ground is accepted as being the safest option. And it is wisdom, the domain of the wise, that is the highest manifestation of this aspect, although there is also a good case for arguing that wisdom comes only with knowledge, maturity and experience.

Saturn sextile Pluto

The capacity for exactness and precision blended with a disciplined, determined and strong will power is common here. There will be little fear of competition or rivalry, as the only player in the game worthy of consideration is oneself. The willingness to push boundaries ever deeper makes this individual someone to be respected and not to be ignored or trifled with. Saturn's ability to concentrate and focus on emerging structures works alongside the Plutonian capacity for psychological effort and Saturn's perseverance coupled with Pluto's resolve creates a lava – like effect that inevitably succeeds, taking its time where necessary but always burning through and leading to great accomplishments at the end of the day. Although the relationship between these two heavy hitters will have a quality of mutual respect, it is never going to be exactly cordial because after all, Saturn did consume Pluto in mythology. The sextile relationship between them does indicate both the ability and the willingness to work alongside and parallel to each other, for the same purpose if not exactly on the same team. It gives the capacity for an objective and detached psychological perspective on both oneself and others, as well as the ability to take both hard choices and actions.

Pluto brings its psychological insight into all of Saturn's structures, both at the personal and the global level, giving them greater depth and resilience, whilst Saturn is capable of man and group management knowing that hard work becomes the ongoing agent of transformation. There can be an element of political intrigue present, which may be both revealing and potentially risky and all situations and developments involving decisions of power should be transparent and accountable for this person to feel comfortable about the process. Over the years maturity and experience breed a degree of acceptance and even comfort with notions of power, leading to a gradual acceptance of one's lot in life and the capacity for steadily rising to the occasion. There will be a deeply perceptive and almost obsessive ability to scrutinise things to the greatest of depth. These people are great at helping others deal with transformation, death and rebirth, they see beneath superficiality and they are excellent at getting the whole picture.

Pluto sextile Ascendant

The Ascendant/Descendant axis governs the relationship that individuals have with both themselves and with significant other, whether that other be in terms of family, friend, professional or personal and intimate. The relationship with oneself involves mirrors, self-analysis, confidence (or lack of) and all forms of self-imagery, whilst the relationship with other involves personal interaction and cooperation at all diverse levels of existence. The basic meaning of the sextile is that of opportunity through work, or working for opportunity and when that opportunity is coming from Pluto then the potential for all relationship experiences to become deeper, meaningful, intense and more profound is amplified. The difference between the sextile and the trine is demonstrated clearly here: the sextile between Pluto and the Ascendant deals with the transformation of oneself through the process of relationship, whilst the trine deals more with the process of the transformation of the relationship with other. The presence of Pluto suggests the desire for all interactions to have substance and depth about them, the sextile encourages the process of transformation and the Ascendant dictates the type of interaction being transformed. If there is not an amount of gravity and purpose to the relationship, it will not last long.

From a Plutonic perspective, no relationship is worth the effort unless it has a quality of integrity, depth and clarity about it from the start. This aspect brings a growing contentment in the relationship one has with oneself, so much so that as the person ages, they realise that the only good reason for being in relationship with anyone else is solely because they want to. Unlike most others, these deep rooted and psychologically sound people are not caught up in the need or even the desire to be with other – an involvement must have merit and reward from the start for these people to even show the slightest bit of interest. They are not attracted by those that need saving or helping but at the same time they are not compromising or in any way subservient. Pluto sextile the Ascendant brings a simplistic approach to relationship patterns as the individual ages, they know what they like, they know what they do not and whilst they are not basic loners, they are OK at being alone and content with biding their time until the right potential presents itself.

Pluto sextile Midheaven

The sextile between these two points encourages Pluto's transformative depths to steadily emerge in a phoenix-like way as the individual ages, especially when it comes to their attitudes towards the acquiring and the using of resources. When young, this position gives a degree of professional adaptiveness and skill from the word go, offering the opportunities for advanced and accelerated growth and development in the outside world. Ideally, the individual will seize these early opportunities and establish themselves in such a way that suggests that in later life they will not need to strive or work so consistently hard. What makes these people different to the others around them in the workplace is their inherent capacity to spot doorways as they open and their ability to get on with all other people around them in an affable yet uncompromising way. This is particularly good for dealing with people in positions of authority and even becoming one of these people as time develops. At the end of the day, it does not matter whether the authority in question is the father, teacher, employer, state or the divine, the individual with Pluto sextile the Midheaven will have an assured and confident way of dealing with them that as they age earns at least the respect if not the admiration of all around them. There is a danger when young of coming across as too self-assured or overconfident, which may engender a minor degree of resentment from representatives of the older generations around the individual. Whilst this position does bring the ability to both handle authority and to rise to prominence through that handling, it also brings with it the internalised awareness that there is an end justification, a result at the end of the day that justifies all the effort and hard work of youth.

There comes a time, often in the mid-late thirties, when that desire to be so apparently successful in terms of external world prominence gradually morphs into the desire to have a more rewarding and fulfilling home life. Here, how the capacity for the responsibility and management skills obvious in earlier career worlds to come into play within the residential and family environment is something that exponentially develops with age. Pluto sextile the Midheaven is thus by default trining the IC, giving a basic good understanding of domestic and familial responsibilities and as the person ages so their standing and status within the family grows. Their ability to understand other people's patterns and motivations without being critical or judgemental is a positive example of how this aspect brings with it an element of wisdom and almost grandparent-like benevolence. And as the person with the Pluto/Midheaven sextile ages and they go through the patterns of career and family, so they learn to blend their unconscious intuitive nature with their desire for success, with the wise ones knowing that success is not just measured in financial terms. In their latter years, this aspect brings greater flexibility towards life's chances, with varied windows of opportunity and stimulus to an ever refining degree.

Squares to Pluto

A square is an angle of ninety degrees, a right angle to the point of origin, when two planets or points are in sharp and challenging angle to each other. A square in astrology is one of the hardest of aspects in that it brings into contact two planets in zodiac signs that are in different genders and elements with nothing in common but plenty in potential conflict. A square links two planetary energies that are not only incompatible but also potentially antagonistic towards each other. Often a square can be seen as two different armies in conflict, where there can be clear indications of both the problem and the solution. But when one of the planets in question is Pluto, issues arise in that it is nothing if not subversive and any challenge made directly to Pluto will invariable end in defeat because of its insidious capacity to absorb and consume and then undermine, go behind the scenes, manipulate and disempower by nefarious and underhand methods. A square to Pluto can bring up a lot of 'demons' from one's own personal underworld and/or it can manifest those 'demons' as being in the individual's outside world. In either case, the square involving Pluto will occasionally force the individual to go head to head with their own notions and ideas of power flowing through their lives, either by dealing with those demons and becoming a person of deliberate and conscious power, or by attempting to suppress and repress those urges. In the latter case this gradually brings over the years an accumulative degree of internal corruption, moral erosion and self-denial that could easily in time become very self-destructive, as well as many different potential conflict situations with other or others in the individual's life based around vague feelings of disempowerment at the emotional level.

It does not matter whether the accompanying elements of phobia, paranoia, compulsion, extremism or intensity that Plutonic squares can generate come from within the person themselves or whether they are attracted from others. The problems are still the same and need not so much to be beaten or conquered as much as understood and allowed expression within the context of the greater whole. A square from Pluto symbolises the repression of fundamental urges that if held in for too long will eventually break free in a way that can be truly devastating and self-destructive. Obsessive behavioural patterns over a period that lack an element of flexibility or tolerance will eventually implode, resulting in times of crisis and/or trauma in ways that are truly life changing and not normally in a positive or easily dealt with way. Often the anger is not expressed openly, instead repressed and over an extended period this can lead to serious illness at some level. Alternatively, on the rare occasion that the person is able to detach themselves sufficiently from what is ongoing around them and observe and act from a totally objective perspective (which with Pluto is fundamentally yes/no, black/white etc.), the square energy from Pluto can be utilised in a way that can seem externally ruthless, but nonetheless is also seen as extremely efficient and practical, transforming situations around them by taking direct actions or decisions that others baulk at.

People with squares to Pluto in their chart are not going to be lightweight, they will carry with them a degree of intensity that can easily burn out the more sensitive or gentle people around them at times, but at the same time they are capable of transforming that intensity into sharp and concise decisions by being absolutely clear with both themselves and with others about where they stand on any particular issue. And there is a positive side to having squares from Pluto in one's horoscope, that being the sure knowledge that no-one can lie to these people for very long at all without it becoming obvious. Their ability to ferret out the untruths and the sordid can make them quite scary in people's eyes, but normally only those with something to hide. This is where the impenetrable Pluto gaze comes into its own, being scarily accurate in determining the truth from the lies. There is no better researcher into buried secrets than Pluto, especially when he is being squared and he has the bit between his teeth.

Sun square Pluto

The Sun represents one's basic sense of identity, uniqueness and individuality; it is the spark at the core of one's being and it is the sacrosanct part of one's nature. The Sun astrologically demonstrates how you carry your energy into every situation of life. Any contact between the Sun and Pluto will invariably bring a great deal of intensity and depth into all diverse types of interactions with other and others, but when the aspect between the two is a square the capacity for challenge is amplified. For example, it may indicate that there will be themes of constantly changing opposition or blockages in the person's life, where as soon as one problem is sorted another of a similar form or nature pops up to take its place. Over the years, by objective and detached reflection, a repetitive pattern of almost self-destructive potential may be seen, represented by constantly similar challenges arising from different environments and suggestive of a refusal to look at the side of oneself that to the rest of the world seems to be glaringly obvious. There is likely to be a recalcitrant attitude to certain situations and the more those situations demand change the more stubborn the individual may become, refusing point blank to change no matter what the cost. And here lies one of the fundamental basics of Pluto, the willingness to self-sacrifice or even to die rather than to compromise, which is all very noble and honourable but can also be seen as shooting oneself in the foot or self-sabotage. It should be emphasised that this behaviour pattern normally only emerges in cases where there have been decades of repression, primarily stemming from the first seven years of life, but there will always be an essence of the potential for elimination in the character which others may see as indelicate, too hard and ruthless towards oneself and others. These are the people who would rather die than surrender and giving up sometimes is just not an option. Bloody minded is a descriptive term that comes to mind…

Alongside this incessant and resolute compulsion to never give up lies different qualities of energy that only become apparent as one grows and matures, not just in age but also in self-awareness and intelligence. The constant desire to prove oneself as always getting stronger/better/bigger needs to be understood for what it is, an almost obsessive primordial urge to purge, cleanse and purify oneself in what may appear to be an increasingly polluted world. One way of doing this as referred to earlier is to be ruthless and eliminative on one's meteoric rise forward, but then the winner of the rat race merely proves to be the biggest rat. Alternatively, the Sun square Pluto brings a more subtle desire for refinement, not so much the aesthetic, delicate or artistic but certainly the focussed, specific and effective. As a good friend voiced: *'From a personal perspective, once I set a goal in place, I find ways to accomplish said goal finding ways to solve for or ameliorate the obstacles. I like to think that I am good at identifying what might be self-sabotage and shifting directions quickly – on a dime usually, but one is always limited when assessing oneself. I have been told numerous times that I am clinical and on the money at evaluating people's actions and motivations.'* This position can get to the very bottom of what is going on and by acting in a dispassionate and clinical way and it can save lives and favourably alter potential futures, albeit in not as gently a way as others might prefer. There will always be an innate urge to act and to do something and if this primal energy wave can be surfed and then subtly channelled, then the individual will become an expert at what they do. The ability to manifest situations through increasingly refined highs and lows can manifest in detailed understanding of all types of criminology, psychology of the difficult sort, or any type of forensic or scientific investigation particularly at the invisible level. This aspect does not bestow psychic ability, but it does give a deep internal sense of simply knowing that can be summarised as gut feel and if this can be both recognised and then consciously worked with, the individual will always be seen as having a clinically good judgement of character.

Moon square Pluto

The astronomical Moon reflects the light of the Sun onto the Earth, so the astrological Moon reflects the light of the Sun out of the individual. The Moon is about one's day by day lifestyle, feelings, emotions, sensitivities and habit patterns. As the Sun represents your individuality, so the Moon represents your personality. Fundamentally, the Sun is seen as masculine and projective whilst the Moon is seen as feminine and receptive. And when that receptive Moon is square to potentially subversive and dark energies from Pluto, all hell (sometimes literally!) can break loose. This aspect is sensitive to emotional undercurrents in the domestic sphere and regardless of gender the person with this aspect may often find that their relationships with important women in their lives will have a profound and difficult impact on their life. It may be a lack of clarity or emotional transparency in the relationship with the main female nurturing influence when young, normally the mother, although often the Moon/Pluto square is common in the charts of people raised by grandparents or family members other than parents. There is the spectre of emotional abandonment here, feeling isolated from an early age with a sense of being uncared for or even worse, unwanted. As a client says: '*I know the feeling of wanting to scream and have learnt to let it out after much putting up with people/situations.*' This aspect is common in cases of emotional (and sometimes other forms of) abuse and in extreme cases of both the square or the opposition of the Moon to Pluto the individual may confuse pain and degradation with love to a degree that becomes almost sado-masochistic. If as adults these people attempt to sweep unpleasant childhood experiences under the carpet, then they may become emotionally fragmented and unable to sustain steady or consistent emotional patterns. This is one of the most common astrologically repetitive aspects in that it can appear in successive generation's charts until eventually one brave soul will face up to the fear and deal with it, ending lifetimes of pain and abuse.

When young, there is likely to be a physical and metaphorical fear of the dark which is a prenatal memory of life in the womb. As the individual gradually matures into puberty and beyond this unconscious fear of darkness can persist until consciously accepted and allowed, often done best in adult years by going into nature alone on some type of purgative and shamanistic ritual. The Moon is about individual feelings and sensitivities; it cannot be explained or experienced in rational and analytical ways. Similarly but different, Pluto represents the psychological and the unconscious, again areas that cannot be rationalised or consciously understood, and when these two deep emotive forces are at war with each other, there will be times of scarily accurate perception that borders on the truly psychic. Equally at the same time there also exists the capacity for that perception to be so skew-whiff that it can only be described as not so much psychic as psychotic. The challenge of the Moon/Pluto square is to face fears knowing and accepting that they cannot be consciously understood, that they can only be felt and hopefully released in a loving and sensitive but also firm and disciplined way. It is the willing elimination of not the childlike side of oneself or one's nature but the despotic infant that is being asked here, to use one's emotional insights for the psychological benefit of all as opposed to just oneself. The Moon square to Pluto can bring a degree of emotional warping and sometimes it is only by asking those few loved and trusted friends and family their honest and true opinion that these people can get real objectivity. Better to scream, cry and release than to fester and become embittered…

Mercury square Pluto

The intensity and psychological depth of Pluto can sometimes be deflected or sidestepped by the trickster-like seemingly superficial nature of Mercury, but when these two planets are square to each other the combination of quicksilver and depth oriented psychology produces highly charged situations. Often when younger, this combination can result in a kind of irrational phobia or other type of deep rooted unconscious fear about something indiscernible, which may result in compulsive mental behaviour patterns towards getting ahead which occasionally in turn can ride roughshod over the feelings and intuitions. There may be an obsessive attitude where the individual will persist in a course of action despite repeated failures, as opposed to changing course. There will be times of extreme concentration and focus to the exclusion of all other external stimulus, which can have its benefits but often is unaware of the presence or needs of others and there can also be an intensity of the mind that is so powerful that burnout can be a real risk, both to oneself and others. This aspect can trend towards mental paranoia, or some other type of fear that has exclusion at its base root. Pluto square Mercury people can convince themselves that their course of action is the right one, even if friends and colleagues all disagree. They are sure that the power of the mind can overcome anything and often the final realisation that this is not the case can bring unfortunate fall outs. This position brings a penetrating insight into the behind the scenes power games that people play and in time it may also bring the discipline and objective intent to turn that insight into something that helps others.

These mental patterns can easily also be translated into the verbal domain. There can be times of nervous, nonstop verbal diarrhoea, as well as a stream of inane banalities designed to keep the mind active and to stop it from facing up to certain realities. This chitter chatter can occasionally verge on the incessant and will then suddenly stop as the individual internalises their processing when the rapidity of words changes from the verbal to the mental and then to the temporarily and acutely still. This is the person who will pick and pick at situations in a way that is both unstoppable and compulsive until they achieve the desired effect. Pluto does not know where or when to stop and when Mercury is being challenged by Pluto it reacts by trying to understand, to logicalise or rationalise as opposed to just trusting the process of the unconscious and the subconscious. Of course, the opposite side to this is that when they do shut up, be sure that they are weighing up big decisions that will be influenced not only by external actions and words, but by internal fundamental beliefs and opinions. Often a period of unusual silence can be followed by specific utterances, complete with deep and unequivocal meaning that is so concise that misinterpretation is impossible. It is hard for these people to willingly change their minds or opinions once they are committed to a course of action; they need to see things through to the end no matter what. Their desire to 'stick it up to' the told-you-so brigade can easily be transformed into simple detachment and removal, keeping one's dignity and not dropping to the level of others. Mercury square Pluto people have an intensity like the sound of an engine in high gear which notifies others that when they are on a mission, do not get in their way.

Venus square Pluto

There is a thin line between love and hate and with Venus square Pluto the potential for extremes of behaviour and sexual intensity can lead to both volatile and challenging types of personal involvements, especially in younger years when relationships are such a steep learning curve. In the younger people with this position, there can be patterns of endless repetition in relationships and these people can have trouble in letting go of the one(s) they love even when the situation is at its most painful. Venus square Pluto can be almost masochistic in nature, occasionally somehow sensing that it is only through the pain of rejection or some other form of emotional torment that life can be truly experienced. Love and power can easily become confused with one another until the realisation as one ages that external relationships reflect one's own inner turmoil, especially around areas concerning value and worth. The other side of the same coin is that as soon as self-respect occurs, it becomes easier to attract a giving, loving person and better quality relationships ensue as a result. The relationship with 'other' will be a direct mirror image of the relationship that one has with oneself. Marriage could occur out of a desire for financial or emotional security or some other form of vague, inconsolable need, although personal security without unconditional love is at least as much a prison as a godsend, if not more.

To control the relationship or other's feelings, there can sometimes be the tendency to turn to underhand methods. There may exist the capacity to be a powerful manipulator, often trying to make things appear a certain way. However, success at this never brings the feeling of having won and this type of behaviour feeds a vicious cycle that one should avoid getting into from the start of a relationship, because otherwise one attracts intense encounters, often with love-hate themes developing as a result. Relationships can bring out one's darker side and inner demons through interactions with other and it is critical that individuals recognize this as their "stuff" and not project it onto their partner, lest transference occurs. Letting go of a relationship can be hard to do and it is sometimes a lot easier to pressure the partner into doing things that save the Venus/Pluto individual from acting, so be careful not to let relationships get to a point where the partner is superfluous or superficial. As a client once stated; 'I *relate this to the end of my marriage. In retrospect I was surprised at the amount of hurt and unkind behaviour I was prepared to endure to stay in the relationship. I think my ex became the same, as they stated*

134

later that they had started to 'enjoy' being manipulative and secretive. I think they eventually realised that my masochistic tendencies were not helping the situation, and following lots of self-justification and blame, they came to terms with being the 'baddy' and also making the eventual break'. With Venus square Pluto, what one wants is often not what one needs, so people who strive to reach their desires may also have to endure periodic degrees of suffering. At times there can be an almost obsessive tendency towards using sex as a device to obtain financial security or material comforts, although again this does not have a realistic long term future as far as personal contentment or happiness is concerned.

Patronising people is a poor substitute for being honest with them, so these people should not make promises unless they intend to keep them. A square between Venus and Pluto suggests that the emotional life may at times be subject to problems, many of these relating to various sexual issues. This aspect is symbolic of intense emotional and sexual involvements and sometimes can manifest as a very debasing influence. At the end of the day, an individual with the Venus and Pluto square in their chart needs to be clear not only with others but also with themselves about the difference between needs, wants and desires and how far they will go to achieve them. Treating others the way one would like to be treated by them is a good start to managing this aspect and keeping things as clean as possible. One can easily go down into a Hadean can of worms with this square, or alternatively aspire to fly phoenix-like into the highest and cleanest forms of pure love imaginable and in every case the latter only occurs after the former has been experienced to its fullest. The lesson here is simple; do not sell your soul for comfort.

Mars square Pluto

This is one of the hardest aspects in the entire zodiac to deal with, in that it can bring up issues of anger, rage and even violence in ways that can lead to feeling out of control if there is not caution. The square between Mars and Pluto always produces a dynamic and forceful nature and semi-regular power struggles can sometimes seem to be a common theme in life, regardless of whom the actual struggle is with. There may be anger control issues, either in oneself or in those around oneself, as if there is a subconscious attraction of that anger. At times, there can be a number of major clashes and sudden changes, often with very damaging results and even violent or aggressive outbursts. As one client so honestly and succinctly states; *'There's a terrible anger, a constant feeling of suppressed rage, with visions of brutality, violence and tyranny at times, especially if attacked, criticised or made to feel vulnerable and weak, which can even turn physically violent at times with those closest. But as time goes on, and with greater life discipline, there's a capacity to manifest more and more strength, but it's always a razor's edge. That strength could so easily turn into self-destructive behaviour, over doing and over giving. Learning when to stop, when to say no is extremely difficult.'*

Mars square Pluto can lead to a very intense and passionate capacity for physical expression, but also brings the potential to sabotage oneself in a moment of extreme passion. This aspect suggests a strong sex drive that may not be well managed at times, especially when younger and inexperienced and brings with it the need to occasionally choose to rein in one's overly assertive nature, otherwise power struggles and control issues may surface in the field of relationships. The interactions that the individual has with their significant other will always reflect the relationship that they have with themselves, in that the better one treats oneself, the more successful one's relationship with other. The approach to love and sex can be quite intense at times and as such the sexual nature can be strong, which naturally adds a very distinct magnetic quality to one's appeal. There is the capacity here for attraction from others to have a quality of near obsession, either to or from the individual, or sometimes both (which can be fun for a brief time, but obsession is usually fleeting). These people, whether they realise it or not, may tend to come across as stronger than they intend even to the point of burning others out and there can be a tendency to impose their will upon others. This can obviously bring severe problems for them when others automatically react in self-defence, normally resulting in both sets of personal boundaries being evaluated and potential conflict situations developing. To quote another client; *'Mars square Pluto is like trying to funnel a nuclear explosion through a straw.'*

There can be a distinctly possessive and demanding streak in the sexual nature, so the need for awareness of one's effect on others is important. Despite the attraction to people who may appear to not have as much vitality as they have, their best compatibility is with someone who is as feisty, dynamic and competitive as themselves. These people will fight like cat and dog with their partner, but they will also both find in each other someone psychologically powerful and hopefully equal. When that happens, the sex will be primal, raw, passionate, powerful and hot. Some people can be really intimidated by this almost primal energy to the point of being put off or deterred from these individual's company, which can cause a degree of uncertainty and even resentment for the individual. This can be difficult to understand until one faces up to one's own issues around anger management, fear of abandonment and boundaries. These people want a deep, soulful attachment on a sexual level and as they do not take rejection well there can be a fear of betrayal and abandonment and this slightly irrational fear can change the way that they see people, making it easy to find something negative about them. Far better for these people to find a way to convince others to collaborate with them of their own free will, on the grounds that it is better to have them pissing on the inside of the tent as opposed to the outside. This is the same principle as keeping friends close, but enemies closer. Mars square Pluto often brings a strong urge to act out fantasies or to live the dream and sometimes to do things that others only talk or fantasise about, but bear in mind the effect of these actions on others and behave in ways that hopefully attracts like-minded others towards you. Take this into the bedroom and there one can find oneself being the dynamic, coarse, abrupt and initiatory, or else someone incredibly sophisticated, fine-tuned, accurate and specialist. The choice is obvious, but the latter approach does have more long term benefits. Would you rather be a lump hammer or a laser? Ask one's partner for the answer to that question…

There is the ability to sometimes perceive the cruel edge in people and understand its source because of recognizing the same potential within oneself, so as the individual deals with their own ruthlessness, they learn how to respond to it in others without risking either their or others physical well-being, but there is absolutely no way that they will easily tolerate a dominating attitude in others. There is respect for power and authority, but only if it is managed fairly. This is the hardest of positions for Mars and Pluto – the individual will have to deal with the nature of power head on and either rise to become empowered or else let oneself become consumed and absorbed by other peoples' power in some way. Yet at the end of the day, despite the challenges that this aspect produces, it also conveys a firm gentleness, the kindness and generosity that comes from a position of strength for example.

Here is the position of the spiritual warrior, the ascetic, the nurturing crusader and the truth seeking pilgrim. Mars square Pluto people learn as they age that the principle of 'loving assertiveness' keeps them sane and everybody else onside. The simple and basic principle in all of one's dealings with others and vice versa should be that 'if you always tell the truth, you never have to remember what you have said.' That way there will never be any form of complication or misunderstanding.

Jupiter square Pluto

On the one hand, this position brings an almost fanatical degree of self-confidence, so much so that it can easily be misunderstood by others as arrogance. It can bring a form of self-conceit and wilfulness that can really rub others up the wrong way, as well as a capacity for exaggeration that can sometimes seem out of proportion to real events. There will always be the desire to do something big, or to be known for something big, but there will also always be the capacity for both over stretching and undercutting, for overconfidence and huge self-doubt. Occasionally a combination of some of these things will sporadically bring things to crunch point, potentially making a crisis out of what is merely a drama or in other ways much larger than life. It is as though the individual is striving to fill an unfillable hole, not realising that whilst sincerity is a noble attribute it does not always feed the family or pay the rent and that every so often altruism must be compromised. This is known as the storm in the teacup aspect, bringing with it often unnecessarily huge upheavals and sometimes massive transformations, but always with a degree of overstatement. There will be an intrinsic resistance to imposed philosophical or religious systems, as one's firsthand experiences over the years tend to nullify the laws and rules of conventional society, instead creating a preference to play by one's own rules. This is a philosophy that often brings either legal trouble or social exclusion although this aspect is bizarrely often found in the horoscopes of the highest churchmen! This square does tend to bring extreme, puritanical or fanatical attitudes towards imposed religion and in oneself there will always be an unmanageable urge to make thing bigger, better, stronger, richer that should be both acknowledged and tempered. A classic example of this lies in the horoscope of Arnold Schwarzenegger, with his desire to always be the best under the hardest of circumstances, both in his celluloid career as well as his political one. Jupiter square Pluto can lead to speculation and risk taking big time and if there are any skeletons in the closet then this type of behaviour can easily bring them out. It can bring either an excess of hedonism or the monastic lifestyle. But these people just cannot leave the biscuit packet half full- it must be all or nothing, even in the bedroom where they can be alternatively abstemious or sexually gluttonous. For example, this aspect features very prominently in the chart of the singer Tom Jones, who despite many infidelities remains married to his first love.

Any contact between Jupiter and Pluto can be potentially complicated – in Greek mythology, from where much of contemporary western astrology derives much of its allegorical origins, Jupiter and Pluto are brothers who upon the overthrow of their father agreed to split the firmament between them, with Pluto taking the underworld and Jupiter the overworld. This brings constant experiences into the lives of people with this aspect that challenge their sense of proportion. There is a need to consciously learn from these experiences so as not to fall into the same old traps and to develop a conscious willingness to look at one's patterns and beliefs, to compare them to the real world and to learn from that comparison. At times, there may be the opportunity to amass huge resources or personal enormous wealth, as well as a deep rooted understanding of how to generate abundance, although whether that ability is used wisely is often dependent on age and experience and especially on whether the lessons of humility have been learnt. Often, these resources can be acquired through unusual ways. Examples of this are found using Plutonian archetypes, suggestive of buried treasure, the mining of the earth for diamonds, gold or oil, or the acquisition of wealth through recycling and reusing processes, although the opposite of this is that these people can also be incredibly wasteful. Yet conversely these can be the panic hoarders, convinced the world is about to end and that they have got to get another sack of brown rice in – quickly! There will certainly be an element of the survivalist with Jupiter square Pluto in some form, sometimes to the point of fanaticism. Jupiter will stick to its principles and philosophies, even when under pressure and this eventually leads to a sense of thriving when going through tough times. There is something of the pathfinder or trailblazer with this aspect, something that brings a kind of forced optimism no matter how big the odds stacked against success are. Even when under the greatest of challenges there will still be an element of faith that the troubled times will eventually come to an end, to be replaced by something more positive. However, as with everything Jupiterian, just because you think that you are lucky does not mean that you are, although at times there can be hidden benefactors or supporters coming out of the woodwork when least expected.

Saturn square Pluto

Saturn square Pluto is a generational aspect often lasting many months and as a result is found in whole sub generations of people. This aspect is associated with lessons of survival and the ability to endure and persist under extremely difficult circumstances, often through separation or profound loss. Nevertheless, it can indicate self-will and persistence to the point of yes/no, black/white in a way that brooks no interference or messing, although there is also an almost pathological fear of losing or being out of control. It pushes the agenda for unstoppable transformation as signified by Pluto firmly up against the walls of fearful and structured authority as symbolised by Saturn, stuck in tradition and unwilling to adapt to the transforming future. Saturn wants everything to stay the same and Pluto wants everything to metamorphose. This version of the unstoppable force (Pluto) and the immovable object (Saturn) can be internally integrated when one accepts the nature of true power as well as the personal disciplines and structures required to manifest that power. Until this need to balance internal power is resolved, there may always appear to be a blockage which can lead to a degree of fear, powerlessness and of being stuck. It may appear to others as though there is a degree of inherent aggression or violence here, especially towards oneself and even in the quieter and less demonstrative people with this aspect there can be an almost fanatical attitude towards self-reliance and self-protection, and anyone who tries to assert any control or dominance towards people with this aspect is metaphorically taking their life in their hands. There may be some difficult circumstances during youth involving authority figures, whether parents, teachers or the employers, government and state, as well as a sense of restriction in social situations and this can make for a recalcitrant attitude towards dealing with authority in later years. Saturn squaring Pluto can also indicate times of collapse when these people's security and foundations at the root core level can be periodically challenged to keep them from complacency.

There is certainly the ability to perform difficult work in a determined and thorough way and self-restraint can be almost compulsive at times. There is likely to be a deep understanding of the inevitability of both personal and global change and transformation and over the years patience will become more than a virtue. Over the course of a lifetime, the main purpose of this aspect is that Saturn in many ways stands for the outer structures such as home and professional security and the inner structures that protect us from straying too far off the beaten track. With Pluto square Saturn both these inner and outer structures will periodically be destroyed or changed, bringing not only a sense of futility but also of the perpetuity of things, just in ever morphing patterns of structure. And as one ages, so the willingness to shoulder responsibility for one's position as opposed to blaming the world grows. It may feel when younger as though one's life is harder than that of one's peers, that the individual may be carrying some type of dutiful or otherwise onerous burden on their shoulders that often does not disappear until midlife. In later years, one's interactions at all levels of society should be characterised by a transparency and a willingness to walk one's talk to avoid unnecessary complications and confusion.

It is interesting to note how many people with this aspect end up in positions of authority or management, so resistant themselves against taking orders that the only realistic way forward for them is to get to the top of the tree themselves, or else to be self-employed. There will certainly be a strong drive to be successful, along with a controlled sense of self discipline and if Saturn's attitude towards ambition and hard work can work with Pluto's attitude towards transformation, then these people can sometimes literally move mountains.

Pluto square Midheaven

Whilst the desire in the individual for personal success can be remarkably high, it can also create antagonism in others when they sense the almost ruthless drive for achievement and alongside it the possibility for public recognition. So, with this position there is a need for making one's own personal success also the success of those collaborating with oneself, bringing a synergetic approach into mutual teamwork. It is only then that there is a sense of not being alone and that two and two can sometimes equal five. There will be a strong urge to remake or remould the world in some way and this can be achieved, but there is a serious need for caution here because the path to this goal is full of personal temptation and power for its own sake will quickly corrupt. There may be periods of love and hate with the public, and if that were to happen consistently then one may rapidly find oneself unsupported, resulting quite fast in feelings of isolation and vulnerability, antithetical to this aspect's desire for public adulation. There will be the desire to influence the world in some way, through the attainment of either a powerful professional position or else as the head of a tribe, clan or family. Pluto here pushes so hard that these people often become high achievers, even if they are not the most popular and they hopefully use that achievement to improve the lives of those around them. At the same time, there is the need to watch out that their interactions with others are open and transparent, lest they attract the negative attention that this aspect is famed for. The desire to control the work environment should be moderated, lest it become constricted through fear of change. There is a need for high personal ethical standards and for these standards to carry themselves both into the professional world and the family home. Pluto squaring the Midheaven will also bring an almost insatiable desire for success that cannot be ignored, but at the same time it needs to be managed in a diligent way lest that desire for success consumes or absorbs oneself, normally resulting in a compulsive urge that will arouse opposition. More than usual, this aspect is found also in the charts of neonatal nurses and palliative carers and other forms of carers of people who are going through near death experiences.

It may be that this aspect sends out a kind of signal that suggests susceptibility to being influenced in inappropriate ways and others, sensing this, will try to take advantage in some way. People with this aspect at times feel as though they are on the wrong planet at the wrong time and that they must make a constant effort to interact with others, both in their professional and their personal life. There will be an element of the reformer with Pluto square the Midheaven, but it must be used for the social greater good as opposed to for personal development to maximise its true potential. People with this aspect are 'cool hunters,' in that they can quickly and accurately calculate the ongoing zeitgeist at any time and in any environment to a precise degree, with laser-like focus and concentration. There may be a family precedent that this individual is supposed to emulate in that the individual may feel that they are being compelled, urged or even manipulated into becoming a success, or following in the family tradition or business. Family status may often play an influence in career decisions. But if the path of 'duty' is followed at the expense of one's personal desire, then the possibility of sacrificing home and family life to ascertain professional success becomes stronger with this aspect, career becomes prison-like and family will steadily be seen as a burden. It is imperative to balance the need for both family and professional success; otherwise one will totally dominate at the expense of the other. This is best manifested in the eyes of others by maintaining an almost fierce attitude towards anyone who tries to intrude upon the private life of the individual and retaining an element of privacy and mystique about themselves.

Pluto square Ascendant

When it comes to the relationship one has with oneself, as signified by the Ascendant, this position brings with it a powerful capacity for self-empowerment but only if this involves also working with and empowering other people. Unfortunately, this aspect is also sometimes strongly associated with people who try to have both powerful and inappropriate influence on others. These people can be convinced of their own righteousness and often it will take until the midlife to exercise a degree of moderate balance, voluntary restraint and quality judgement. If told that they may be being obsessive, then this too can be seen as external interference and thus ignored. It may be seen as being one person's world with everyone else being role players, and this degree of fanaticism about one's own omnipotence will inevitably bring conflict with various levels of authority. Pluto square the Ascendant individuals will always experience difficulties in accepting orders or for that matter any chain of command and as a result there can be a degree of insensitivity to other people's needs or requests. These are the people who will persist even when it is clearly demonstrated that they are going in an incorrect direction, simply because it is so difficult for them to accept that they might just be wrong.

Pluto square the Ascendant also has a great influence on the relationships that one has with 'other,' whether that other is personal and intimate, friend, social, family or professional. At times, there can be an almost antisocial attitude, preferring instead to 'go it alone' and it is surprising how many of these people do go through divorce at least once in their life. The willingness to compromise is sometimes noticeable by its absence with this position; it is much more the all or nothing approach to relationships that works, although at times it does seem that all relationships patterns are cloying and a burden, only to be replaced by feelings of longing and yearning for that personal touch once alone. Yet at other times, there is the potential for composure under the most challenging of difficulties from other people, along with the determination to win through no matter what the cost or effort. There can be a tendency for one partner in the relationship to become more powerful than the other, with the dominant partner trying to mould or otherwise change the other instead of themselves and for one partner to overreact to the other, especially in sexual situations. But power struggles that persist in the relationship over a period normally indicate that the compatibility levels are low and that there is unlikely to be any easy or willing compromise. If either partner feels constantly under pressure to be anything or anyone other than who they are, problems in the relationship will either surface to be dealt with or be suppressed, leading to major breakdowns.

Trines to Pluto

A trine is an astrological aspect of one hundred and twenty degrees, one third of a circle. The trine links two planets that are in zodiacal signs of the same element, with different behaviour patterns and methods but similar motivations and aspirations. It is commonly accepted in contemporary astrology that the trine is the most beneficial of aspects in that it seems, at least on the surface, to offer nothing but positive energies with a natural and complimentary enrichment organically occurring between the planets in question. In addition to the single trine effect between two planets there is also the Grand Trine, which is a triangle composed of three one hundred and twenty degree aspects around which energy constantly revolves in a recurrent, harmonious and flowing way. The trine creates the pathway of easiest flow and brings into the chart the capacity for a more flowing attitude towards art, music, creative pursuits of all types and easy going relationships with other and others. It is a feel-good aspect that brings internal confidence, strength and comfort into the areas governed by the planets in a trine aspect. If there is anything non-positive about the trine it is that it can and often does lead to complacency, where placid being is accepted instead of creative doing. The artistic genius on the one hand is the wasted alcoholic on the other and the trine does bring awareness of both extremes and of the difference. There can be a sense of never fully using one's potential, regardless of external situations or other people's viewpoints and in the chart of someone who finds it difficult to motivate themselves the trine can be seen as the pathway of least resistance and thus to an extent the easy cop-out.

Pluto by nature is not considered an easy going planetary energy to deal with by most astrologers and it is not known for its flexibility or tolerance. Pluto is accepted in astrological parlance as being a major heavy hitter in terms of effect, regardless of its size or astronomical status and thus when involved in a trine aspect should bring an element of psychological fortitude and deep and persistent determination into the proceedings. Pluto's presence in the trine aspect provides a kind of psychological underpinning into the individual's personal affairs and situations, a sureness that their psychological well-being is sound. On its own, a trine from Pluto will not bring any specific issue to a position of enhancement, but it will bring power and strength into that which already exists. It adds a degree of gravitas, depth and meaning which no other planet (except for Saturn) brings as well as a quality of strength and self confidence in a way that exudes self-empowerment. Of course, being a trine sometimes none of this can manifest, instead remaining latent in the background and only being sensed in terms of deep dream or imagination. It takes an element of conscious effort to activate a trine's energies and when Pluto is on one end of the trine in question, then it will be immediately clear that nothing can ever be done by half measures. It will be all or nothing, but because the aspect is a reactive trine, there is a greater chance than of any other astrological aspect to Pluto of the result being nothing, simply because of the lack of urge, impetus or incentive.

Sun trine Pluto

It is accepted in astrology that the Sun is that part of oneself that is unique and solo and that governs words like individuality, identity, personhood and uniqueness. Any trine to the Sun is going to function as a powerful conduit for positive transformative energies and when the planet being trined is Pluto then the capacities for in depth self-analysis, ongoing soul searching and self-development are limitless. These people make for great psychotherapists, counsellors, tarot readers or other forms of unconscious facilitators. Because this aspect is a trine the combination of these two powerhouse points must be taken in a more social context, with the desire to actively contribute into society in some way. It certainly enhances perception in a way that is often seen by others as being scarily accurate and these individuals are not willing to put up with pretence or superficialities in any way. Ambitious in terms of self-development, they are incredibly good at accepting that sometimes (rarely) they are wrong, there is no sense of self-delusion here. While these individuals do not always agree with those around them, they will fight to the death for the right for that person to hold their opinion.

With Pluto trining the Sun, a sense of strength in identity is gradually built on as age develops until by midlife the individual will be able to safely plan the rest of their lives in ways that people without this aspect just will not have the confidence to do. There is always going to be the desire for the individual with this aspect to 'make something of oneself,' they are goal focussed and as they grow older, they become more comfortable with the idea of being 'out there' or on view. Pluto here will add depth, weight and meaning into anything that the Sun individual will try and do. It adds a degree of stamina, resolve, resourcefulness and drive that empowers the individual into ever greater effectiveness and efficiency. At the same time, it will bring significators, or 'omens' into one's life in a way that defies coincidence and promotes a different view of the universe to most. As they age these people realise that there is nothing to fear except fear itself and by working with this knowledge they can empower others into making the same realisation.

When this aspect is reversed and taken as the Sun trining Pluto instead of Pluto trining Sun there can be a different point of view. The Sun brings light and enlightens the darker areas of Pluto's domain (remembering that Pluto is lord of the underworld), adding heat and light to the ongoing alchemical transformation that lies at the heart of every Plutonic influence or operation. These people encourage others to live life to the fullest and by doing so themselves function as conscious examples for the rest of humanity. As a client says; *'I have always had a very strong work ethic and the feeling that I have to do the absolute best that I can, even to the point of excess when in reality a little bit less effort would have worked just as well, but I always have to go that extra mile or three'.* There is an element of the strident about these people, it is as if they consciously need their sense of purpose to have greater meaning or depth than most because otherwise life is not worth living. To promote this feeling and to make it real they must walk their talk or as is said in the UK 'they do what it says on the tin.' They have an extremely acute insight into what it is that motivates people to behave the way they do, although they are not always that forward in sharing this information. When they do say something they normally mean it and the word profound applies strongly here. Over a period the capacity for a kind of enduring stamina here is at an all-time high.

Moon trine Pluto

With any contact between the Moon and Pluto there will be an element of intensity accompanied by the potential for emotional extremism that simply put, cannot be found in any other planetary combination. Yet because the aspect in question is a trine, the most harmonic and flowing of aspects, the opportunity for these two deeply emotive planetary energies to work together is strong and hopefully healthy. There will always be a conscious emotional focus, which accompanied by an element of intensity can sometimes put other people's backs up (those with something to hide). There will also be a fascination and deep attraction to the unknown and the unknowable with an acceptance of and a willingness to embrace the challenges involved in this area of emotional research. Sometimes this can manifest as a caring and nurturing nature, especially with people who are either very young or very old, although as with all contacts between these two planets there may always be an element of obsession or other similar forms of compulsive behaviour lurking somewhere in the background.

With Pluto trining the Moon there will always be an added quality of depth to the emotional situations in life along with the basic understanding that still waters do indeed run deeply beneath the visible surface. It may seem to others that on the surface there is an initial caution when dealing with new emotional situations and similarly a degree of reticence about sharing one's feelings with others until they are established friends, although this does not run to the level of caution that other Pluto/Moon aspects can engender. These people are only attracted to other individuals who have a quality of emotional gravitas and sincerity about them. Pluto trine Moon people really do not care about the superficial, it is not physical appearance or financial wealth that attracts them as much as it is emotional depth and the willingness to look at and embrace the deeper and more emotive sides of life. Pluto here adds in specific ways to the Moon's tenacity by always being willing to look at problems in increasingly diverse ways until eventually the right approach to resolution is found. The only condition of Pluto's help here is also found in every Pluto/Moon contact, that being the need to deal with people and be dealt with by them honestly.

Whereas when this aspect is reversed and seen as the Moon trining Pluto a slightly different slant appears. It is as though the reflected light of the Moon casts a pale shadow of itself into Pluto's dark domains illuminating a particular trait or talent that can be brought back to the land of the conventional in a way that aids psychological comprehension, both of oneself and of the world one inhabits. As a client puts it: *'there is deep feeling and urge of having a wisdom to share, but this has to be allowed to gradually unveil in conjunction with the lessons and tests to be passed on the denser levels of reality, however constant emotional niggling there is if living out of tune with developing this path'*. Another client states: *'It reminds me how much I "feel" through thinking, and "think through" feeling. Sharing thoughts and ideas is where I build the trust needed for that in-depth relating, not necessarily through "friendship" but through thinking together.'* It is difficult if not impossible to rationally understand how the Moon and Pluto work and dance with each other in terms of logical and rational words. When that search is aimed at feeling as opposed to understanding it all becomes suddenly clear, accompanied by a new, stronger sense of emotional security. The trine from the Moon empowers Pluto to have a greater, deeper and more profound all-encompassing experience than most suggestive of higher and more sophisticated intuitive and spiritual development as one ages, along with a genuine desire to help those less able to help themselves. In addition, there will be a craving for a level of in depth intimacy which if not met will be totally abstained from. Here the trine does not detract from the basic eliminativism of Moon/Pluto, which says that if it cannot have the quality that it wants then it will happily go without as it wants the best or nothing.

Mercury trine Pluto

The trine between these two planets is ambiguous in that it describes different scenarios, all intrinsically linked to the different forms and patterns of media and communication that either come from the individual or else go towards them and the quality of psychological depth that these communications patterns have. The trine links Pluto's capacity for in depth research with Mercury's ability to process information resulting in a potential for quality investigation that leaves no stone unturned along with a diligence that misses little if anything. Normally, a contact between these two disparate energies can be fractious. Pluto, representing all that is dark and hidden within oneself at the primal and subconscious level is normally resentful of Mercury's incessant twittering and constant desire for more information. Mercury, the logical, rational and analytical communicator, is fascinated by Plutonian depth and simply cannot leave things well alone, being determined to bring everything to the surface. This can manifest as visible versus invisible, conscious versus unconscious. However, when these two forces or energies flow as they do in a trine, there is the blending of mental word, innate feeling and primal urge in a way that integrates the individual mentally and helps project an image of quiet solidity, stability and reliability into the outside world.

With Pluto trine Mercury an added degree of mental intensity and depth is always present in some shape or form, a quality of concentration and focus that makes the individual incredibly hard to hoodwink. There will be a capacity for concentrated focus and mental effort that stands out when compared to other people and the willingness to mentally persevere until the desired result is achieved, along with an almost but not quite ruthlessness that gets results at the end of the day. Although because the aspect in question is a trine the methods used to get the results will always be above board and transparent. As a client states; *'I am very much a truth seeker and like to research subjects slowly over a period of time – I gather the facts and then store the information in my brain for whenever it may be needed.'* There will always be the capacity with the balancing trine to analyse motives objectively, whether those motives are one's own or those of other or others and there will always be an innate understanding of the law of reciprocity and how like affects and attracts like.

Alternatively or sometimes as well, with Mercury trine Pluto, there will always be an insatiable curiosity about the underlying cause and nature of things and events. It is as though the individual will never be satisfied with superficial or mundane explanations if there is the slightest inkling that there is more to be discovered or unearthed, they will always get to the point of origin concerning a problem or challenge. It is this capacity that makes them such great problem solvers. There is a basic inquisitiveness about this position that will drive the individual in question into greater and greater efforts to uncover all that needs to be revealed, no matter what the cost or effort. And when all is done, these people have the internal mental patience to sit back and contemplate for a long time before drawing conclusions, they are good at playing the waiting game. Mercury trine Pluto people are constantly aware of the mind's deeper processes that cannot be detailed or analysed but are equally comfortable with these processes knowing that they are the hard wiring that lies underneath the more superficial mental, intellectual and communicative mind.

Venus trine Pluto

The trine formed between Venus and Pluto in an individual chart shows the capacity for an intense romantic nature with an intrinsic fundamental faith in life and an innate optimism that all will work out well in the end. It gives similar indications to the sextile, although whereas the sextile is a more proactive aspect the trine sets out situations where the possibility of personal transformation is more likely to occur through emotional experiences of a higher and intense kind, especially through the shape and form of personal one to one relationships. There will be the feeling that higher values are essential in interpersonal relationships, as indicated by the ever more refined desires of Pluto for purging and cleansing to a high degree. The individual with the Venus/Pluto trine will try to embody these higher values in their own life, expressing them in ways that adds to the quality, duration and consistency of their relationship. It may help to look at the similar elemental sign of the zodiac that this trine occurs in to get a broader understanding of the interactive dynamic pattern. They will need to resonate with their partner in an unconscious way, where they naturally dance around each other in different areas of life. If a relationship becomes an effort over time, it often will not last.

With Venus trining Pluto, there can be the need to avoid the tendency to interfere in others' choices and instead let them find their own way, even when it hurts to do so. This is one of those aspects where the individual will meet people and instantly feel as if they have known them all their life if not longer, there can be instant and immediate recognition. This is not about waiting for Mr. or Ms. Right or the desire for one's soul partner, but this aspect does give the ability to recognize a fated quality of interaction and attraction when it occurs around oneself. This belief in the goodness and synchronicity of life can be 'contagious' and there may easily an attraction towards sharing one's personal approach or philosophy of life with one's significant other, especially if that significant other is also looking to grow and evolve through the relationship. There can be a 'fascination' with other that can have the hallmarks of falling in love at first sight which is perhaps an indication of the intense romantic nature that this aspect generates and something that one needs to be aware of.

Similarly, with Pluto trining Venus, there exists a greater capacity and willingness than normal for sensing and seeing that the bedrock of a partnership (apart from mutual love and affection) is deep. In it lies in qualities of commitment, transparency, honesty, integrity, responsibility to mutual obligations and the allowing each other the space to express his or her own unique nature with a degree of both autonomy and privacy. Pluto loves this degree of autonomous interaction, where one feels both trusted and independent within the confines of a committed relationship, because it feels the desired quality of both shared depth and personal freedom within the boundaries of what hopefully becomes a long term settlement. The Pluto/ Venus person will not scatter their energies loosely preferring instead to take the high ground and only involving themselves in relationship patterns that hold a quality of moral integrity with an element of spiritual purpose as well. Pluto here seeks to refine the Venusian experience and transmute its baser lust into a cleaner and purified feeling of the highest calibre, constantly aspiring to a more sophisticated and refined form of love.

Mars trine Pluto

Pluto trine Mars creates an initiative-taking situation that links two planets with not dissimilar energy fields. The main difference is that Pluto's energy is coming directly from the underworld and is normally couched in terms of psychology, subversion or other forms of undercurrents, whilst Mars, being overtly and demonstrably in one's face, is anything but. Both planets have a lot to do with power and the flow of that power through one's life and both are driven in an unconscious way to make their presence known in one's life in ways that simply cannot be ignored. Both Mars and Pluto have an affinity with Scorpio, which explains the common association of these two planets with sex. The trine aspect here takes out a lot of the potentially more violent or aggressive potentials that the harder aspects between these two warlike planets can sometimes symbolise and replaces it with the potential for a flow of regular stamina in a way that is unstoppable once the head of steam is built up. The trine also encourages these two surgical operatives to blend and fuse together in a resourceful and powerful way that makes for a growing sense in invulnerability as one ages, matures and develops.

With Mars trining Pluto, the emphasis is on the placing of physical exertion and effort into managing the unconscious and subconscious, often through rigorous exercise, regular sex or some other form of consistent and rhythmic physical expression. This creates a naturally healthy flow of vital energy within the body and makes the individual a passionate person capable of generating a commanding aura and with a strong degree of confidence about their own talents as well as giving the capacity for applying tremendous effort to anything that one attempts. A trine between Mars and Pluto enables the individual to draw on deep reserves of energy to get through any crisis and the physical and sexual drives and desires are likely to be not only strong and intense much of the time but also controlled, directed and purposeful. Romantic connections have deep meaning and interest and will not be entered into lightly as these people do not do light-hearted flirtatiousness, finding it superficial and vacuous.

When this aspect is reversed with Pluto trining Mars there will be at least a semi-conscious acceptance of one's own personal power and immense energy as well as an acknowledgement of one's more assertive nature. There will be a knack for uncovering things and bringing up things from the underworld or from the distant past and these people are excellent at exposing secrets. This makes them great natural investigators or researchers, private detectives or investigative journalists, forensic accountants or criminal psychologists or anything that exposes anything rotten or corrupt. Pluto here makes the individual relentless in pursuit of their goals and they will never give up, steadily persevering over the years although when difficulties arise, they prefer to avoid conflict and confrontation in favour of more peaceful or subtle methods of resolving problems. However, even here clear boundaries will exist and there needs to be a clear acceptance from others of the fact that the furthest that Mars trine Pluto will go is halfway because any further would be surrender and it is more their style at that point to just walk away with head held high. There will be the ability to act quickly in any emergency and to make far-reaching decisions and commitments that others may require a long time to consider which is perhaps one of the reasons that this aspect is relatively common in the charts of fire-fighters, police officers and paramedics or other similar occupations that require immediate decision making ability. To quote a client; *'I have always coped extremely well in emergency situations, and made quick and big decisions when needed. In fact, all the major changes in my life have happened so quickly that looking back it seems strange that I can 'um and ah' about seemingly insignificant things in my life for ages.'*

Jupiter trine Pluto

Here the big brothers of the astrological solar system play harmoniously with each other. As equal and opposites in the Greek pantheon they balance each other in a way that is normally mutually complementary and sometimes even helpful. Often the blend of Pluto's more subversive nature with the Jupiterian urge to enlarge and grow can lead to situations where rampant and unabated growth can suddenly develop with inevitable consequences. When the aspect in question between the two is a trine that potential is ameliorated significantly being instead replaced with elements of both fatalistic acceptance and dark humour. A trine between Jupiter and Pluto links them both in a way that suggests commonality and similarity in approach if not in direct action. If there is always a degree of integrity and openness about one's dealings there should never be any of the legal or moral issues that are commonly associated with this combination in a harder aspect. As a client says; *'I cannot lie or cheat, mainly because this is doing myself down, and harming others as well.*

Faith and insight are what enables me to be resilient. In times of stress and hardship, I suddenly get a 'knowingness' of what needs to be done, and always follow my instincts in that regard. I feel supported and guided, it is just a question of remembering to tune in.'

Jupiter trine Pluto brings a natural and organic flow of growth, light and exuberance into all of Pluto's darker domains and creates an element of transparency and hopefulness that transforms potentials into real creative possibility. It really helps inspire others to achieve their potential and is seen as a boost to one's own sense of inner confidence especially when it comes to business or financial matters where this aspect comes into its own. Pluto's deep inner resources combine well with the Jupiterian desire for expansion resulting in high aspirations and a strong desire to achieve one's goals. Jupiter trine Pluto people have the capacity to constructively focus and direct their willpower in ways that minimise output whilst maximising return. They are naturally quite charismatic with powerful leadership ability which when combined with their natural understanding of what it is that makes others around them tick creates excellent counselling skills.

Pluto trining Jupiter on the other hand is a definite help when it comes to providing fortitude, resilience and high standards of behaviour. Pluto here brings the capacity for depth, resourcefulness and strength into Jupiter's more authoritarian side and creates the potential for a person with substance and leadership ability. There may be the desire for political or religious achievement and if this is for the benefit of the larger group more than personal aggrandisement there will be no problems. Pluto will amplify Jupiterian humour and add a dark twist to it, as demonstrated by one client with this aspect who works in a cancer ward and puts it well; *'Cancer is still one of those illnesses that doesn't always have a happy ending, but having a gallows humour helps both them and me get through it and it is cheaper than going to see a shrink'*. Certainly, the capacity for faith and insight is strong and can prove unbreakable in times of challenge and there is the ability and the willingness to correct any situation that has gone wrong quickly before it gets any worse.

Saturn trine Pluto

These two astrological behemoths are never going to be the best of friends even though symbolically in Greek mythology they are father and son. There is always going to be an element of the unstoppable force for complete and thorough transformation of Pluto up against the intrinsically solid and immovable roots of Saturn and normally this combination simply does not work that well. It commonly creates intransigence and inflexibility along with an element of bloody mindedness that can often prove terminal in some shape or form. When these two opposing and sometimes conflicting powers blend and meet through the auspices of the trine aspect, an uneasy truce can be declared allowing an interaction to occur that theoretically should benefit both parties. It is as though the normally rigid boundaries of Saturn will slightly begrudgingly allow Pluto's transformative energy to enter and influence its domain, whilst at the same time Pluto will condescend to let Saturn bring an element of structure into its otherwise formless nature.

The trine from Saturn to Pluto brings a degree of structure and boundary into the way that the individual with this aspect carries themselves in the outside world. They will be experienced by others as someone who thinks things through thoroughly and then takes decisions and actions only after forethought and planning, an attitude that brings a much higher probability of success eventually. Normally these people operate to the letter of the law knowing that by doing things both properly and transparently they can only benefit. Saturn will seek to define and regulate Pluto's transformative energy in a way that will not be seen by Pluto as being dragged kicking and screaming into the light but that will be recognised as having an organising functionality and a necessary form. Saturn will allow Pluto to remain occluded knowing that by doing so to a degree yet by also bringing an element of definition into the purpose and intent of this interaction, the blend of these two planetary energies will make for a more powerful force for progress than either of them could achieve on their own. This aspect generates a kind of specialised and focussed concentration to the exclusion of all other when the need arises.

By turning this aspect on its head and making it Pluto trining Saturn the meaning is subtly changed. Here the regenerative and transformative energies of Pluto will slowly sandpaper away at the more intransigent boundaries of Saturn, gradually encouraging him to become slowly and gradually more flexible whilst at the same time maintaining resilience and resistance to radical or sudden change. Pluto here reminds Saturn that to show tolerance and adaptability when it is not required is the mark not only of confidence in oneself but also of wisdom and maturity. Pluto brings a quality of internal psychologically sound conviction and strength into what Saturn forms, making for something that is like hard rubber, impenetrable but flexible to a degree. Should Saturn ever need firming up the trine from Pluto is one of the best aids for this purpose as it imbues the individual with a sense of internal assuredness that cannot normally be found or demonstrated. It also creates the necessary drive and urge to push through needed reforms and in this light sub generations of people with this aspect can be seen as major social reformers. Pluto adds an element of scrutiny and intensity to Saturn's more pragmatic side, which can sometimes be very helpful both to self and others when dealing with issues of loss, transformation and passage, knowing intrinsically, instinctively and intuitively when to let go and when to persist.

Pluto trine Ascendant

The difference between a trine and a sextile is subtle but significant: a sextile combines the virtues of hard work and effort with the potentials for self-development whilst the trine is a less direct aspect, not bringing anything directly to the table but instead just offering background support and goodwill, as well as assistance when needed. The trine may be seen as a latent positive energy whilst the sextile is the more potent. When Pluto is an element in this mix it could be said that a Pluto trine will be seen as more influential in the background whilst a Pluto sextile will be more dynamic in the foreground. When the point in question being aspected is the Ascendant, it is the interaction with other at the one to one level that needs to be considered as well as the relationship one has with oneself. In terms of the examination of oneself there can be a critical eye regarding one's appearance and bearing with an almost microscopic approach to presenting oneself into the outside world as effectively as possible. This will be accompanied by a measured way of dealing with others that presents a safe and impenetrable face into the outside world. Pluto trine the Ascendant encourages the individual to delve into their own personal psychologically deeper states and many of them will use some type of psychological approach in their work. These people are not 'scared of the dark' but they certainly do not like dealing with those who are and they will always express their opinions forcefully in a way that tolerates no misunderstanding. Strangely, for such self-determined individuals they do attract followers, people who see them as inspiring or with leadership material. As a client so adroitly puts it: *'Better to be feared than loved.'*

When it comes to one to one relationships Pluto trine the Ascendant considers itself something of a specialist. Whilst it is certainly slower than many other aspects in developing relationship patterns it is one of the most thorough and once this individual makes their mind up and is committed to any type of relationship they will see it through to the end no matter what the challenge, as long as there is nothing hidden. They bring a quality of strength into those relationships they do commit themselves to, assuring both their partners and themselves about the willingness to see things through. It provides and brings stamina and endurance into relationship patterning, creating a safe base for solid growth and expansion. Pluto trining the Ascendant does not have too many problems when it comes to attracting the quality of support that they sometimes need, although this only becomes apparent when older. As one client states; *'When younger, I was never interested in easy going, regular types. I wished I was, but I wasn't. Now I'm looking for transformation through the power of lovingness, not narcissistic jerk types!.*

This is one of the few aspects about which it could be said that once they finally make their mind up, they are truly excellent romantic and relationship material as long as they are partnered with somebody who, like themselves, has an underlying desire to be a positive agent for transformation in a rapidly changing world. The word transformation is not used lightly here – as a client puts it; *'if the transformation event is not recognised by both parties, the change in emotional involvement can be sudden and irrevocable. One moment they can be everything, and the next nothing.'* If there is no recognition or awareness of this dynamic for ongoing regeneration of relationship purpose, both in personal terms as well as what the relationship brings into the outside world, it will not last long.

Pluto trine Midheaven

The Midheaven is the point of the sky at the time of one's birth that rules words like public image, career, ambition and success, at least at the external level. Pluto brings the basic urge for ongoing death and rebirth, the ongoing purgative but transformative process which constantly refines and renews, whilst the trine aspect between the two ameliorates the starker qualities of these points and helps them flow well.

Pluto trine the Midheaven brings a greater degree of depth, resourcefulness and stamina into the way that one projects oneself into and onto the outside world as being, especially in the professional domain. It adds an underlying element of substance and gravity into one's performance and carries the message into one's external community of clarity of process, in that everybody will know instantly where they stand with this individual. The aspect conveys a kind of no-nonsense approach to dealings in the public domain, an approach that often in time leads to considerable acceleration and fast tracking into positions of responsibility or authority. When younger this individual may find themselves sometimes playing the role of 'hatchet-man;' doing the types of difficult jobs that no-one else has either the taste or the guts for. When into the second half of life, if the desire for professional development is still there then it can only be at one's own behest, in that this individual must be captain of their own ship or not at all, because the mundanity of just 'doing their job' will never fulfil them.

Pluto trine the Midheaven encourages the individual with this aspect into going into some type of work or profession that encompasses a greater degree of depth than most other types of work or career. These are often represented as the 'strong, silent types,' who can maintain a resolute and firm but at the same time quiet stance which emits a sense of solidity and strength that is resolute and permanent. These are the people who can undertake mammoth research tasks that involve digging up lots of old facts or going into specific research areas, knowing that their work may take years. The blend of the public and professional Midheaven with the depth and darkness of Pluto means that these people can not only see any hidden corruption, but they can also root it out and replace it with their naturally good organising ability. They apply themselves with a kind of determination that is persistent and thorough in all its endeavours and that cannot be shaken off or deflected without a great deal of effort. Even then these people do not forget and they will always eventually return to get things sorted, although that may take time as on their pathway they will try many diverse options, always seeking to improve themselves through their work.

Oppositions to Pluto

A planet is deemed astrologically as being in opposition to another when they oppose each other in the heavens from a geocentric perspective, for example with one planet rising on the eastern horizon just as another sets on the western. The opposition in astrology links two planets in opposite signs and houses and in a difficult angular relationship with each other. Until very recently there has always been an energy of conflict ascribed to the opposition by astrologers and it has only been in the last two decades that a willingness to also see it as a powerhouse of determination and resolve has begun to circulate in astrological circles. The old dictum 'opposites attract' may apply here although not for the original reasons of the anonymous authors. It can be safely stated that oppositions in an individual's horoscope show both the nature of extremism within the individual as well as their intelligence as perhaps signified by their willingness to take the middle path and deliberately choose not to go to extremes. If the Plutonic urge for ongoing transformation is denied here, then over a period of time pressure for change will build up to such a level that inevitably there will come a sudden release often accompanied by crisis and trauma, although it should be emphasised that this is only normally evident in cases involving denial. In some cases, Pluto oppositions are more common than average in the charts of people who have been through harrowing experiences involving powerlessness, whether emotional, mental or physical and those that survive these traumas learn quickly about what it is that they do not want.

When one of the planets in the opposition is Pluto the nature of and the potential for extremism of all types is only going to be emphasised. Pluto is nothing if not extreme at times and is not known for his general willingness to take the middle path. Therefore, oppositions to Pluto are going to be no nonsense affairs with no room for doubt or misunderstanding and a great deal of focus on specific issues. Whichever planet or point is being opposed by Pluto will come sharply under the anti-spotlight and find that all the dungeons, cellars and cavities that they would prefer to stay hidden will be exposed and brought to the surface. Yet at the same time, out of the seemingly impossible oppositions of two completely different perspectives and opinions comes a kind of alchemy where the pressure for change becomes so intense that there is a transmutation, a shift in the nature of problems in an almost cellular way into a form that can be more easily managed, wrenched, twisted and shaped. Similarly to the conjunction with Pluto the opposition is a 'do or die' aspect that does not really deal in half measures and will not compromise, preferring to go down fighting rather than surrender in any form. Normally, a combination of incisive subtlety at the right moment coupled with the ability to persevere when under pressure arrives at a point where everybody can be content, if not happy and that is a starting point for Pluto to weave his transformative web which if allowed to deliver will normally yield a regenerative energy of the highest order.

Sun opposite Pluto

The Sun represents that part of oneself that relates to individuality and identity, one's sense of being unique and alone as oneself. An opposition to the Sun will bring a forced element of challenge and change into the way that the individual tries to lead their life and it will inevitably bring difficulties and even confrontational issues in certain cases in the ways that they define themselves in the world. When the planet doing the opposing is Pluto the challenges will not be transparent or clear and they may well be coming from a behind the scenes or underground or otherwise subversive origin. However, God help anyone who tries to point these potential challenges out to the individual. They are constantly aware of their own foibles and inadequacies and do not need other people's reinforcement of these patterns. An adage here is 'the brighter the Sun, the darker the shadow' and Pluto is the shadow in this context, yet many people with this position cannot see their shadow so will deny its existence and as a result live either shallow and/or vacuous lives. Here is found the person to whom inexplicable occurrences happen, who then asks 'why me? What have I done to deserve this?'

With Pluto opposite the Sun the individual may resort to their own patterns of coercion and persuasion, both of themselves and of others, which depending on the individual's ethics may or may not be clean and open. Pluto here can undermine one's best attempts to be 'up front' and sabotage the best of efforts. But this is not 'Pluto' doing this, merely Pluto acting as a symbolic agent for one's own capacity for foot shooting or other forms of self-sabotage. There can be difficult relationships with male role model imagery here as Sun opposite Pluto people do not really do orders, but they do like to have some type of boundary to push at or something or someone to fight against.

Sometimes this person's worst enemy is oneself in that the subterranean urge of constant purging and cleansing can be taken too far; the individual does not know when to stop and as a result they burn out everyone else around them and end up isolated and alone.

With the Sun opposite Pluto there will be an ongoing and permanent urge to go deeper and leave no stone unturned in one's own self exploration regardless of how difficult some of the difficulties and challenges found within are. There will always be the desire to refine, cleanse, purge and eliminate that which is toxic or redundant from one's nature whilst at the same time resonating with a level of self-loathing about those same toxins within oneself. This self-dissatisfaction is what drives the individual into ever greater transformative processes of refinement. When it comes to relationship patterns this individual will either accept the fact that they have a strong personality and thus will attract similar types or else end up in relationships that have an element of domination or manipulativeness or other forms of subversiveness about them. The key to this aspect is the acceptance of the need for ongoing transformation and regeneration and the accompanying aspiration to reform oneself into something constantly purer, higher and more refined.

Moon opposite Pluto

As shown elsewhere in this book, aspects between the Moon and Pluto are potentially more emotionally volatile than with any other planetary contact. They bring an intensity of feeling into every emotive interaction and when the aspect in question is the opposition then extremes of all types will easily apply. The key to working with the opposition is to understand the cycles of loss and gain, death and rebirth etc and to allow the ebb and flow of these cycles in one's life. As these individuals age, they steadily learn a greater tolerance for the foibles and failures of mere mortals and find room in their hearts for forgiveness although this normally only comes after austere or difficult personal emotional experiences. They are all truly psychic in some shape and have no problem collaborating with those delicate individuals at the very start or the very end of life.

From a Plutonic perspective this aspect unleashes a large amount of 'dark' energy, dark not in terms of content but in terms of working with the unknown and the unknowable. During youth it can bring a sense of disempowerment in the family life and from an astrological perspective Pluto opposite the Moon is one of the most common aspects prevalent in cases of emotional abuse, neglect or abandonment and it is surprising how many of these people are adopted or orphaned from an early age. When older this aspect denotes similar extremes but in a more controlled way, either for detrimentally manipulative purposes or else for regenerative transforming processes.

Fear of betrayal or other forms of emotional loss can scar the individual so much that often they prefer to deal with life's more primal challenges alone, knowing that they can only truly rely on themselves when it comes to the bottom line. Their penetrating insight makes them scary in other people's eyes as does their ability to see right through people. They cannot stand rejection because to them it is a symbol of their low self-worth and they will never forget. They need gentle managing at the emotional level, their ultra-powerful yet incredibly delicate and sensitive emotional patterns respond best to consistent and regular emotive support and in return they provide an element of backbone that is unshakeable and unbreakable.

When viewed from a Moon opposite Pluto viewpoint the capacity for compulsive behavioural patterns that are rooted in early childhood to still have a powerful effect in later years is strong. There can be a direct refusal to change one's standpoint or a degree of obsessive and persistent action even when it is obvious that it will result in failure. These people can attach themselves to others limpet-like to the point of surrendering their own sense of individuality and finding that they have become absorbed or consumed into others' lives. This is part of their deep inner emotional craving to belong, which if it becomes insidious can result in these people becoming emotionally addicted to other. Moon opposite Pluto people wrote the rule book when it comes to sulking and brooding, with lower types of people using guilt techniques and plotting revenge and the more evolved types letting go in time but never forgetting. There is a need to bring old emotional wounds to the surface for elimination, much like a boil rising. By doing this the individual can escape years of being scapegoated and the subsequent self-degradation thus freeing themselves of old emotionally ingrained patterns and truly giving themselves a chance to begin again, a guilt free zone and unhindered by anybody else's emotional hopes or expectations of them.

Mercury opposite Pluto

Normally Mercury's androgynous nature gels well with the more transpersonal side of Pluto and creates an in-depth approach to life through all facets of communication, an approach that gives sharp and perceptive insight into other people and their reasons and motivations. However, when the aspect in question is the opposition there will always be an added degree of intensity about the communication methods and processes that whilst constantly sharpening the intellect may also engender an element of caution or even challenge from others, even though this aspect is the best there is at keeping secrets. There may always appear to be an element of motive inherent in the individual's actions and communications and the person with Mercury opposite Pluto should go out of their way not to be seen as trying to convert people. If the paranoia that this aspect sometimes produces in the first thirty years of life can be channelled appropriately and the mind corralled into a healthy and consistent focus then the potential for unswervable concentration and ultimate personal success is guaranteed, although the amount of mental effort required for this is not minor.

When viewed with Plutonic eyes there will always be various levels of perceptive awareness ongoing at the same time. The natural caution of this aspect tends to make the individual more reticent than most in coming forward but on the occasions that they do, their content will always have significant depth and weight to it as well as the capacity for a form of dark humour. As a client puts it; *'Sometimes I do deliberately come forward, but more to inject some humour with the desire to lighten things – which of course brings me a lot of attention too!'* Pluto opposite Mercury people are so aware of the potential for the dark side in others to emerge that they are not as astonished or appalled as everyone else is when on many occasions their suspicions are found to be correct. Not so much psychic as sharply and accurately intuitive at the mental level, they have an uncanny ability to read people's minds or at least it can seem like this at times. Fantastic researchers who leave no stone unturned, these natural investigators of the hidden, the 'taboo' or occulted and the invisible will always get to the bottom of things no matter how painful or what the cost to their stability, prestige or sanity. Pluto opposite Mercury affects not so much the words but what it is that lies behind them. This is the philosophies, concepts, ideals and urges that from behind the scenes empower individuals into defining their life through communications.

With Mercury opposite Pluto, the emphasis switches into the more superficial mind and the type of communications and experiences it attracts. There can be a lack of patience inherent in this aspect both with oneself and with others, something that needs to be moderated to retain an element of community in one's life. Here can be seen the terrier-like person, who once they get hold of some titbit or piece of information will worry away at it until all is revealed, no matter how long the process takes or how deep one must dig. As another client states: *'I have certainly had to do some digging in my time. I do like to get to the bottom of things and get things resolved though with age I have not done it so savagely as I used to when younger.'* Also here is the frenetic and incessant worrier, the mentally ruthless, the deeply contemplative and the mercilessly neutral, all representative of how the mind works and what quality of psychological self-empowerment underlies the superficial day by day trivia. The speech can sometimes be incessant or at other times abrupt or terse, to the point and without decoration and at the corresponding mental level there can easily develop an almost obsessive attitude which once established is difficult to relinquish. What this aspect lacks in terms of tact, diplomacy or subtlety it makes up for with insight, sharpness of perception and an unnervingly accurate bullsh*t filter.

Venus opposite Pluto

'Well, I've kissed a lot of frogs!' says one client with this aspect. On the surface level these superficially lonely souls can seem to be constantly concerned with different levels of intrigue and trust and over the years associated with long term relationships they have to learn and accept the need to let others have the upper hand occasionally, so that they can satisfy themselves that they are not being a total control freak. Even here there is never total surrender, as another client states; *'There is always an element of control – the upper hand is only given when it concerns something that can be let go of – not something important.'* They do not do lightweight people or partners; they do tend to go for the deep thinkers of the zodiac, people with substance, depth and solidity. At the root of their fear lies the issue of abandonment, so the sensible ones with this position partner themselves with someone who can be strong for

them when they cannot do it for themselves, someone who will help them manage their anger and then still be there to hug and cuddle them regardless. Secretly they ooze passion and sensuality but they need to feel safe enough both with self and with partner to express it and that safety takes a secure environment and the stability of years of experience. Pluto takes a long, long time to trust someone thoroughly and consistency and reliability are the quickest way to earn that trust. As another client so succinctly puts it; 'Liars and cheats make my blood boil, as do superficial and political types.'

In the bedroom Venus/Pluto can play the role of the tramp, the gigolo or the surrender junkie with ease, although at times it may seem as though they will be anything their partner wants them to be in order that they feel accepted. It makes for a sensitive and emotional disposition that on the challenging side tries to remould the partner into something more to the individual's own liking as opposed to compromising and meeting partners halfway. The opposite and positive side of this is the ability to help both partner and self go through the fear and pain barriers together and emerge through real teamwork into a synergy of strength. The true and deep love offered by this position will always bring a symbiosis at the intimate level that takes the interaction way beyond that of a normal relationship. This position often has clear definitions with sex. It is either a quick and functional need being met and/or brief desire being sated, or else it is the deep, committed and passionate loving experience of which sex is only the physical but this experience can and often does take years of both practice and trust to evolve into.

Venus opposite Pluto has a kind of Scorpionic feel to it that on the surface challenges others to understand what is going on underneath, a kind of 'I dare you to work me out' game. It likes to drag partners under the quilt or sheets and pretend that they are in a cave, or even better to be not pretending and in the real thing. There is a temper, as a client states; *We can be like little volcanoes or summer thunderstorms, a short, sharp jolt of discord, then normally all is forgotten and well again, although there is the occasional 'biggie' or meltdown that has accumulated over many months, when I take half the planet with me'*. This aspect has a degree of the extremist about it but not so much in a threatening or challenging way as much as in a seductive and suggestive way that is never clear or transparent. The nature of Venus and Pluto in opposition is to look for the crevices where dirt can be hiding, to go the extra mile to uncover and find out about a partner and to insinuate itself into everything around itself, to have a little awareness of everything and everyone in the immediate environment. It helps make these potentially paranoid people feel safe, as though they have a grip on the situation. Woe betide anyone who pokes too deep into their personal lives without permission and when dealing with these highly charged and sensual people, never ever kiss and tell or be prepared to be frozen out for life if you do. What can come across as secrecy is the need for privacy born of past experiences of deceit and mistrust. This position truly can be that of cold ice, the unbreakable and the involatile with an impenetrable wall being the only possible interface between them and the people they distrust. It can also be the most passionate and loving when it feels both safe to do so and wanted at the same time.

Mars opposite Pluto

This aspect is one of the most challenging of all in terms of anger management, physical expression and the accompanying transformational processes of life. Most people with this position are likely to have experienced a significant level of difficulty with one or both parents in the early years, often leading to suppression of one's true feelings. Unless acknowledged and dealt with early in life, this repressed energy then builds into a resentment against all forms of imposed or disciplined structures, all the way from the parents and the teacher to the employer. As a client puts it so well: *'I contained myself until the age of eighteen when I could finally escape to University. Freedom for me was everything; I engaged in big drama projects endlessly, first of all because it was my passion and second because I could then avoid going home in the holidays under the pretext of being on tour with a play. This disappointed my parents, I know. However, I saw it as payback time, for all I had not been allowed to do and express when I was growing up. Plus, I valued my freedom too much. Home was a restriction and boredom for me.'* This is not the position of the rebel fighting for a better future but more the position of the destroyer or nihilist willing to bring down the old to see if something new and better comes out of the mix. Mars opposite Pluto does not really do words except in short sentences. It works on the principle that whilst constant and regular events are the desired outcome, where and when necessary specific actions will always speak louder than words. This capacity for incisiveness and direct action is normally only activated by evolving situations of external pressure and it is a measure of the person's maturity and evolution as to whether they express this action in ways that are either destructive or transformative. Parents of children with this aspect are advised to get them into a type of assertive and projective martial art on the grounds that it will train and guide them into self-discipline from an early age not only physically but also mentally. Children of parents with this aspect are advised to suggest to them that some type of passive and receptive form of martial art, such as Tai Chi or Qigong would bring an element of balance into their lives.

In the outside world, Mars opposite Pluto manifests in many ways, but the single common factor is that of an unstoppable drive towards whatever the person considers to be success in their life. If untrained or repressed this energy of volatility can emerge into the world in challenging ways from surly and resentful behaviour to almost aggressive attitudes. Commonly, these people work alone if only because they burn a lot of people out and most others cannot keep up with them. These are the people who if they can focus and train their energy away from anger into specialisation can become true masters and artists of their ability. There is a need to recognise that this is a formidable force that can be quite 'petty tyrant' like when young but dynamic and projective when older.

But when there is no vehicle for focus the Mars/Pluto energy can turn inwards and fester, occasionally erupting in acts or words of irrational and unconscious anger or over a long period of time coming out through inflammatory illness. These are the people who go in for marathons or similar other forms of pushing their boundaries via will power and pure determination. If they can divert their energy into their work by doing something as a career that is representative of the Mars/Pluto urge for purgative and eliminative in depth action, they can transform both their own and potentially many other people's lives as well for the better. The challenge here is not so much that of finding one's specialist niche because that will occur one way or another in the course of time: it is knowing when to let oneself stop being that specialist and sit back and smell the roses and the coffee. The biggest danger to oneself here is that of burn out, of not knowing when to stop, as much as it is that of alienating others through a lack of tact. As a client states; *'It's taken me all of my life to realise that I am the most important person in my life, including my children, because how can I help anyone else if I'm not in good working order myself?'*

In the privacy of the bedroom Mars opposite Pluto will have any different number of expressive forms but none of them will be passive for that long without wanting to act. These people are not going to be content with sex as a mechanism for just sharing love. To them sex is a quick way into the state of consciousness where they can feel and surf the flow of the true vitalised power of life although what they do when in that state of feeling is dependent on their personal moralistic code. Here lies the aggressive and violent, the manipulative and the coercive as well as the selfish and amoral attitude of the emotionally corrupt or unevolved based purely and solely on power over others as a survival mechanism. Here also lies the aspirant grail knight who purges and purifies themselves of all that is corrupt and dirty, who constantly seeks to transform their raw lust and desire and regenerate it into something far more refined and sophisticated. There is a need for physical expression at a constant level with this position whilst at the same time struggling to live within one's own boundaries as opposed to those imposed by others and this physical expression, whether sex, athletics, martial arts, violence or other will inevitably become the vehicle of personal transformation, hopefully in ways that help the individual evolve instead of devolve.

Jupiter opposite Pluto

This opposition can take the individual to heaven or it can take them to hell, but it will not ever let them sit on the fence. It is a classic 'all or nothing' aspect that comes across alternatively as either ice cold or else explosively volatile. The potential extremism of this position needs managing carefully as to these people the middle ground is often a far-flung and foreign country. This is one of the aspects associated with extremist viewpoints or perspectives whether financial, religious or political, which is great if done with a degree of social responsibility for the common good but not so good if it concerns the imposing of one philosophy for another. Jupiter's constant search for truth, higher understanding and meaning normally equates well with Pluto's ongoing quest to transform and regenerate all that it encounters but when these two arbiters are in opposition there may be an ongoing conflict between one's higher philosophical truths and the more mundane lower daily truths.

The challenge here is to be able to 'walk one's talk' whilst deliberately choosing not to go to extremes.

When viewed from a Plutonic perspective this aspect can lead to or indicate a strong potential for underground or subversive actions and situations, suggesting a clear need for these people to be transparent in all their business dealings and to only deal with likewise transparent others. Jupiter opposite Pluto does bring the capacity for hardnosed, ruthless attitudes in financial and professional circles but it also brings the basic urge and desire to not only compete in the market but to also succeed no matter what the effort or cost. There will be times of moral or ethical judgement calls that can cause considerable thought and/or heartache and the individuals' attitudes towards social ideology and practices will say a lot about their political stance. Long term personal policies will be dictated by direct individual experiences over the years as opposed to imposed dogma or theology. There may be strong personal religious ideas and Pluto opposite Jupiter easily understands what it is that drives individuals into fundamentalism of all types.

When taken from a Jupiterian viewpoint the eternal potentials for undercutting and overstretching whilst always there in the background will occasionally arise to the surface in ways that simply cannot be shrugged off or denied. From one end of the spectrum this is the ascetic monk or nun, solitary, silent and remote, seeking perfection through isolation and refined denial whilst an opposite alternative to this is the macho bully boy regardless of gender who will succeed no matter how many people are walked on and is utterly and fanatically convinced of the righteousness of their ways. In many cases there can be a holier-than-thou attitude, an autocratic demeanour that treats everyone else like staff, whether intended or not. Quite content to be alone rather than compromise beliefs, these people feel almost destined to do something big whether that is a bank robbery or running a world health programme.

Saturn opposite Pluto

Although this sounds as though it should be a difficult aspect, it is a generational pattern that can last as little as four weeks or as long as ten months thus affecting whole sub-generations of people and affecting people as much at the group level as it does at the personal. However, when it does affect individuals, it will not be gentle. The first thing to look at is the houses that the opposition falls in and to apply the unstoppable force (Pluto) against the immovable object (Saturn) rule and identify the blockages and issues in question and then to find ways to transmute these blockages into smaller, more manageable packages which can be individually transformed and then re-united into a larger, more healthy whole. Once the opposing sides of one's nature have been brought to heel they can be forged into an unstoppable force for transformation, ideally for the right reasons. There will be an intrinsic drive to create stimulus and revolution in the world and the lives of those around oneself but equally there is also a strong capacity for resisting change.

This aspect is often accompanied by ongoing periods of destruction (Pluto) followed by reconstruction (Saturn), a cycle of constant ending and new beginning that only over a period shows signs of steadily becoming more refined as the process evolves. There will need to be an element of self-dedication and perseverance to get the best from this aspect; otherwise, depression and constantly giving up on the point of success can be all too common. The willingness to sacrifice oneself for the benefit of others is very noble but no-one will say thank you and this can leave the Saturn/Pluto individual high and dry, feeling used, abused and taken for granted.

Self-restraint is a feature of this aspect but unfortunately this restraint can be detrimental as opposed to positive if taken too far. Saturn opposite Pluto can in extreme cases lead to cruelty, either towards others or towards oneself although the forms of that cruelty cannot be determined by this aspect alone. Remember that these are fundamentally different principles, in that Saturn seeks to bind, regulate and structure everything it meets whilst Pluto governs the formless part of one's nature, the part that simply cannot be regulated. When these two equal forces are in opposition, something must give. Normally the individual will go through some type of crisis of confidence every seven years or so but as they age so the impact of this lessens. This is the individual who needs to end up in control of their own life and no-one else's, who takes responsibility for their actions and who can manage large amounts of authority in a mature and adult way.

Pluto opposite Ascendant

The Ascendant is the start of the new day at the place and moment of birth. It gives the outside world its first glimpse onto the newborn child and vice versa and as one ages so the Ascendant becomes the armour that the individual puts on as they go outside the front door into the outside world, it is the way they are at the moment by moment level in their daily life. Oppositions to the Ascendant brings challenges, not only in terms of how the individual manifests their life at the daily level but also in terms of the people they are regularly involved with. When the planet doing the opposition is Pluto there is always going to be an element of either subversion, transformation or some other form of intensity in all interactions with 'other' regardless of the status of that other person.

When this aspect is looked at from the perspective of having Pluto opposite the Ascendant there can be complications in terms of defining a regularity of identity to oneself. Certainly when young the tendency for revamping or remodelling oneself is a constant theme, it is sometimes as if the appearance, the dress sense and the bearing that one presents to the world are nothing but a canvas for the individual to try out their emergent ideas of what identity really is. There can be an intense dislike of one's appearance when young with drastic changes at times. These people can change their intensity levels at the switch of a button when needed from placid and quiet to full on and extreme and back within a few minutes, making it hard for others to comfortably co-exist around them unless these same others also have the urge for constant reformation and transformation. However as these intense and occasionally obsessive individuals get older and wiser they realise that it is not the appearance or the outside world that needs transforming as much as it is one's own internal world view and personal aspirations. When necessary, there will be the willingness to make oneself go the last extra mile that no-one else can do and to force oneself to make the last step to get things done. This position may have an almost compulsive streak but it is also great at getting things done in a final and permanent way.

When this aspect is looked at in terms of Pluto conjunct the Descendant, the influence of other or others comes much more sharply into the picture. It is not others at the collective or group level here; it is others at the singular, one to one relationship level that is being considered, whether that relationship is family, friend, professional or personal and intimate. Here can be found the potential obsessive in relationship patterns where in the worst case scenario people put up with all types of degradation or abuse rather than be alone or where they can fixate almost leech-like on another as the answer to their prayers until the inevitable disappointment when their golden angel turns out to be only human. Sometimes the Pluto/Ascendant person finds that their relationships with other become the battlefield for personal development and that it is only through exposure to others at an almost primal level that the individual can really learn about how to truly be themselves in a relationship. Every so often the relationship with their significant other must be purged and cleansed from the inside out to see if it is still valid and a true agent for change. There is one absolute golden rule in all relationships with this position, this being that not only must the individual be sure that they are constantly in receipt of the truth even if they do not like it but they must also ensure that they are telling the truth so that there is no tripping up later on down the line.

Pluto opposite Midheaven

The Midheaven (MC) has three different archetypal roles in astrology, these being the relationship the individual has with all authorities ranging from God, state or employer through to teacher and parents; one's attitude towards career, goals, ambition and work; and words like status, profile, visibility and public image, the way one presents oneself into and onto the outside world as being. When there is an opposition to the MC all or any of these facets of life will come under fairly constant challenge until an accommodation is reached and when the opposing planet is Pluto that accommodation will not be reached easily without significant change and almost pain like experiences leading to phoenix-like renewal, albeit through the alchemical fire on its way.

In the area of career and professional goals, the opposition of Pluto to the Midheaven will invariably bring degrees or elements of jealousy, manipulation or other forms of subtle or not so subtle behind the scenes tactics. Power struggles such as these are unfortunately common and very hard to avoid without a clear understanding of the deeper dynamics that are empowering the situation. It may be that superiors are fearful for their job or contemporaries worrying about parity in some shape or form, or alternatively it may that that others in one's professional environment may be concerned about the Pluto/MC individual's movement forward, worried that if one individual is changing for the better then that raises the bar for the group. Peer group pressure ranging from the subtly persuasive through to the manipulative to the downright threatening can feature, making it difficult for the individual to operate in a group environment. Sometimes the only way out of potentially subversive situations is for the individual to face down protagonists, preferable in public, state what they are doing, why they are doing it and what their intentions are and then ask the protagonist for either their help or at least their advice. Whether that help and/or advice is given or not, at least the individual will know where they stand regardless of whether it is black or white, yes or no, which is hugely preferable to being left in the dark or uncertain as to the nature of things.

This situation may also be replicated within the boundaries of the close family in ways that can be equally if not more difficult. There may be a heritage issue where a line of tradition has pervaded over generations, with the family intent for this to continue regardless of personal wish. Commonly this aspect has about it an element of family obligation where care of older generations or acceding to others wishes at the expense of one's own can be consistently seen. It may be that family obligations whether to older people, similar generation or younger children can stymie and block individual aspirations and that at certain critical junctures in life the individual will potentially walk away and start again free of obligation to anyone except themselves. It is only at this point of extremism, whether professional or family, that the individual can really say to oneself what it is that they want, what it is that is still of value and worth as they emerge into a steadily transforming world. Inevitably there will be family responsibilities, obligations and duties but there is also a moral duty to oneself. It is fine to be a good child, partner and parent but eventually the time comes where the individual asks 'what do I get?' To which one of the obvious answers is 'well, how can I be of help to anyone else if I'm not first of all in good working order myself?' Sometimes putting oneself first is not selfishness, it is self-enlightened interest and with Pluto opposing the Midheaven an individual's priority must be to oneself. In this light the single best thing that an adult can do with this position is to find themselves a secure and private residence. If the home is solid everything starts from there. If the home is wobbly, everything else will be wobbly too.

Section Three: The Theoretical

8

Working with ideas of Pluto in today's world

The information in the following two sections about Pluto in the natal chart and Pluto by transit is derived from my own personal astrological client files as much as if not more so than from contemporary astrological thought and in that light should not be taken as statements of fact. It is up to the astrologer at the time to use and adapt this information as they best see fit, not to blindly follow what others may say. However, any astrologer who attempts to understand the nature of Pluto in a mechanical or logical way is not going to 'get it' whilst those astrologers who use Pluto in a psychological way are also not going to make the best of this energy because they are looking too deep and sometimes missing the obvious. Pluto cannot be consciously worked with because it represents everything that is in the realms of the unconscious and to a lesser extent the subconscious, the realms of oneself where thought and objectivity cannot go. Pluto deals with the transpersonal outside of individual rationality and its energies can never be brought into any clear or manageable form. It deals with energy in terms of one's primal urges and instincts and can never be simply understood or rationalised. It can be sensed, felt, intuited and known in an unconscious way, but it cannot be defined. Here perhaps Pluto's existence is an excellent metaphor for the difference between understanding and meaning.

Pluto in the natal chart

When working from an astrological capacity with the natal position of Pluto in an individual's horoscope chart, there are many factors to consider.

Obviously, there is the house position of Pluto to consider as well as the individual aspects that Pluto may make to other planets in the chart and their strengths or weaknesses. Pluto's closeness to the angles (Ascendant, Nadir, Descendant and Midheaven) should also be considered. From my own astrological perspective, it is primarily the aspect pattern that Pluto makes to other planets that is the main indicator of meaning and the translation of this meaning should always be based on aspect first, house position second, at least as far as Pluto goes.

Because Pluto's speed geocentrically relative to the other planets is the slowest when viewed from the Earth, when it does make an aspect pattern to the other planets in the solar system those aspect patterns are in place for many months if not years. For example, since the late 1940's to the current day Pluto and Neptune have either been in a sextile aspect to each other or very close to it. It is easy to bring this to a basic astrological translation of Pluto being transformation, Neptune being the imagination and the sextile being the aspect of opportunity. Therefore, it could be said that Neptune sextile Pluto in a horoscope brings the opportunity for the transformation of the imagination or the opportunity to bring imagination into or inside the transformative process. However, this aspect has been in place for seventy years and everyone born in that time frame will have this aspect in their charts, so obviously this is not going to be a major feature when translating or explaining the individual's horoscope. Similarly, when Pluto makes an aspect to Uranus, it will last for more than a year. The conjunction of Uranus and Pluto from 1964 to 1967 lasted four years and it could be said to be a very strong astrological significator when it comes to explaining the radical social changes of those times. When that conjunction is weighed in an individual horoscope the power of it will only come through and be obvious in the life of the individual in question if there are other aspects as well from/to the more personal planets or points in the chart in question. Similarly the sextile between Uranus and Pluto in 1995 and 1996 brought a number of global opportunities for the merger between humanitarian innovation and the drive towards transformation but for this aspect to be significant in a natal chart there would need to be other aspects from Uranus and Pluto to the personal planets. There is the Uranus/Pluto square of 2012-2015 to consider with the rights of the individual as symbolised by Uranus in Aries being directly challenged by the transforming needs of the state systems worldwide as symbolised by Pluto in Capricorn. Individuals born at this time with this square strongly aspected by other planets in their horoscope will have to integrate the notion of personal freedoms with that of national or other forms of organised structure to grow and expand healthily.

When Pluto is in aspect to Saturn, the aspect in question will always last for at least a year, so the effects of an aspect between these two planets will not be seen as personal. However, when supported by strong aspects from other planets, these aspects between Saturn and Pluto can go a long way to defining the roles of power management and the structures in the individual's life. It definitely could be said that the trine and sextile between the two aids the sense of depth and regularity in one's personal boundaries as well as bringing a reliable sense of knowing when to move and when to stay still whilst the square challenges the consistency and reliability of those same boundaries and structures that forces them into occasional periods of critical self-examination. The opposition and conjunction play a different role in that they bring specific issues of authority, challenge and order into conflict with each other, with the house(s) in question showing the fields of operation.

When the planet aspected by Pluto is Jupiter, the situation is different. Normally, any transiting aspect between these two will only last a few weeks and the influences will be found as much at the personal level as much as they are at the generational or sub-generational level. The trine between the two brings the talent and ability for good business skills whilst the sextile adds the gift and opportunity of people management and negotiation to those skills. The square between Jupiter and Pluto is the angle of the pressure cooker, with the potential for (hopefully controlled) explosions at any time or in any area although the house position of natal Jupiter is a good guide here. In the cases of both the conjunction and the opposition between these two astrological heavy hitters, although it could be said that the opposition tends to polarise the power issue whilst the conjunction tends to concentrate it the houses really do have to be taken strongly into consideration. For example and depending on other aspects, Jupiter in the fourth house opposite Pluto in the tenth will have a much stronger impact than Jupiter in the sixth house and Pluto in the twelfth, or Jupiter conjunct Pluto in the seventh or second house will have a greater significance (again, dependent on other aspects) than it will in the third or the eleventh houses.

A dissimilar experience is offered by Pluto in aspect to planets inside the orbit of Jupiter as these planets tend to go round the Sun a lot faster, resulting in their transits through the signs of the zodiac and the houses of the individual's horoscope being much faster and potentially more significant as a result. With the inner planets and the angles, the sign and house position of the planets that Pluto is transiting can be as important as the transiting aspect itself.

When the planet in question is Venus or Mars the obvious background dynamic is that of sex, relationship patterns and the psychological undertones that power those patterns. The sextile is a positive aspect bringing a natural curiosity about sex and sensuality in a healthy and well balanced way as well as the opportunity to express that curiosity. The trine between either of these planets with Pluto gives a bonus to the depth, shared qualities and empathic moments of intimacy. However, a square between Venus or Mars with Pluto can bring up a degree of primality in certain cases that must be expressed, ideally through either by a robust external physical environment with lots of action and exercise or through some form of disciplined approach to sexuality, i.e., tantra. In the cases of people who are not consciously aware of these influences, cyclical power struggles within family, career and relationship will constantly surface and there can be a tendency to feel 'out of control' when it comes to relationship potentials. The opposition of Venus or Mars to Pluto can sometimes create such a high energy that it completely eludes the day by day life of the individual, being so strong as to be almost invisible until inevitably at some time in one's life the buttons get pushed in areas to do with control, power, dominance and subversiveness, all within the context of relationship dynamics and the individual will have to make choices about their future. Similarly, the conjunction between Venus or Mars with Pluto brings such a high focus into certain specific areas of life as to almost eliminate the drains on one's attention from elsewhere. As the individual with the conjunction or opposition ages they seek a more refined, sharp and pure way of expressing themselves preferring to move away from the drudge of the power games of life. The conjunction or opposition is the power angle that creates the relationship dynamic here: the signs of the zodiac it involves will show the way that the aspect manifests in the individual and the houses will show in which areas of the external life environment this comes out through.

With Pluto/Mercury aspects, the emphasis is less on the emotional and instead more towards the objective, analytical and informative. The trine between the two as one ages brings a sense of permanent self confidence in one's own psychological stability and the willingness to go into the dark when necessary, knowing that there is nothing there to be worried about. The sextile actively encourages the individual to develop the research capacity inherent in this aspect in a way that is transparent and clear but that also is no fool and cannot be duped or deceived. The square between Mercury and Pluto can be a bit like the incessant mental worm, always going into those dark holes. What can be the paranoia of youth turns into a willingness to undertake extensive investigative work as one ages with Mercury's sign and house giving an idea of the area in question. The opposition can bring a degree of intensity at the mental level that can border on obsessiveness but at the same time it can also bring an amazing capacity for completely isolated and concentrated focus and specialisation again indicated by Mercury's sign, house and other aspects. The conjunction of Mercury and Pluto can be one of the strongest astrological aspects of all if responsibly managed but when young the sheer power of the mind can drag it down into the Hadean depths and induce not only paranoia but also phobia. Only with age and a willingness to look at one's own internal depths, to deal with the potentially compulsive and repetitive side of one's nature does the true strength of the conjunction emerge into the capacity for determination, thoroughness, resolve and depth, all manifested in a no-nonsense way that will not deviate nor brook interference. Again, the house and sign of the conjunction give clear indications as to which areas of life and in which ways this energy manifests into the individual's life and the outside world.

I have had a decade or more direct experience of working the positions, aspects and meanings of some of the major asteroids and whilst the research is too new to begin to analyse let alone summarise it, one or two specific points can be hypothesised relating to the largest asteroid Ceres, the Roman equivalent of the Greek Demeter and its relationship with Pluto. It has become increasingly clear in the last decade or so that Ceres' key function has to do with the concept of nurturing. Nurturing covers many fields and ages but it primarily governs the way one is nurtured as a child and the conditionality of that nurturing especially in the first seven years of life. It is the nurturing that one gives as an adult to others in forms of a bed for the night, food, clothing, money, hugs and reassurance etc. It is the way one nurtures oneself primarily through lifestyle management, nutrition and diet and it is the way one allows others to nurture oneself, or not. Initial observations clearly show that when Pluto is in opposition or conjunction to Ceres for approximately for one month out of every twenty six and that there are also other astrological contributing factors then issues concerning neglect, abandonment, emotional isolation and feelings of being totally alone are fairly common in youth, being replaced as one ages by an almost pathological need and desire to both nurture and be nurtured. Female role model imagery can be extremely powerful here, often for the wrong reasons. The reader here is reminded that this is speculative and ongoing work based only on my own extensive research.

Pluto in aspect to either of the angles (Ascendant and Midheaven) will go a long way to describing how the individual interacts at the day by day level with the outside world. Aspects to the Ascendant pertain more to the individual's own direct experience *of* the outside world whilst the Midheaven's aspects relate to the individual's direct experience *in* the outside world and in both cases, Pluto brings an element of intensity. The trine from Pluto to the angles indicates that the individual comes across to others as solid, mature and reliant, even if the individual does not actually feel those qualities, because the trine gently but solidly advertises the resilience and placid strength of Pluto into the world in an unassuming and non-challenging way. The sextile between Pluto and either of the angles amplifies this attitude but also adds a degree of effort, direction and occasionally pervasiveness into the equation. This prides itself on its effectiveness but at the same time in an understated way subtly ensures that the path ahead is clear by nipping potential opposition in the bud. Individuals with a square from Pluto to either of the angles will find that they both attract and repel specific types of people much more quickly and obviously than most. This is because either of the angles in question function as a point of expression for the Pluto energy that is normally used to behaving in a more behind the scenes way so when it is thrust forward into the world then a level of intensity and sometimes an almost obsessive attitude towards thoroughness can be evident. The quality of this intensity can sometimes be gauged by looking at the mode that Pluto and the angle in question are in, whether cardinal signs (active), fixed (determined) or mutable (flexible).

The opposition of Pluto to the Ascendant or Midheaven brings an element of depth and intensity into all relationships with other right across the board, an intensity which if managed properly and consciously then leads to the individual becoming an agent of change and catalyst both for themselves and others in a positive and regenerative way. Alternatively it can seem that these people are so dogmatic or single minded that they attract opposition at every turn. Here especially the other aspects to Pluto and the angle are significant as is the strength of the opposition by orb and the house Pluto occupies to a lesser extent. The underlying dynamic here is the unfathomableness of life where some things normally visible to others are simply occluded to this individual and they must arrive at their conclusions via different routes than most. These routes are often via some form of symbolic passage through their own intuitive darkness before emerging healed and purified from the other side but that passage does involve an element of metaphorical death and rebirth not seemingly evident in most people's lives. The difference between the opposition and the conjunction involving Pluto and either of the angles is that invariably the opposition brings in the power challenges of Pluto as reflected through the interactions with other or others whilst the conjunction is almost unilaterally focussed on the relationship one has with oneself and the effect one has in and on the world. With the conjunction of Pluto to the Ascendant or Midheaven there can be such a degree of single mindedness as to make the individual seem a specialist and/or a loner in everything that they do. It is not that they are lonely or crave for company, it is just that they are on a self-appointed mission to save themselves, others and the world and only they have the power and foresight to do it, thus making themselves ever more alone as opposed to lonely. They simply will not tolerate deception at all; they never, ever forget and some will never forgive either. In return for trust and transparency coming their way from those they care for, these all or nothing Plutonian warriors will maintain their strength to the end to protect what is under their self-appointed aegis and will quietly and willingly shoulder greater responsibilities and make immense fundamental choices when needed.

Pluto in aspect to the Sun is a truly alchemical mix, being the openness, heat, light and life of the Sun interacting with the dark, mysterious and hidden Hadean depths of Pluto. Regardless of the aspect in question, any contact between these two quite different astrological forces is going to have a profound influence which will lead to either total transformation or annihilation because with this combination there can be no middle ground. Admittedly this capacity for extremism is only one trademark of this combination but one that is common. It is not so noticeable by trine or sextile, with the trine bringing a sense of physical solidity and the capacity for endurance and steadfastness, a resilience and stature that bends but never breaks and is always there. The sextile builds on this and encourages exploration and expansion of that stature both up and down. It will bring the occasional opportunity for chance encounters with random other or others in ways that defy statistical rationality and within minutes that encounter with 'other' will have achieved a depth and profoundness that with other people never happens at all. The square between these two often has such a penetrating gaze as to make others feel distinctly uncomfortable, but only those with something to hide. It has an incessant nature that just does not give up until it has achieved its original desire and sometimes this can be so focussed as to not see the people it is treading upon in its unstoppable urge forward. Similarly to Pluto with the Ascendant and to a lesser extent the Midheaven, the opposition and conjunction of Pluto to the Sun are like two different sides of the same coin. The opposition will bring situations of challenge in an almost impossible way to manage, constantly pushing the individual to change and transform their ways of seeing problems to overcome them, whether those problems are through other people or situations or else in their own psychological makeup and then projected outwards. It will seem to the individual as if the outside world is a kind of inverse mirror of their own inner state at any given time. Whereas the conjunction unifies the light and the dark, the ice and the heat and brings with it the potential for a true alchemical transformation although normally only through a type of almost shamanistic purging and cleansing of one's soul at a fundamental level. The conjunction of the Sun with Pluto is the single strongest aspect in terms of determination and willpower and will not be beaten, it will die first. Indomitable is a word that comes to mind.

When Pluto is aspecting the Moon there will always be an element of primality about the individual and their emotional states and the type of aspect will suggest the ways in which that emotive primality is expressed. The harmonious aspects of the trine and the sextile between the Moon and Pluto will give the individual a sheen like the archaic Celtic word 'glamor,' to weave charm and allure into a veneer of power, emotional strength and not a little magic. The trine illuminates a quality of emotional depth that permeates all that the individual does. It makes for someone emotionally solid who can deal with the dark sides of life in a matter of fact way and who implicitly trusts their gut instinct more than the thoughts or the superficial feelings. The sextile takes these attributes and complements them with a more proactive stance, the making of windows of transformation as opposed to the trine's just waiting for them to occur. The sextile imbues the individual with the regenerative and transformative urge in such a way as to bring a quality of stimulus into all that they do. What this is will be determined by the sign of the Moon, the houses of the Moon and Pluto as well as other aspects to these points, but the power of creative depth is there and fertile in people with this aspect. The square between Pluto and the Moon is one of the hardest aspects in astrology and the sign, house and other aspects to the Moon will go a long, long way towards determining the emotionally responsive capacity of the individual. There can be a real fear of trusting people even after years and an almost phobic attitude towards the privacy of one's own personal feelings. There may be considerable challenges at the emotional level stemming from the first seven years of life often resulting in compulsive and almost unconscious habit patterns such as eating disorders, nail biting, scratching etc... However, a square not only brings challenges, it also brings the requisite energy to turn those challenges into gifts over a period and with application. In many people with this aspect their willingness to go into their own personal dark and face up to ingrained psychological issues dating from early childhood empowers them into a position of both self-empowerment and emotional invulnerability. Occasionally this is done by eliminating the emotional content of one's life because it is simply too overpowering and dominant but usually this emotional abstinence is eventually transcended and becomes a powerhouse of true intent, feeling and emotive power.

The conjunction and opposition of Pluto with the Moon is a mirror image aspect that holds no equal in terms of power. Individuals born with either of these aspects in their horoscope will find that periodically they must go through times of intense emotional experiences that can border on the extreme especially when young. There can be an almost compulsive need to have 'control' of one's life and emotional states which necessitates the 'control' thus extending into personal environment and sometimes the lives of others around the individual. Woe betide anyone who attempts to get too close to this person's emotional boundaries without subtlety or kindness. The Moon/ Pluto opposition particularly has an obsessive streak about it sometimes clearly demonstrated by the sign and the house that the Moon occupies. It is 'the devil made me do it' aspect, driven into compulsive and repetitive emotive patterns even when it is obvious that this is the wrong way or that the outcome will not work. There is a 'do or die' attitude that never surrenders under any circumstances. These people sometimes push themselves through the literal fires of hell to get to what they see as the bottom of their own personal emotional depths as well as the deep underlying reasoning for external developments and actions. The repetitive nature of the opposition can be refined and transcended once the process has been undergone enough times and the individual has had their fingers burnt but has somehow survived and purified into the epitome of sanctity, purity and intent that this aspect offers, but the pathway to these aspirations is littered with temptation. The conjunction of the Moon and Pluto fuses the opposite ends of the emotional spectrum into a single driving force that will not tolerate opposition. Yet there is an almost subversive attitude of subtle underplay here in that these people, especially as they age, become increasingly aware of their own invulnerability (sometimes, unfortunately, brought on by aloneness) and in a quiet and normally understated way they exude strength and emotional solidity that just simply will not be misdirected. With both the conjunction and the opposition of the Moon with Pluto, one particular facet of these aspects jumps out, that once these individuals have gone to the very bottom of their soul and dealt properly with all of their fears and phobias, whether imagined or real (mainly imagined), they become so assured and integrated at the emotional level that they never have 'emotional problems' again.

Pluto by transit

Since astrologers have consciously been placing Pluto in horoscopes since the mid-late 1960's the meaning of it from an astrological perspective has been both developed and statistically consolidated in recent decades. Clear and definitive meaning can be ascribed to the astrological placement of Pluto in an individual's horoscope via the sign and house that it occupies and the aspects that it makes. Similarly in the last half century astrologers have observed the transits of Pluto through individual horoscopes and seen how influences in the person's life at the time of the corresponding Pluto transit have defined a form of meaning for that transit. It is rare in the middle of the second decade of the twenty first century to find astrologers (apart from the traditional schools) who do not use Pluto extensively, both natally and by transit.

Recent astronomical developments in the last twenty years have proven to astronomers' satisfaction that Pluto is not a 'planet' in the same sense that the Earth, Mars or Uranus is a planet, but despite this unalterable fact, the energy of Pluto still manifests as a more conventional planet would, both natally and by transit. Astrologers know what the essence and energy of Pluto is in the horoscope and they also know how the energy of Pluto manifests by transit. Where the dichotomy comes in is when astrologers attempt to explain or even understand how Pluto works in such a strong way when it is so fundamentally different from any other astronomical body used in astrological parlance and this apparent dichotomy is addressed elsewhere in this book. One of the beauties of astrology is its inherent capacity to blend symbolism and metaphor with geometry and mathematics, add a little intuition and – hey presto! Astrology is a blend of science and art from which over the years, centuries and millennia astrologers have faithfully recorded statistics and derived accurate meaning from them. Regardless of its physical nature or the absence of, there is some type of energy field that emanates the transformative potentials as indicated by the transits of Pluto and that the field in question comes from the same geocentric point in the heavens that Pluto appears to occupy. The following sections concerning the influences of Pluto by transit are solely born of my own first hand and direct experience of dealing with client's Pluto transits over the last three decades or more and should not be taken as gospel.

It will quickly become apparent to the practising astrologer that Pluto by transit conjuncting one person's Mars will be a different experience to the next persons. In some cases, a transit of Pluto sextiling a person's Jupiter may go almost unnoticed whilst in others it can be hugely significant. Regardless of the planet being transited by Pluto or the nature of the transiting aspect the effects of the transit in real terms will be influenced by other factors as well. These include the other aspects in the natal chart to the aspected planet, whether the aspected planet is in a sign or house that it is comfortable or uncomfortable with, other ongoing transits to the aspected planet in addition to that from Pluto, and each and every one of these factors is different according to the individual in question. It is the art and skill of the astrologer in both synthesising these factors and emerging with a functional rationale for the Pluto transit that is most required, and this only comes with practise and experience. By necessity, the following assessments of Pluto by transit is thus generalised and the reader is reminded that every chart and life experience is different.

Pluto in transit to the outer planets (itself, Neptune and Uranus) very rarely if ever can be directly attributed to any type or form of measurable or manifest effect without there also being considerable other influences as well. These transits will last at least a whole year and, in many cases, more and relate to such deep transpersonal issues as to be completely outside of the realm and range of most people's consciousness. Pluto itself brings a very deep and profound eliminative and regenerative energy that defies rational explanation and the generalised nature of all the outer planets in terms of horoscope analysis is that of the dark, mysterious, unpredictable and deep, so the potential for making logical and clear sense of these combinations is less than zero. In my personal experience, unless there are significant aspects to the aspected outer planet any transit from Pluto to the outer planets will go unnoticed at the personal level. As detailed elsewhere (Pluto in Capricorn) when Pluto makes long term aspect to the outer planets in the heavens or makes an aspect to a previous outer planet conjunction powerpoint the significance of Pluto's long term of this is sometimes much clearer on the global scale than it is on the personal.

Any definition of Pluto by transit to the planetoid Chiron or the major asteroid Ceres must be hypothetical as neither of these points have been in astrological usage for as long as Pluto which has less than a century's pedigree. However initial observations suggest that similarly to the natal aspect pattern of Pluto with Ceres, transits of Pluto to Ceres by conjunction or opposition bring issues concerning neglect and nurturing into the equation and that this is similar but different when Chiron is involved, with the conjunction or opposition by transit from Pluto bringing up similar issues but with the spectre of abandonment being thrown into the mix as well.

The significance of transiting Pluto to natal Saturn is normally not of major importance unless Saturn is either conjunct or opposite the Ascendant or Midheaven or strongly squared to one of the personal planets in which case either the willing or the forced transformation of boundary is going to be a central theme in the person's life for a year or so. The trine or sextile from transiting Pluto to natal Saturn brings a more flowing energy into the smoothing of boundaries and borders with a blend of strength and flexibility. The square inevitably brings challenges from other people in the individual's life at certain times, challenges that may not be intentional but that certainly involve a need for determination and resilience or else total surrender and release. Transiting Pluto opposite natal Saturn has an element of closure of old patterning about it in ways that suggest permanence and the conjunction also has a degree of finality bordered with incisiveness. Of course the houses in question need to be considered, but even here the influence will be at least partly generational and only majorly affecting a person's chart if their Saturn is otherwise strongly aspected.

The transits of Pluto to Jupiter can have a varied manifestation. In one person they can really push the individual to look at their conscience, their integrity and their dignity and cause the person to re-evaluate all of their morals and ethics, whilst in another person the same aspect can cause the Jupiterian person to not care about the ethics and to either go for broke or completely yield in certain areas of their life, preferring the material to the moral. Obviously, the aspects to Jupiter and its house position affect these choices but transits from Pluto tend to accentuate them significantly. The trine from transiting Pluto to natal Jupiter in theory adds a shine to the individual's business talents and ability, giving them an apparent edge of confidence and verve in a way that is seen as generally focussed and grounded.

The sextile takes this latent ability and turns it potent and looks to project oneself as being astute, wide and knowledgeable about as many diverse areas as possible whilst still retaining focus and concentration on the core matter. The square between the two takes the natal potential of being the pressure cooker and translates it into a temporary but acute period of inflatedness often signified by the house area of Jupiter, which when influenced by other and brief transits can suddenly roar like a lion only to immediately shrink again afterwards and should be noted for its capacity to over exaggerate. The opposition of transiting Pluto to Jupiter has the effect of making one's capacity for the 'all or nothing' attitude painfully obvious, the individual will not be able to be wilfully ignorant of their own capacity for extremes and the wise amongst these people will deliberately choose the middle path with a red hot yet icily sharp focus and determination that will endure no matter what. The passing of Pluto in the heavens over one's Jupiter by conjunction places the person firmly between the devil and the deep blue sea. They will be very aware of the potential for radical growth and sudden and dramatic twists and turns. There is such a strong potential here for growth but equally such a strong capacity for self-sabotage through excess or impulsiveness. The other natal aspects and the house position of Jupiter will determine the person's capacity for extremism; Pluto will merely amplify and exacerbate it for a year. Quality always works better than quantity, especially when it comes to one's own personal philosophies.

Pluto by transit to Mars brings the individual head on into direct contact with the physical sides of life in ways that simply cannot be ignored or pushed under the carpet. Inevitably at times this can in some people lead to situations of potential aggression or other forms of confrontational behaviour whilst in others the same influence can be seen as a refined and sophisticated way of getting things done in a quiet but assured way. Channelling the raw power of this combination into a focussed and directed channel in a way that is projective and with a quality of loving assertiveness is the ideal but learning how to forecast and deflect oncoming challenges becomes a skill as the individual ages. The trine from transiting Pluto gives an added degree of stamina and physical capacity as well as a greater element of personal magnetism and charisma, even if only for a year. The transiting sextile to natal Mars from Pluto brings an added assertive energy that announces to the world with confidence that their glass is half full at least and that they are actively looking to increase that amount. It is the transit of Pluto square natal Mars that is difficult because it forces the individual to engage with their physical nature or their lack of it in a way that brings power and control issues strongly to the fore in their lives, probably in areas indicated by the sign and house position of Mars. There is no option here sometimes but to metaphorically close one's eyes and step blindfolded into the darkness, trusting in one's own self-preservation instincts alone. Here lie the personal encounters with power unlike any other aspect and despite the environments that this square is set in, the real issue here is the ongoing power struggle one is having with oneself around being assertive. Other external environments are at least partially acting as a mirror image for this process.

The conjunction and opposition to natal Mars by transiting Pluto bring an entirely new dynamic into the equation. Here one cannot avoid the need to engage with both oneself and with other(s) in a way that has at least a degree of assertive and projective behaviour in it and if not careful also the capacity for over-reactive and seemingly confrontational behaviour as well. The transiting opposition to Mars invariably has an element of 'backs against the wall' about it where no matter what the circumstances the individual will feel alone or even isolated and that only they can make the strenuous effort needed to get them to the place that they want or need to be. They can make the mistake of misinterpreting other people's actions or intentions as opposition although this is rarely the case. A simple 'yes or no' question or two normally sorts any problems out before they get to become serious. Transiting Pluto opposing Mars calls for the individual to create or manufacture something to fight against for them to find out how strong they are, as though they need an element of opposition to struggle against. Pluto passing over natal Mars normally has a very galvanising effect where it brings the person a period of abundant physical drive, a healthy libido and the self-confidence to assert oneself comfortably into and onto the outside world although the manner of this approach will be dictated by the sign and house of the natal Mars position. It is less likely to attract any problems from others than the opposition is but at the same time the conjunction does carry a single mindedness about it that sometimes is so fully engaged with their own self-appointed mission that they do not see the toes they tread on during their headlong push forwards.

Pluto working in transit with Venus is like the way it works with Mars except in more receptive and passive ways as opposed to the Martian assertive and projective mannerisms. Pluto and Venus have an insidious relationship with each other with neither of them completely trusting each other's wiles and motives but agreeing not to disagree for the sake of the common good except in certain cases. They both relate to value although Pluto is concerned more with depth and profoundness whilst Venus is seen as more valuing the material or sensual. Of course, with Pluto ruling Scorpio and Venus ruling the opposite sign of Taurus, there is always going to be an element of challenge between these two different but similar value systems. The beneficial experiences of transiting Pluto to Venus are seen as some of the nicest experiences one can go through. The trine brings a positive and transformative energy into all of one's values, enriching the individual's experience and adding an element of increasing quality to the person's life through this transit, often through better quality and calibre people. The sextile from transiting Pluto to natal Venus amplifies these attributes and adds an element of conscious volition, creating an almost magnetic ability to attract what is right for them at the time and both the transiting sextile and the trine to natal Venus brings a better quality of experience in all of one's relationships with other and others. It is as though the people around oneself suddenly appear more sophisticated or reliable, more down to earth and grounded, and if this is happening it is because the natal Venus individual is putting out these qualities themselves and the other people are naturally being magnetised in because like attracts like. The square by transit from Pluto to Venus is one of the most difficult transits of all as it can potentially unleash hidden or repressed demons in several unusual ways. These are likely to be indicated by the sign, house and other aspects of natal Venus but on its own the transiting square from Pluto can take any inherent obsessive tendency or attraction and twist and wrench it out of shape, making much of the time for painful re-evaluations of the need or the reasons for relationship and deeply questioning the value of ongoing interactions.

The opposition by transiting Pluto to Venus is one of those transits that simply cannot be ignored. The natal Venus individual either accepts that their value systems are out of date, redundant and in need of radical transformation or they do not. If they do accept that fact, then the metaphorical death and rebirth process is easier and those relationships which are an honest expression of both the relationship and the individual in question will not only survive but prosper. If the person does not want to face the fact that their relationship patterns are becoming stale then they will have to deal with an element of ending that can be quite traumatic ranging from the obsessive denial and refusal to let go to the metaphorical ice scalpel coming down and everyone from the past immediately becoming yesterday's news. Via manifestations in the lives of people immediately around them, this transit normally asks of the individual 'what is it that you still want?' and 'what is it that is still of value and worth to you'? The conjunction of transiting Pluto to natal Venus dispenses with the roles of 'other' or 'others' and instead focuses purely and solely on the needs and wants and occasionally even the desires of the person in question. It raises the question of value through every level of direct personal experience whether financial, moral, relationship, ethical or personal. These values are some of those that are permanently transformed and hopefully regenerated by this aspect. Pluto transiting over Venus will eliminate the unsubstantial and the irrelevant and ensure that those values, people and situations that pass through this transit in one piece are of value and worth for the long term future.

Pluto transiting Mercury is seen as a favourable aspect in all its manifestations except for the square and possibly the opposition. Pluto's capacity to bring hard and permanent endings whilst at the same time breathing new life into projects and situations blends well with the more objective, detached, impersonal and methodical side of Mercury. Mercury's penchant for communications of all kinds welcomes the attentive and fastidious energy that Pluto sometimes brings and helps channel it into something specific and focused. The transiting trine from Pluto to Mercury is one of the nicest transiting aspects of all in that regardless of the individual's age Pluto will gently but firmly grab the mind and intellect of the natal Mercury person and gently massage it into something sleeker, more adaptable but at the same time something much more efficient, confident and assured at the mental level in ways that grow to be permanent. The sextile takes these attributes and adds to them by bringing an element of incentive and aspiration into the mix, using the more depth oriented perception that the transiting Pluto and natal Mercury blend has naturally and creating something profound, deep and meaningful out of it. This impresses the individual into and onto the world as a person who always gets to the bottom of things and leaves no stone unturned but who also manages to persuade everybody else that they thought of things thus leaving the person in question to get on with stuff in the background quietly and efficiently whilst others are taking the limelight. When Pluto in the heavens squares Mercury there can be problems. This square can lead to dogmatic or obsessive thought patterning where the individual refuses to give up or change their mind even when it is painfully obvious that they are doing things the wrong way. The actual ways in which the communicative challenge is manifested is normally indicated by the sign and house position of natal Mercury along with its other aspects, but a general rule of thumb here is that this is a time of zealous, overly concentrated and almost compulsive attention onto one or two situations or people in the person's world to the cost and detriment of most of the rest of their life. The inflexibility and refusal to change one's mind that often comes with this aspect can lead to the person feeling ostracised by a world that is in radical disagreement with them over most things, so these individuals really do need to know when they are barking up the wrong tree and when it is time to quit. When they do quit and reverse positions it is so sudden and dramatic as to beggar belief in such a dramatic change of mind, such is the absolutism of Pluto transiting Mercury by square.

The opposition of Pluto by transit to Mercury can create such a radical shift in the individual's mindset as to completely change one's programming or at least this is how it may appear on the surface. It can create such a 'brainstorm' that the individual can suddenly appear to change their mind about everything in their life and suddenly go off on a tangent in ways that no-one could have guessed prior to this transit. The natal Mercury person may suddenly exhibit a very strong single minded concentrated focus into a particular subject or theme which is not necessarily a bad thing but they can also concentrate this focus into an obsession towards something or someone which then becomes difficult to manage in a rational and logical way. Fanatical thought patterns along the 'might is right' pathway can be evident although this is not normally permanent, just seen for the duration of this transit. The house positions of the natal Mercury and the transiting Pluto will help in defining the areas being affected here. Similarly, the house position of transiting Pluto and natal Mercury in the conjunction between these two points will be of immense use in helping to understand the psychological dynamics behind this conjunction. Pluto here will concentrate the power of the mind and the communication as represented by Mercury and helps to create a powerful sense of mental focus, clarity and direction. It is an extremely good transit for studying a subject and mastering it within a year when under normal circumstances the same subject would take two or even three years to learn because the attention span is concentrated and directed with little fear of distraction. Pluto in transit conjunct natal Mercury can also create the equally strong potential for obsessive and compulsive behaviour towards the ideal of getting an object or goal to the exclusion of all other stimuli. At the end of the day Pluto in transit to Mercury does not dictate what the mind thinks or how the communication develops but it does talk about the power with which it is delivered and the ability to influence others by the intellect and the speech.

The Ascendant/Descendant and the Midheaven/Nadir axis relate primarily to the interface and interaction one has in and with the outside world from the moment one leaves the safety of the home to the way one addresses large groups or crowds. These axis', whilst having an influence in the natal chart in terms of defining characteristics in the individual, create a set of fixed points when it comes to relating to the world outside of oneself. So, when Pluto comes along and transits these fixed points a challenge to the nature of fixedness and resilience is issued, a test of the viability of one's ongoing external interactions.

Pluto by transit to the Ascendant or rising sign directly influences the interactions that the individual has with people in the outside world at the one to one status as well as how the individual behaves at the minute by minute and day by day level. The Ascendant represents the armour that the person puts on as they go outside the front door, it is the way that they are in the outside world in terms of moment by moment interaction. Any transit from Pluto to the Ascendant creates a kind of veneer around the individual making them seem to the outside world as though they are not to be trifled with without caution and care. The transiting trine from Pluto to the Ascendant brings the opportunity for other people in the person's life to suddenly step up to the mark and acquire a degree of substance. It should denote other people coming in who have a degree of gravitas and profoundness about them, not in any way lightweight and it always helps sort out the wheat from the chaff when it comes to defining who in one's community is reliable under pressure and who is not. Pluto by transit sextiling the natal Ascendant shifts the emphasis from the role of others in the person's life to the way that the individual in question impacts upon other people's lives. It makes the person come across to others as being more solid, stable, deep and reliable than previously presumed and it gives them the ability to make and take far reaching decisions without screwing up. The transiting sextile makes the opportunity for relationship developments and other types of profound meetings to have a greater potential for success than usual and should be seen as an aspect of positive transformation. The square from transiting Pluto to the natal Ascendant makes for difficult interactions with certain others in the person's life. It helps create a confrontational or pushy attitude either from the individual or towards them but in a way that is not given to willing compromise. It can bring about some very intense encounters with others and if so, there is a need to behave in above board and transparent ways, regardless of how others are behaving. It can occasionally attract subversive behaviour from other people and the attraction to this type of energy can be quite strong but should be resisted lest the person become just like those around them who are trying to drag them down to their level.

Pluto transiting opposite the Ascendant is primarily related to the patterning in all of one's relationships with other at the one to one level, normally but not necessarily that concerning personal and intimate relationships. It is almost inevitable that during this transit an element of extremism or other similar form of intensity will enter one's personal life often because of developments in the lives of those very close. An eliminative response to difficult relationships is often evident at this time in that the individual will often just shut the door and walk away never to return if they feel that this action is justified. On the one hand this transit leads to a much more incisive and decisive attitude towards one's personal relationships in that situations quickly become reduced to a yes/no, black/white situation where although the options are stark, the individual will quickly know where they stand. Alternatively, those relationships that withstand the intense scrutiny and testing that this transit brings will emerge out of the alchemical crucible in a way that is seen as solid, invulnerable and sustainable for the long term future. The conjunction of transiting Pluto to the natal Ascendant is a different thing altogether. The Ascendant is seen as one of the most important points in the horoscope being the point of reference into the world outside of one's body and personal life so to have the behemoth that is the astrological Pluto on top of it brings immense change. The compression of power and energy that is generated by this time is one of the strongest of all transits and no-one exits this time the same way that they entered it. Here Pluto metaphorically wipes the slate clean and eradicates old and worn out patterns of behaviour and social interaction, replacing them with a far greater capacity for streamlined and effective attitudes and behaviour. This period can also bring the impression to others that the individual may be on a power or control trip during the length of this transit which is not actually the case but the person will exude an element of challenge at this time. Inevitably during this process, the nature of relationship patterns both with other and with oneself will go through massive upheavals and irrevocable change and the person undergoing this transit may go through a major makeover, changing their appearance, lifestyle, the works. Pluto conjunct the Ascendant is one of the biggest astrological aspects of all in terms of transforming one's life, both internally and externally.

When Pluto by transit interacts with the Midheaven/Nadir axis a similar degree of intensity is experienced as with the axis of the Ascendant/Descendant but the areas of manifestation are usually different. Whereas the Ascendant primarily deals with the relationships that one has with 'other' and with oneself in the outside and measurable world the Midheaven deals with issues concerning the peaks and bases of life, the ambitions, goals and public life on the one hand and the home and family situation on the other. Pluto transiting the Midheaven is as strong if not stronger in terms of direct influence than it is when aspecting the Ascendant in that it rarely if ever fails to symbolise times of great personal change and transformation in the individual's life. When Pluto in the heavens is trining the individual's Midheaven there will be a sense of growth and development apparent in one's external professional world as well as the feeling that one has the implicit support needed from those near and dear. It gives a form of maturity blended with confidence regardless of physical age into whatever one is doing in the world outside of the front door and brings a strong public profile to bear, where one is externally seen as being able to oversee big decisions and large areas of responsibility. The sextile from transiting Pluto to the natal Midheaven creates a degree more impetus where the individual will commonly take the initiative and consciously project themselves into either larger situations of responsibility or similarly, more visible public life whilst at the same time ensuring that a significant minority of their energy and output is held in reserve for other eventualities. This reserve of energy is often stored in either property or other forms of home and family environment which also prospers in a background way through the transiting sextile. The square from transiting Pluto to the natal Midheaven/Nadir axis can be difficult to anticipate. It can manifest equally through both home and professional circumstances, or it can register just at one end of this axis in a powerful way. It can bring direct challenges from people in positions of authority and power in one's life whether they are parents, teachers, employers or any other form of dominant authority. Equally it can bring challenges into one's own reasons for staying in those environments especially when the pressure is on. Pluto square to the Midheaven can create an energetic field that is not conducive to compromise and the individual is best advised to work alone on a project where they will not burn others out or to be aware that the capacity for effort during the period of this transit is unlikely to be matched by others, which can lead to a lot of frustration and even anger.

Pluto by transit in opposition to the Midheaven and by extension in conjunction to the Nadir is one of the most powerful transits in astrology. In certain ways it will bring an element of permanent closure into the individual's life. This can relate to ancient possessions being lost, old properties crumbling or people who are already showing clear signs of being elderly and/or infirm getting ready to pass. It can bring certain situations to prominence in the person's life in ways that cause them to reconsider all their priorities in life from the family to their own long term career. This transit can precipitate a permanent and lifetime change in the ways that one wants one's home environment to be. This transit can involve a large-scale residential move or major renovation or other form of building work on the home, all designed to solidify and establish one's long term base. Pluto passing here distinguishes for the individual the difference between house and home in that one is where one lives and functions, the other is private and where one feels safe. Pluto passing in opposition to the Midheaven will also bring the spectre of challenge into the way that one interacts with people in positions of authority over oneself and potentially brings situations of either professional breakdown or breakthrough to a head. By the time that this transit is over the individual will have a much clearer idea of where they stand both in the family hierarchy and in the professional world in ways that will be both clear and permanent. Pluto passing in conjunction to the Midheaven has many of the same qualities as the opposition but the emphasis is always going to be on different outputs and outcomes. Pluto on the Midheaven will see family and home situations as distractions to the main theme in life at the time of the transit, the attainment of professional achievement and hopefully success. Pluto here will ask the individual to redefine to themselves what it is that success consists of and what they want to do with their life in terms of ambition and goals. With the Midheaven's region of influence being at least partly that of public image, status and profile, there is a need with this conjunction to avoid walking on other people's toes even inadvertently, because the headlong rush to the top may not be as subtle as one would like and there can be the potential for alienating or antagonising others in the workplace. It may also be that at this time the individual undergoing this transit may feel as though they have simply had enough and need a radical change of focus and career or a major life makeover in other words. There is the potential with transiting Pluto conjunct the Midheaven for arguments and disagreements of a large and permanent nature with employers, parents and authorities of all types and this is something that needs to be watched out for.

When Pluto transits the Sun the whole notion of identity undergoes various forms of regeneration and transformation. The cognisance of one's own identity goes through an alchemical transformation akin to a metaphorical shape shifting where even the physical appearance can change significantly. What one previously thought of as being one's identity and individuality will be seen as only a cocoon, a preparatory stage for the fully functioning and mature being that invariably appears after Pluto-Sun transits although the process of transformation and its nature can be varied by the transiting aspect in question. Pluto trining the Sun by transit brings a greater degree of comfort than usual with one's physical body as well as enlivens and heightens one's physical actions and responses. It brings a high energetic output over the course of a year and aids and assists any ongoing course of rejuvenation or rebirth that is happening. It brings a gentle but unbreakable strength into one's life that is not transient or temporary, a strength that once it is developed then plateaus and becomes consistent and permanent. If transiting Pluto is sextiling the Sun, there is an added impetus and stimulus to 'get out there' and make things happen knowing that the potential and power for transformation is within the person's grasp for at least the year that this transit lasts. It brings windows of opportunity but not the obligation to take them although chances taken at this time will work out better than normal. Whilst there is no compulsion to take these windows of opportunity or chances as they occur they do not come along that often to the quality that Pluto sextiling the Sun brings so when this happens the individual should strive and aspire to some type of refined rebirthing experience, probably in the areas signified by the Sun's house position.

Pluto squaring the Sun by transit is one of the most turbulent of times in that it potentially unleashes a great deal of energy and anger from the depths of one's subconscious and unconscious and creates patterns of behaviour that are at odds with the individual's normal ways of being. It can easily manifest as some type of direct challenge to your personal power or status within the family, career environment, social world or relationship situation to the point where it may seem as though other people in one's life are deliberately trying to block or stymie movement forward. It can generate extremely powerful emotional states which in the cold light of day do not add up to anything but in the heat of the moment may become a life or death situation. Pluto squaring the Sun by transit can also create a pattern of self-examination to such a critical degree that self-loathing can sometimes be the result at least for the duration of this period. The need for self-control both in external situations and internal self-assessment is strong to avoid becoming either a tyrant or a victim. A healthy physical expression over the year of this transit is recommended in that the more physical one is the less the chance of anger outbursts. There will be an eliminative streak present which if used dispassionately can be extremely effective in clarifying one's priorities.

Pluto opposing the Sun is an aspect that will only affect approximately 35% of the people alive on planet Earth at this time, because it takes so long to go around the Sun. It is only really people born from late Capricorn to early Cancer who will have experienced this transit. There is no mistaking the effects of transiting Pluto opposing the natal Sun; it has a direct and permanent influence on the way in which the individual interfaces both with others and with the larger dynamic. It is an 'all or nothing aspect' where once decisions or actions have been taken and confirmed then nothing but nothing will stop the individual from conducting their appointed task or mission. It can have a potential for fundamentalism about it which can border on extremes of behaviour in certain areas, often indicated by the house position of both transiting Pluto and the natal Sun. During this transit it may seem to the individual that it is not enough to just think or feel something strongly but that the urge to do something remarkable and memorable, hopefully in a way that breeds a clean conscience, may well come to the fore and dominate thus creating the impetus for action. Invariably this transit is symbolised by endings in some form often in ways that seem out of the individual's control. Indeed, an element of powerlessness is often evident, as though the person suddenly loses all their solidity and instead just gets swept along with the tides. In this combination the opposition is different from the conjunction. With the opposition there will be an inevitable tendency to flow with the ongoing tides no matter how compulsive or obsessive those tendencies, urges or impulses may be. But with the conjunction those same impulses and urges are generated from within as opposed to coming from without. Transiting Pluto conjunct natal Sun is the single biggest transit of all in terms of sheer personal power. It creates a blockbuster of intensity and unstoppable drive especially in the areas governed by the house that the conjunction falls in. It generates stamina and determination and keeps going when everyone else falls by the wayside. In fact, transiting Pluto conjunct natal Sun is an aspect that is best experienced alone because there can be a tendency to burn other people out with what they may see as an almost fanatical desire to get ahead and succeed. There will be an eliminative tendency towards most that the individual does as they will be of the opinion that they do not have time to waste on fripperies or losers but at the same time they will need to remember that they are not a permanent island and that they can afford to spend just a little time remembering who their friends are. It is a 'kill or cure' aspect and no-one comes through the alchemical crucible the same way that they entered it.

Transiting aspects from Pluto to the natal Moon are the strongest aspects of all in terms of a transit that expresses itself through the unconscious and subconscious levels of feeling and emotion. Pluto always goes to the extremes of depth and when it engages with the Moon and its emotive and feelingful way of dealing with the world, then the individual in question will surely find that indeed, still waters do run deep. The Moon is about one's sensitivity levels and emotional states, one's moods, feelings and day by day lifestyle choices and any type of Pluto transit will have a thorough and scrutinising influence. If the transit in question from Pluto is a trine, then the capacity for trusting one's internal gut instincts, feelings, hunches and intuitions is going to be stronger and more reliably accurate than normal, without going to extremes. Pluto will add and then augment a level of emotional confidence in oneself, the ability to trust one's feelings without doubt or insecurity. Linking Pluto and the Moon together by being in the same element of both sign and house for the duration of this transit, the surety and innate strength that this trine bestows can carry the individual forward in a way that is seen as powerful and dependable. The sextile takes this transformative and stimulative capacity and turns it from latent into potent, giving the individual the impetus and the drive to become the agent of change for themselves and to actively catalyse their lives by willingly taking on a much deeper psychological way of seeing and dealing with the world. The transiting sextile from Pluto to the natal Moon stirs up the deep waters and creates a purposeful flow that has intention and strength, if not clarity.

It is the transiting square from Pluto in the heavens to the natal Moon that should carry a health warning as it invariably stirs up one's feelings and emotions to the point of turmoil at the very least. Relationships with women will go through major transformations, some of them in quite difficult ways. There can easily be an element of emotive manipulation, guilt tripping or some other similar form of unconsciously coercive behaviour, normally towards the natal Moon individual but occasionally emanating from them as well especially if they are not fully aware of their own emotional conditioning. Any developing emotional power struggle needs to be either walked away from with finality and incisiveness or else managed in a totally transparent way without resorting to the power games of others. However sometimes this transit produces these challenges with oneself as opposed to through the medium of others and it does call for a great deal of effort and willingness on the part of the individual to face up to their own personal caverns and deal with what might be in them. Normally the fear of dealing with one's own unconscious feelings is far worse than the actual process itself, it is as though the fear is not of anything tangible, but what might be, a fear of being afraid, almost phobia. Any upcoming psychological issues at this time should be met and dealt with and not swept aside or hidden, because they will only come back later in a far more powerful way. The main reasons psychological issues come up for people at any given time is because they are mature and adult enough to deal with them.

Pluto in transit by opposition to the natal Moon is sometimes known as 'the devil made me do it' aspect in that it can produce powerful and extreme urges emanating from deep within one's own subconscious that cannot be denied and will be expressed. It is the manner of expression that is at question here, not the need for the emotive expression itself. There may be powerful conflict issues during this transit with older members of family, tribe or community, or there may be internal conflict about the nature of one's own roots and foundations at the emotional level. Often there is an accompanying element of emotional angst that accompanies this transit and it is quite common for people at this time to exhibit brief but strong patterns from the first seven years of life. This is obviously them eliminating these patterns but sometimes through the medium of playing them out through their adult interactions, which can be disconcerting for those around the individual if they do not know what is going on. Pluto transiting opposite the Moon is not a good year for making long term, objective and emotionally detached plans. Instead, it is time to surf the emotional extremes and then by choice head back to the safety of the near middle ground. Whereas Pluto transiting in conjunction to the natal Moon is very different. Dependent on the house and sign that the Moon is in, Pluto will intensify and accelerate the emotional processes of the Moon in ways that may come across to others as being yes/no, black/white and in others ways very selective or even eliminative about the quality of experience that the person wants in their life. Any dishonesty or lack of transparency will be simply removed permanently from their lives without a backward glance. These people need loyalty and trust, not game playing. It brings the capacity for lifetime internal emotional rebuilding and reformation; the emergence butterfly like into true emotional maturity. However sometimes the birth process can be painful and needs to be embraced and taken seriously so that the long term influences and effects of this transit are not forgotten.

9

The transformative future with Pluto

Discoveries in astronomy and developments in astrology within the last fifty years have completely transformed and revolutionised our concepts and understanding of the solar system, its component parts and how those parts interact with each other. Using the model of the solar system as a metaphor this same conceptual revolution has also manifested in the ways that individuals, communities and countries live and share together. There is a common link in all these events, a link that has become its own movement in recent years and that is based around the principle of accelerationism. This accelerationism can be demonstrated in many ways.

I was born in the middle of the 1950's when the population of planet Earth was somewhere in the region of two and a half billion. This has tripled within the last sixty years to a current figure of some seven and a half billion, with a projection of ten billion by 2040. As Serena Rhoney-Dougal points out in her seminal book 'Where Science and Magic Meet,' when a host body such as a microbe, bacteria, planet etc attracts a virus, that virus will cover the surface of the host, consume all its resources and then both the host and the virus will die. Regardless of the size of the host, the coadunate number of collective viruses leading to that terminal trigger is ten to the power of ten, or ten billion. Humanity's population is now at ten to the power of nine point seven five, well within range of that ten billion figure. As Serena also points out, in some cases at this point of life and death the virus will mutate from single celled organisms into multi layered organisms with cells combining in certain ways, becoming concentrated with less mass, and requiring less food and hopefully creating a symbiosis between host and virus where each can support the other. Using this host/virus analogy and stretching it to the question of humanity the accelerationism of these times in terms of the population explosion can be clearly seen and from this can be extrapolated a time around 2040 where unless there are fundamental changes to the ways in which humanity lives on and shares the planet and its resources, some type of challenging conclusion to this accelerationism will inevitably occur. Elsewhere in this book, under the section of Pluto in Capricorn are inferences to the years 2017 and 2018 when Pluto in the heavens will conjunct the degree of the Uranus/Neptune conjunction of 1993 and earlier potential resolutions might be postulated. As one eminent astrologer stated about the nature of Pluto in connection with population growth; *'More and more souls are coming here now, because they know that Earth is on the point of a magnificent leap in consciousness that they want to be part of. But to be a conscious part of this process requires the ultimate surrender of the individual to the deeper side of their being and the willingness to trust their instinct and intuition as much as if not more than their conscious mind and feelings.'*

Within that same time span of the last sixty years the technological revolution has accelerated beyond anyone's capacity to predict. From the small black and white televisions and the family car of the late 1950's to the colour televisions and transistor radios of the 1960's to man on the Moon in 1969, the pace of revolution in the sciences developed exponentially. The 1970's and 1980's brought the advent of digital watches, personal computers and incredible advances in both the military and the entertainment worlds and of course the advent of the internet at the end of the 1980's ushered in a major leap in technological innovation, a leap that is still being explored today. It is commonplace and taken for granted in 2014 that any information, music or other form of electronically registered information can be available at a moment's notice on a number of different devices at anytime, anywhere. If the principle of accelerationism is used here it can clearly be seen that from small valve driven black and white televisions in 1954 to the instant download facility of 2014 is a massive leap forward, one that is exponentially developing and leading humanity into ever stranger futures. Humanity has gone from thirty miles an hour to ten miles a second within the space of fifty years. Within the near future this desire for increased technological innovation will lead us into smaller and more highly evolved systems which will diversify into two separate pathways. Nanotech is becoming a steadily more crucial tool for the future, ranging from microscopic robots building new structures for people to live and work in, to these same robotic microbes being used in surgery to a degree of accuracy incapable of by a surgeon. The development of neurotic technology, creating the first stages of a cyborg-like humanity with an active interface between thought and machine can also not be ruled out, especially in the face of ever increasing environmental degradation. When Pluto is added to this mix the question is whether this process of technological transformation will lead humanity into a greater and harmonious coexistence with each other and the planet or will it symbolise a Dystopian and fragmented future?

If this accelerationism is viewed solely through the accelerating developments in population and technological capacity, then the prospect for the future of anything but an increasingly robotic system denuded of human feeling or emotion is looking bleak. Fortunately, there is another type of accelerationism that is also on the increase, that of spirituality. Within the last half century and the corresponding development of global communication networks a more knowledgeable and informed attitude towards theology, religion, dogma, philosophy and individual relationship with divinity has grown into the world of today where there are as many religions as there are people. As the rigidity and strictness of existing religions in both the eastern and the western world has left them behind in the accelerating consciousness movements of the last fifty years, the need for more realistic alternatives has become more urgent. The patriarchal attitudes of most contemporary religions are now seen as dinosaur-like and have directly contributed to the rise of the feminist movement in the last fifty years. More people than ever before are now searching for their own relationship with whatever it is that they call the Divine having given up with the old conventional order. Recent scandals involving priests from every religion since the turn of the millennium have contributed massively to the decline in organised worship and the corresponding upsurge in fundamentalism as a direct reaction to that decline. As both population and the demands upon individual time grow exponentially, so perhaps also does the concept of individual psychic space and the need for people to have their own direct line to God. This trend is accelerating in ways that match both population and technology. The purpose of Pluto in this aspect of accelerationism is to push people individually into a deeper and more psychologically oriented focus on the need for a greater sense of collective unity in their lives.

It can be clearly seen from the above paragraphs that the proposed accelerationist principle in human evolution exists and that the speed of this accelerationism is not linear but is exponential. It can also be seen how Pluto can be used as an allegorical reference in all these scenarios. Up until the time of writing Pluto remains hidden and occluded, a mystery awaiting discovery and this is clearly shown as evidential in human society by its refusal or inability to see the accelerationist perspective and not plan for the future. The imminent unravelling of at least some of the Plutonian mysteries may indicate a symbolic wakeup call in humanity to the immediacy and urgency of its problems as a species regardless of internecine squabbles. One thing is absolutely certain however and that is that population is not going to decrease, technology is not going to stand still and neither are attitudes towards spirituality and divinity. All these things are set to continue their exponential growth in the coming few decades in ways that without tweaking or managing will inevitably lead to some type of sudden downfall. Exponential growth in any form is not sustainable so the question has to be asked – what happens when that exponential growth curve reaches prime vertical? Also from an astrological viewpoint, how can astrology help?

When the hypothetical exponential graph curve reaches prime vertical, one of only two things can happen. The pace of acceleration can become suddenly unsustainable; the pathway of the exponential curve turns in on itself resulting in a sudden crash and the whole process beginning again, this time in the opposite direction to the past. In this eventuality, a Dystopian future of a soulless population living on processed food, chemical drugs, antibiotics and endless superficial media in an increasingly polluted environment only leads to a mass pandemic. Alternatively the exponential curve can do the opposite and instead exceed the parameters or boundaries of the graph. This could mean a greater symbiosis with the Earth and an advancement into the emerging soft technology in a way that embodies spirituality as opposed to the mechanist attitudes of the old hard technology. It will also require more holistic attitudes and a willingness to allow the conscious and unconscious sides of our nature to combine, both personally and globally, as well as a more balanced attitude towards environmental situations, feminism, art, human rights etc, and to quote Terence McKenna '*if these things are not a part of our future, what kind of future will it be? We didn't cross the ice sheets for this — we crossed the ice sheets to go to the stars.'* It may well be that in the future astrology and particularly that branch of astrology that helps people understand themselves better at a psychological level will become a common language between humanity and the cosmos that it lives in and with.

Within a year, the New Horizons spacecraft will have passed the Pluto system and humanity will hopefully have a vastly unique perspective on this most distant of objects, both from an astronomical and astrological perspective. Our collective view and understanding of Pluto will be quite different although he will not give up all his secrets willingly. If the outcome of the mission is successful, Pluto will at least temporarily come out of shadow and into the light and hopefully the transformation process that is so necessary for human evolution will be more readily entertained and understood.

Section Four: 2023 Perspective

Postscript

This postscript is being written in late May and early June of 2023. In the ten years since starting this book, and nine years since finishing, many of Pluto's secrets have come into the open, both physically and metaphorically.

10

Developments in astronomical and geological understandings

The New Horizons probe, launched in mid-January 2006, made its closest fly-by to Pluto on the 14th of July 2015. A journey of nine and a half years for a visit of a few hours seems a waste of time and expense when viewed dispassionately. However, the large amount of information and photographs that were obtained in those precious few hours vastly expanded humanity's knowledge of Pluto, which was the last planetary member of the Solar system, until in their infinite wisdom, in 2006 the International Astronomical Union (IAU) downgraded it to a dwarf planet.

The visit of New Horizons probe revealed much in terms of Pluto's geology. The photographs obtained by the probe's brief fly-by revealed that Pluto is a planet with mountain ranges, huge ice sheet deserts and even an atmosphere. These photographs also show that Pluto's terrain has a number of assorted colours, some quite dull and others very bright. Of the considerable number of photos sent back to Earth, one of the most striking was that taken just before the closest encounter, showing Pluto in its entirety. It is clear from this photo that Pluto is covered by a mixture of mountainous dark terrain and by brightly coloured huge ice sheets that flow right up to the mountain edges in many cases. The fact that the mountainous areas of Pluto appear dark in these photos and the ice sheets appear predominantly white, add to the existing ideas of Pluto as being a planet of extremes of black and white from an astrological perspective. The most visually striking photograph of Pluto shows the area of the Tombaugh Regio or as it has been nicknamed, the 'Heart,' at one edge of the largest ice sheet on Pluto.

From the information gathered so far, the ice sheet plains of Pluto consist of around 98% nitrogen ice, with small traces of methane and carbon monoxide. But unlike deserts on Earth, Mercury or Mars, the ice sheets of Pluto are not uniform – they do not flow in a glacial way. Instead, they are comprised of polygonal cells bringing water up from the subterranean depths and then carrying those floating blocks of water ice crust towards their margins and up against the foothills of the mountains, which in turn seem to be composed primarily of water ice. It is worthy of note that there appear to be no craters on Pluto, or at least the New Horizons probe did not discover any. Scientists suggest that this shows that the surface of Pluto is young, indicating that it is less than ten million years old. To quote the New Horizons' science team: *"Pluto displays a surprisingly wide variety of geological landforms, including those resulting from glaciological and surface–atmosphere interactions as well as impact, tectonic, possible cryovolcanic, and mass-wasting processes."* Beneath Pluto's icy surface, contemporary scientific thinking is that there lies a subsurface watery ocean, ranging from 100-200 kilometres deep, which in turn is surrounding a silicate core. Upon leaving the Plutonic environment, the New Horizons probe had one last magnificent surprise for us all. Turning its cameras backwards as it headed into deep space, the probe took one last picture of Pluto occulting the Sun, and the resultant picture showed the dark side of Pluto encased by a thin bright blue ring. This proved beyond doubt that Pluto has an atmosphere, composed primarily of nitrogen, methane and carbon monoxide, like much of the ice on its surface.

Prior to the New Horizons visit to the Pluto system. all that was known about its astronomy was based on observations from land and orbital telescopes. It was known that Pluto and its main Moon, Charon, orbited each other and that they were in a barycentric relationship with each other – Charon's mass was substantial enough to pull Pluto away from a fixed point in its orbital pattern. So whilst Charon orbits Pluto, Pluto itself orbits a void. Charon's orbit around Pluto takes 6.4 Earth days, and one Pluto rotation on its axis (a Pluto day) takes 6.4 Earth days. As a result of this, Charon neither rises nor sets, but hovers over the same spot on Pluto's surface, and the same side of Charon always faces Pluto, whilst the same side of Pluto always faces Charon – this is called tidal locking. The only other example of this known in our solar system is the similar relationship between the Earth and its Moon, but there is a major difference here as whilst our Moon always shows the same face towards the Earth, the Earth does not always show the same face to the Moon. The astronomical reasoning behind this is that Charon is so close to Pluto – 12,160 miles or 19,570 kilometres – and that it has half the diameter and one eighth of the mass of Pluto, that it could be seen as a binary system as opposed to a planet with its Moon.

There are four other Moons of Pluto – in order of closeness they are Styx, Nix, Kerberos and Hydra. In preparation for the journey of New Horizons, NASA scientists used the Hubble space telescope to research other Moons of Pluto to calculate orbital pathways that avoided collisions. Nix was found in June 2005, and Hydra in August the same year. Nix was named after Nyx, the Greek goddess of night and darkness and the mother of Charon but was deliberately spelt Nix to avoid confusion with the already prenamed asteroid Nyx. Hydra was named after the Lernaean Hydra, the nine headed lake dwelling beast that battled Heracles (Hercules), who was the nephew of Pluto. These names were also chosen for their starting initials, N and H, as resonant with the New Horizons probe, much as Pluto's naming was resonant with Percival Lowell, the astronomer who initiated the search for Pluto. Kerberos was discovered in June 2011 and was named after Cerberus, the three headed dog who guarded the gates of Hades and was of similar parentage to Hydra. It was named Kerberos instead of Cerberus as, similar to Nyx, Cerberus was already a prenamed asteroid. Styx was discovered in July 2012, and was named after the river Styx, the river that bordered Hades and was the boundary between the land of the living and the land of the dead in Greek mythology. Styx herself was the daughter of two of the Titans, but during the Titanomachy aligned herself with the Olympians instead of the Titans. After this, to honour her choice, Zeus/Jupiter made all oaths made by members of the Olympian pantheon binding upon drinking the waters of the river Styx. Charon was, of course, the ferryman who carried souls across the Styx from the land of the living to the land of the dead, with the journey downstream on the Styx taking longer depending on how blamelessly one had lived their lives. It should be noted that both Kerberos and Styx are miniscule compared to Nix and Hydra.

What was known but not confirmed until the New Horizons probe passed through the Pluto system was the existence of accurate ratios between Pluto's lesser Moons. Styx, Nix and Hydra are in a three body resonance with each other: the respective ratio of orbits is 11:9:6. This becomes exact when orbital precession is considered. This means that in a recurring cycle there are eleven orbits of Styx for every nine orbits of Nix and every six orbits of Hydra. This degree of accuracy, along with the barycentric and tidally locked relationship between Charon and Pluto, should be enough to keep geometrists, numerologists and astrologers busy for decades to come.

11

Astrological developments of Pluto in the last decade

Reviewing the astrological content of this book, nine to ten years after I originally wrote it brings a sense of pride. To add to my writings on Pluto in the signs and houses of the zodiac would not warrant any significant or deeper relevance and understanding of its nature than has been already stated. Similarly, I feel that the content of the natal chart aspects to Pluto to be a standalone quality of work that needs little if any update. I draw little comfort from my comments, written in early 2014 in the final two paragraphs of the first edition which I reproduce untouched here – '*When the hypothetical exponential graph curve (of evolution) reaches prime vertical, one of only two things can happen. The pace of acceleration can become suddenly unsustainable; the pathway of the exponential curve turns in on itself resulting in a sudden crash and perhaps the whole process beginning again, this time in the opposite direction to the past. In this eventuality, a Dystopian future of a soulless population living on processed food, chemical drugs, antibiotics and endless superficial media in an increasingly polluted environment will only lead to a mass pandemic*', although I also paint the potentially opposite better picture with '*a greater symbiosis with the Earth and an advancement into the emerging soft technology in a way that embodies spirituality ..... and requires more holistic attitudes and a willingness to allow the conscious and the unconscious sides of our nature to combine...*

When I wrote the above words, I had been studying astrology for about thirty five years – now it is forty five. At the time of this book's original publication, Pluto had been in Capricorn for three to four years – it is now moving into Aquarius. At the time that the internet burst into the collective consciousness, I was fortunate enough to have already studied astrology for twenty plus years. It seems to me that astrology and the internet were made for each other. Since the emergence of internet technology, awareness and acceptance of astrology in the mainstream has amplified massively. What was a fringe subject twenty five years ago is now firmly established in today's rapidly changing world.

The downgrading of Pluto's planetary status by the IAU in 2006 has not and should not be reflected in modern translations of Pluto's astrological significance. I am aware of astrologers who refuse to use Uranus, Neptune or Pluto, let alone Ceres or Chiron in their chart readings – this is anathema to me. I could not consider constructing and delineating a horoscope without using Pluto. A repetitive and consistent theme in my understandings of Astrology is that as a planet is 'discovered,' so its archetypes and meanings come into the collective consciousness. Without Pluto, we would not have any recognised astrological reference point to psychology, our understanding of the compulsive and obsessive, our notions of extremes and intensity of behavioural patterns, let alone our notions of cleansing, purging and detoxing which in turn leads to transformation, regeneration and rebirth. We would not have any meaningful relationship with our own internal ideas of 'the dark.' Put bluntly, we would not know ourselves anywhere near as much as we currently can with the advantage of the astrological Pluto in our birthchart. This is a good place in this narrative to suggest that anyone who wishes to explore the astrological Pluto to any depth would benefit from buying and reading 'The Idiot's guide' or 'The Dummies guide' to psychology, or some other simplified handbook or guide to the different forms of psychology currently in use.

I own my own inability to be objective here. One cannot simply 'unlearn' elements of Astrology. In the last decade, mainly due to my studies of the astrological Pluto (and Chiron, also) I have come to a much greater comprehension and acceptance of the true nature of Astrology that is my own, that works for me and that I would not expect any other astrological practitioner or student to accept. Through regular and constant working with positive Plutonian archetypes of metaphorical death and rebirth, along with positive Chironic archetypes of holism and integration, I have come to the ongoing conclusion that death as we collectively have been led to understand it as being is a fallacy. This fallacy has been imposed upon us over millennia by vested interest groups who use the threat of heaven and hell as a form of control. I suggest that instead, the physical death of the body releases the soul into another dimension where time as we know it in this world does not exist. That there is no death, just a transition of consciousness. I suggest that liberating oneself from traditional mental understandings of death can bring a significantly less fearful approach to dealing with Pluto, seeing the planet as a gateway phenomenon instead of the finality often associated with it.

At the same time as coming to this ongoing conclusion about the nature of death, I also went through a personal revelation about the nature of Astrology. Simply put, I stopped seeing Astrology as an 'it,' and started seeing Astrology as a 'she.' With that acceptance in mind, it is a small step further on to realise that people do not find Astrology, but Astrology finds people. And if Astrology has found you, dear reader, it is because she wants to work with you.

It is only a short step from these assumptions on my part to seeing the uni/multiverse as having a form of sentience. If this is the case, then we as a species are made up of 'star stuff', i.e. atoms, electrons, protons and neutrons it is easy to see ourselves as volunteers on planet Earth at this time, with clear mission statements and purpose as defined by the position of the planets and stars in the sky at the time of our physical birth. It follows that those of us who study Astrology and work with it have the honour and privilege of not only passing that gained knowledge onwards, but also developing that knowledge for future generations.

With these sentiments in mind, I find myself in 2023 with no real choice when it comes to working with Plutonic archetypes and energies. To go along with the mainstream of scientific and astronomical thought and accept it is impossible for a dwarf planet that is smaller than Earth's Moon and over four billion miles away to have any effects would make sense in an ordered world. Yet I have tens of thousands of statistics and thousands of client feedback comments that totally contradict this. I cannot explain in scientifically acceptable terminology how Pluto works from an astrological perspective. Yet I know it does.

Pluto/Hades is the eldest of the children of Cronos/Saturn. He spent the longest time of his siblings 'in the dark' after being ingested by his father. The mythology of his youth (or lack of) goes a long way to explaining his astrological archetype, of operating in ways that defy rational or logical explanation and always having a psychological basis. One cannot understand, explain or rationalise Pluto. There is no logic to it. However, one can sense, feel, envision and know Pluto in a way that defies all conscious explanation but that is absolutely verified by our own internal instincts and experiences. I suggest here that experiencing the astrological Pluto is akin to an energy field that manifests strongest through our gut instinct as opposed to any conscious thought or feeling. Intuition is a human construct, centred and originating from the solar plexus and then heading north. Instinct is an animal construct, centred inches below the navel and then heading south. Pluto deals with instinct, not intuition, intellect or emotion. This is obvious in the horoscope, where individuals with a strongly aspected Pluto always have strong 'bullshit filters,' where they instinctively know when something is wrong or right, or when someone is lying or telling the truth. It is easy to ignore these instincts, instead relying on mind and feeling to qualify the world as being the way we want it to be. But by using Plutonic energy, we can see the world as it really is, even if we do not like what we see.

12

Transits of Pluto

Little can be added here regarding Pluto's transits to the other planets and points in the individual horoscope that have not already been expressed. However, since this book was first written a greater comprehension of how Pluto works by transit has developed within the astrological community.

The single biggest factor here is the inexorable urge that is becoming increasingly associated with the transits of Pluto. When Pluto hits one's chart in a strong way – primarily through a transiting conjunction or opposition, but to a lesser extent by a transiting square – the individual undergoing the transit WILL go through an intense year or two. The only negotiation here is whether the individual allows Pluto to work with them and 'flows with the go,' or whether they are dragged by Pluto kicking and screaming into the transformative process. There are often strong lessons to be learnt about the difference between being powerful and powerfilled. Those who seek power, especially Plutonic power, normally end up trying to control themselves, Pluto and other or others, in any order. This results in the individual blocking the flow of power through themself and creating a block in the Plutonic outlets. The power then, unable to flow cleanly, turns within and spirals downwards, creating a potentially corrupt and paranoid energy. Alternatively, those people who see themselves as powerfilled recognise that they don't own Pluto's energy, that they are merely the conduit for it, and by empowering others they also empower themselves.

The trines and sextiles of the transiting Pluto are easier to manage, as they are less confrontational, either with oneself or others. They still retain a level of intensity in them that makes it clear that the windows of opportunity that these transits offer for positive transformation and rebirth can only be ignored at one's peril. Without change there is entropy, which leads to decay. Because the gentler Pluto transits of the sextile and trine do not force the individual into making changes, it can be easy for the person to ignore them, or at least attempt to ignore them. But to do this is folly, as the opportunities for the massive harmonious psychological upgrade that these transits bring is something that will normally occur only once or twice in an average lifetime.

13

Summary

As an astrologer with over forty five years of study and well over thirty five years of consultative experience, and as a mature adult human male who in all probability is over eighty percent of the way through his life, I care little for long winded explanations or justifications – I like simple. And although Pluto can be seen as having an incredibly complex and deep astrological resonance, I think that in a way, Pluto likes simple as well. In my dealings with clients, I find that if I spend too long going into the Hadean depths with them, either their eyes glaze over and/or they become uncomfortable with all the long winded explanations. So in the following three paragraphs, I hope to summarise the qualities of Pluto concisely as I see them from an astrological viewpoint in the middle of 2023, hopefully without being superficial or derogatory towards this most misunderstood of astrological energies.

Viewed from a challenging perspective, Pluto can be seen as obsessive and/or compulsive, intense and extreme, and bringing periods of crisis and trauma into one's life. It can symbolise major power struggles in our lives, normally through contact with other or others in ways that can be quite confrontational. This is not to imply violence, at least at the physical level, but individuals with difficult or challenging aspects to Pluto in the personal horoscope will inevitably engage in emotional, psychological or mental struggle with others at various times in their lives and the tactics used can be very underhand. This can be manipulative at many different levels, coercive, subversive – it can attract jealousy, guilt tripping, shaming etc. Common catch phrases here, for example, are 'but if you love me you'll...' or 'but you should....' It is as though there are individuals out there who have a vested interest in holding the Pluto person back. If the Pluto person makes changes in their lives, then others around them will also have to change, or else lose the Pluto person. Most people do not want to make these changes, so it's easier for them to hold back the Pluto person on the grounds that if no-one makes any changes then the status quo can be maintained.

From a neutral perspective, Pluto simply – gets things done. Pluto in one's chart can be totally detached and impersonal, to the point of seeming uncaring. People mistake this for the capacity to be mercenary, or merciless. The correct word is ruthless. Mercenary is cruel, callous and uncaring, whilst ruthless is seen as being yes or no, black or white, with no room for compromise or negotiation. When viewed neutrally, this ruthless quality is not only useful, but can be seen as a prerequisite when necessary for purging oneself, detoxing, cleansing, eliminating all diverse types of toxins and purifying. This can be done in a number of ways, none of which is necessarily better than any other, but in my astrological experience the best way is through sweat. Whether it is through strenuous physical effort, down the gym, in the sauna, doing marathons or treadmill activity or on the dance floor, sweat generated through repetitive motion and physical exertion seems to have a powerful cleansing and purging effect. Alternatively, other purifying techniques, such as yoga or fasting can also result in a kind of 'deep cleanse,' where the Pluto individual feels as though they have scraped the bottom of the barrel of their own personal experiences. Many times, I find myself saying to clients that under a Plutonian influence they have no real choice but to go into the caves at the bottom of their soul and deal with what they find there. Often, the imagined fear is just that – imagined. But it is only by going into one's own Hadean depths that true cleansing and elimination can take place, leading to a feeling of redemption for those brave enough to go to rock bottom and then return with a sense of psychological invulnerability.

Viewed in a positive light, Pluto is seen as the caterpillar turning into the butterfly, exhibiting a kind of psychological metamorphosis that refines and extols one's own personal inner strengths. Another metaphor for the same experience is that of the snake shedding its skin, leaving one's outer shell behind and instead contracting on allowing the inner being to become purified and lighter. Both metaphors suggest a form of transformation at many different levels, not only physical but also mental, emotional and psychological. The transformative process of Pluto resonates with the idea of 'shape shifting,' which embraces a level of shamanic development. With a well aspected Pluto in the horoscope, the individual will often exhibit changes at the physical level, especially in the potential to suddenly lose weight. There is a regenerative impulse here, with the individual constantly trying to improve themselves in a multi-level way. The idea of 'rebirthing' oneself is never far from the consciousness, in fact as the individual ages so the rebirthing urge becomes more and more important. The end goal of all these transformative and regenerative experiences seems to be the idea of the phoenix arising from the ashes, lighter in one's soul and less attached to the density and materialism of the world we live in.

14

Pluto and the dark feminine

As we as a species approach the quarter way point through the current century (according to most, but not all the world's calendars) it is worth reflecting on astrology's relationship with the outer planets. Uranus, Neptune and Pluto are outside of naked eye range, which is one of the reasons why they astrologically represent the deeper and less transparent sides of human nature. Since the discovery of Uranus in 1781, it has completed nearly three orbits of the Sun. Astrologers are now becoming more confident in explaining and using its energy patterns. Since its discovery in 1846, Neptune has completed just over one orbit around the Sun, passing through every sign of the zodiac. Astrologers are just beginning to draw clear assumptions about its meaning. Pluto was discovered in 1930 and will not complete its first orbit around the Sun until 2178, so there is yet no clear understanding on its influence in half of the signs of the zodiac.

Since the New Horizons probe sent back clear images of Pluto, both astronomers and astrologers have rapidly advanced their understanding of it. We now know that Pluto is a mixture of black and white, with traces of orange. We know it has an atmosphere. And in the last two or three decades, new translations of Greek mythology have suggested that Pluto is not the dark, broody, misogynistic abductor that was being suggested until recently. Pluto in the birth chart and by transit makes you go to the depths of your soul and encourages you to transform and expel any old residual poison that lingers from the past. By doing so, you cleanse yourself in such a way that creates a degree of both psychological purification and confidence, to the point of becoming psychologically invulnerable. Pluto encourages us to accept ourselves as being who we are, warts and all, whilst at the same time striving to consistently transform and regenerate ourselves into becoming better than we have been. It is for this reason that I suggest an emerging archetype of Pluto being a force for integration, assimilation and holism in our approach to self determination. That capacity for personal growth and self-development does not come from mechanistic or patriarchal roots, instead it comes from our capacity for compassion, empathy, intuition and kindness. This is why I suggest that as Pluto gives up its secrets and we as astrologers continue to define its attributes we should embrace and encourage the philosophy of Pluto as being representative of both the divine and the dark feminine.

15

Postscript to the Postscript

Nine years ago, when I finished the first edition of this book, the final paragraph stated '*Within a year, the New Horizons spacecraft will have passed the Pluto system and humanity will hopefully have a unique perspective on this most distant of objects, both from an astronomical and astrological perspective. Our collective view and understanding of Pluto will be vastly different although he will not give up all his secrets willingly. If the outcome of the mission is successful, Pluto will at least temporarily come out of shadow and into the light and hopefully the transformation process that is so necessary for human evolution will be more readily entertained and understood.*'

Now, in June 2023, Pluto is on the threshold of moving into Aquarius, something I feel that we should collectively embrace. But this is not all. By the middle of 2026, Pluto will have moved into early Aquarius, Neptune into Aries, Uranus into Taurus and Saturn into Aries, along with Neptune. Indeed, Saturn and Neptune will conjunct each other in February 2026 at zero degrees of Aries, the very start of the zodiac. Viewed heliocentrically (as opposed to the normal astrological way of looking at things geocentrically) there is a day where Mercury, Venus, Mars, Jupiter, Saturn, Uranus, Neptune and Pluto are all in the very early degrees of their respective sign – for the curious among you, it is the 11th May 2026.

There has never been a time in astrological history where all the major planets move signs within a year or so of each other, let alone all of them moving from feminine signs into masculine ones. I suggest that we as a species are on the point of the biggest evolutionary leap we have ever made, a revolution in consciousness as much as in soft technology. We were born for this time. To quote Terence McKenna, *'not a moment too soon.'* I genuinely believe that by gaining a deeper and more powerfilled perspective on our own psychology, we are ideally poised to break free of thousands of years of struggle and grow into maturity. Thank you, Pluto, and bring it on.

9th June 2023

www.ingramcontent.com/pod-product-compliance
Lightning Source LLC
Chambersburg PA
CBHW022356280326
41935CB00007B/201